THE NEW
MONASTICISM

THE NEW MONASTICISM

An Interspiritual Manifesto
for Contemplative Living

Rory McEntee
and
Adam Bucko

ORBIS BOOKS
Maryknoll, New York 10545

ORBIS BOOKS
Maryknoll, New York 10545

Fathers and Brothers
MARYKNOLL

Second Printing, October 2016

Founded in 1970, Orbis Books endeavors to publish works that enlighten the mind, nourish the spirit, and challenge the conscience. The publishing arm of the Maryknoll Fathers and Brothers, Orbis seeks to explore the global dimensions of the Christian faith and mission, to invite dialogue with diverse cultures and religious traditions, and to serve the cause of reconciliation and peace. The books published reflect the views of their authors and do not represent the official position of the Maryknoll Society. To learn more about Maryknoll and Orbis Books, please visit our website at www.maryknollsociety.org.

All interior art is the work of Deborah Koff Chapin. We extend tremendous gratitude to her for making her art available for our use. The drawings were produced with an original methodology called "touch art," most of them during presentations on New Monasticism during the international conference *Dawn of Interspirituality*. For more of Deborah's work please see: ww.touchdrawing.com/.

Published by Orbis Books, Maryknoll, New York 10545-0302.

Manufactured in the United States of America.

Library of Congress Cataloging -in- Publication Data
McEntee, Rory.
The new monasticism : an interspiritual manifesto for contemplative living / by Rory McEntee and Adam Bucko.
          pages cm
     Includes bibliographical references and index.
     ISBN 978-1-62698-126-3 (pbk.)
  1. Monastic and religious life. 2. Monasticism and religious orders.
  3. Spiritual life – Christianity. I. Title.
  BX2435. M396 2015
  255– dc23   2014039837

To Griffin, my son,
my ground in this world,
this is a song for you . . .
Rory McEntee

To New York City's Homeless Youth,
Whose courage continues to be
one of my greatest teachers. . . .
Adam Bucko

Contents

FOREWORD

Llewellyn Vaughan-Lee

The spiritual or mystical journey is the heartbeat of humanity, always present even if hidden beneath the surface. It is the most primal calling of the heart, the song of the soul going back to God, from the outer world to the formless Truth that resides within each of us.

Over the centuries this journey has been woven into the fabric of our history, imaged in icons, written in prayer books. It has taken on different forms, been followed by Zoroastrian priests and Sufi dervishes, Christian nuns and Buddhist monks. Each pilgrim makes the solitary soul's journey from the alone to the Alone, and yet also in the company of fellow travelers, of others who have been called by Truth, by the heart's desire for what is endless and eternal. Each form of this journey, whether that of the Desert Fathers or the Beguine women mystics, of a Himalayan yogi or a Zen monk, is colored in the images of the time and the place: the austerities of the desert, the mystical passion of medieval women, or the empty begging bowl of the monk. In the following pages we will see this journey told anew, in the colors and images of the twenty-first century, full of freedom and joy as well as the simplicity of the heart's calling. Always it is a journey from words to silence, from images to emptiness and yet at the same time it needs to speak to us in a language we can understand, a call to prayer we can hear and recognize.

Adam and Rory have responded both to their heart's calling and the need of the time. With the sincerity of true pilgrims, they have shared their map of the journey with fellow travelers. Here is the path from separation back to union with God told once again, in a language both ancient and modern. It speaks to the present day, of a "new monasticism" without the walls and regulations that are too limiting to most of today's seekers, but with the same spirit that sounded in the cloisters of earlier centuries. It is interspiritual, referring to a contemporary movement that looks beyond any one form to a sharing of the wisdom that lies at the root of all religions, to the "mystic heart," to quote Brother Wayne Teasdale. It celebrates the single human family to which we all belong, and the unity that lies at the root of all our diversity.

Reading their words one can hear God's call to the soul and our response. They show that this journey is always alive, that it is as essential and needed in the cities of today as in the monasteries and hermitages of an earlier time. Their new monasticism is not an escape from life, but a celebration of what it really means to be alive. It comes from the deepest core of our being—humanity's need to experience the Divine.

This spiritual calling is like a primal stamp within all of humanity, and yet for each of us it is unique, and nothing is more intimate than our relationship with God, our partnership with the Divine. It is our own innermost being that speaks to us. The authors state that the new monasticism is about honoring one's own unique path, cultivation of one's unique relationship to life, to God, in trust, fidelity, and partnership with the guidance of the Holy Spirit. One of life's wonders is the uniqueness of everything that is created, every bird and every butterfly, every cloud and every raindrop. The Great Artist has made everything different—no two brushstrokes on life's canvas are the same—and each moment is new and never repeated. On the spiritual journey this uniqueness is embraced and lived—it is the journey from the alone to the Alone. No one else can make this journey for us: it is *our* heart that cries out, *our* feet that bleed. And yet this unique path takes us into the realization of the oneness that is at the core of our being and within all of life. All is one, and each cell embodies and reflects this primal oneness—the unity of being. The journey home, of the soul back to the Source, is a journey back to unity, to the mystical realization that we are the Divine Oneness.

And so we discover that what we thought was our individual journey, is in fact just an expression of the one great journey—there can never be more than one. The real story, in fact the only story, is that of the Divine awakening within the soul. Within the heart of every pilgrim is this calling to return home, and yet we are already home and there were never two. The relationship to God *is* this secret of divine oneness—lover and Beloved are one—there is no other. And this intimacy is always alive, even if hidden deep within the heart, as the Sufi mystic Rumi exclaims:

> It is he who suffers his absence in me
> Who through me cries out to himself.
> Love's most strange, most holy mystery
> We are intimate beyond belief.

Every moment the Divine is coming into manifestation, and every moment the Divine is returning home. Each breath sings the song of being and nonbeing. We head to the mountain and we return to the world, only to realize the simple truth that there is neither mountain or world—there is not even a journey, just the unfolding mystery of the Divine.

New monasticism is a way to live this mystery, to breathe this primal breath. It is both a call and a response: a call to prayer, to the interior journey, and also a response, a path to follow. But rather than the tolling of the monastery bells for matins and vespers, the canonical hours and strict observance of prayers, Adam and Rory offer a set of principles, of blessed simplicity, contemplation, spiritual friendship, and an awareness of the inner values that belong to the core of what it really means to be a human being. They also stress the grounded need for psychological work, an essential part of the transformative journey that takes one toward spiritual maturity. This is an organic, evolving vision that speaks to the need of the time, of a moment in our human history when the spirit is coming alive in a new way. It is a doorway to walk through into sacred space.

PREFACE

Mirabai Starr

It is an honor to be invited to offer a few words at the beginning of this important book. I have been following Adam and Rory for a few years now, although they seem to believe they've been doing the following. This is a perfect example of what the authors mean when they speak about "dialogical dialogue." Although I am older and have been on a spiritual path for longer, ours has been a horizontal conversation that has transformed each of us. As you will see, Rory and Adam are very wise, and this book is a transmission of the perennial wisdom reimagined for an emerging globalized world. The vision they share here is both practical and exalted. They use language with precision, offering a masterpiece of scholarship unencumbered by jargon. *The New Monasticism* is lucid and soaring, arcing gracefully between the landscapes of theology and love poetry. It is invitational. When you read these pages, you step into a world you have always hoped was possible and find your own place there.

At least I did.

If you, also, are a seeker drawn to a committed spiritual life and yet do not feel at home in any one of the established religious traditions, you are not alone. You are probably a new monastic—a member of a growing tribe of interspiritual beings who draw from the many wells of the world's timeless mystical teachings, and with these mingled waters cultivate the garden of your soul and feed the hungry. This is a process that involves discernment, patience, and faith in the invisible life germinating underground. It is an endeavor that comes with no manual, though there are many teachers who can offer guidance on plowing or planting, weeding or deadheading, harvesting and feeding. The journey of new monasticism requires deep quiet, deep listening, deep dialogue. It is not for those who are looking for predictable questions and reliable answers. It may yield blissful moments, but it is not feel-good spirituality. It is a ferocious devotion to Love itself.

If you are this fierce, tender, curious, broken-open kind of being, you are probably a new monastic.

Here is another attribute that may sound familiar: you are as dedicated to the well-being of all creation as you are to your own awakening. Maybe even more so. In fact, the distinction between action and contemplation is a nonissue for you. When it comes down to it, you do not actually perceive yourself as separate from other humans, other animals, or the earth itself. You recognize your participation in the intricate web of life, and you celebrate that interconnectedness. At the same time, you strive for authenticity. You take the advice of the Buddha, who suggested that we be lamps unto ourselves and cultivate our enlightenment with diligence. You treat the spiritual elders you are fortunate to meet with deep regard. And then you test the truth of their teachings in the crucible of your own soul.

A new monastic is not afraid of annihilation. You stand ready for direct connection with the holy and prepared to be transfigured by the encounter. You do not select the belief systems that make you feel safe and comfortable, nor engage spiritual practices that prop up your ego. You want nothing less than union with the One, and you will do whatever it takes to alleviate sorrow in this world. The fruits of both of these aspirations ripen through fire.

A new monastic is also a new contemplative. That is, you maintain a vigilant alertness to the presence of the Spirit in all things, everywhere, all the time. Even as you have labored to build a solid foundation of silent sitting practice, you do not limit your experience of the sacred to a fixed set of conditions necessarily removed from the demands and distractions of life in the world. For the new monastic, as for Krishna in the Bhagavad Gita, everything is a prayer. Every act, each thought, all efforts are divinized and blessed when dedicated to the Holy One. You see the face of the Divine in the poorest of the poor and at the heart of your own most vulnerable moments.

A new monastic may not even believe in a personified deity. You may bristle at God-language and resist ritual. Nevertheless you drop to your knees in awe of the beauty of the natural world, and you experience the suffering of children in war zones faraway as if your own body was being poisoned. A two-minute conversation in line at the hardware store opens your heart and changes you forever. You catch glimpses of the perfect order of the cosmos while serving soup, brushing your lover's hair, bearing quiet witness to a friend who is grieving. You are in love with the Great Mystery itself.

The call to this new way of abiding with the Holy and repairing the broken world is an urgent one, but it is not grim. It is prophetic, but it isn't grandiose. It is about fully engaging with life while actively cultivating contemplative space. The journey of the new monastic brings the body along and the psyche, with its shadow and its innocence, and it welcomes enigma. New monasticism does not separate itself from politics, economics, and the arts. A new monastic says yes to unknowing and no to divisive dogma disguised as revealed truth. The new monastic resists the impulse to otherize, embraces his or her own ordinariness. and willingly steps up to the invitation to usher in a world of voluntary simplicity and radical lovingkindness.

This book is moonlight spilled on the water, illuminating a path that guides us home to the place where we remember we are one, and energizes us to act accordingly.

INTRODUCTION
Beginnings

The religion of humankind can be said to be spirituality itself, because mystical spirituality is the origin of all the religions. If this is so, and I believe it is, we might say that interspirituality—the sharing of ultimate experiences across traditions—is the religion of the third millennium. Interspirituality is the foundation that can prepare the way for a planet-wide enlightened culture.[1]
—*Wayne Teasdale*

By our fidelity we must build—starting with the most natural territory of our own self—a work, an opus, into which something enters from all the elements of the earth. We make our own soul throughout all our earthly days; and at the same time we collaborate in another work, in another opus, which infinitely transcends, while at the same time it narrowly determines, the perspectives of our individual achievement: the completing of the world.[2]   —*Pierre Teilhard de Chardin*

May this practice, this intention, this seed of realization, take root in us all and lead us into greater freedom, generosity, and change, culminating in a new human order: a civilization with a heart![3]   —*Wayne Teasdale*

MAN, WOMAN, AND LANGUAGE

First, let us begin with an editorial note on gender language: Traditionally, "monk" or "monastic" can be used to refer to both men and women contemplatives, and we use it throughout the book in a gender-neutral sense. We make use of both personal pronouns "she" and "he" throughout the book, staying consistent within individual paragraphs. Finally, you will see a number of quotations from other authors. Many of these authors wrote in a time before sensitivity and understanding of the gender bias inherent in much of our language arose. We have chosen for the most part not to change the original words of those authors, e.g., substituting "[Human]" for "Man." There are a number of reasons for this. The lesser reason is stylistic, as reading passages constantly splattered with brackets can take away from one's experience of what is being expressed. A more important reason is a hesitation to change an original author's words, which can lessen their transmission, even if they are writing with an unknown and unseen bias.

Another important reason is a potential negative side effect, that of hiding the *real* problem, which is that most of the theological and philosophical frameworks we have inherited reflect the masculine experience of the world. Changing "Man" to "Human" does nothing to change this, and we must own up to the fact that woman's experience of the world is not always reflected in these frameworks. Even the great women mystics, St. Teresa of Avila or Julian of Norwich, still interpreted their experience and wrote their treatises within the framework of Christian theology, the vast majority of which was developed by men and hence reflects the masculine experience of the world.

We mention this at our Beginnings because we feel that articulating frameworks that speak specifically to a woman's journey is one of the most important undertakings in our contemporary age. To have women express their own paths, in their own language, and to be able to compare notes and build on the experience of other women, is a great gift for us all. To give but one example of this, Beverly Lanzetta's *Radical Wisdom: A Feminist Mystical Theology* recounts the spiritual journey from a woman's perspective, speaking of a path she dubs the *via feminina* which has its own particularities, including a "dark night of the feminine"—an apophatic process (or way of negation) that allows the feminine to free itself from the conceptual frameworks of the world, many of which inflict a subtle violence deep in women's souls. We are also very encouraged by the work of V. K. Harber and her practical rearticulation of new monasticism from a feminist perspective in her booklet "New Monasticism: A Feminist's Perspective on an Engaged Contemplative Life."[4]

We fully support and actively encourage this emergence. To it, we humbly offer our hearts, prayers, and gratitude for its bounty, a blessing to us all on our journey into a more mature humanity.

WHY "NEW MONASTICS?"

"The monk is a lay person. . . . An order of monastics is essentially a lay order. Some monks may live in monasteries, but increasingly the majority will live in their own homes or form small communities—a monastic order in the world."[5] These words were spoken by the Catholic monk Bede Griffiths toward the end of his life. He went on to express a new vision for monastics, one in which communities and individuals live spiritual lives independent of religious organizations or institutions, independent of celibacy and overarching rules and dogmas—free to follow their own conscience and guidance of the Holy Spirit in living a sacred life, yet united in the common cause of building a sacred world. We envision these "new monastic" lives as being fully engaged in contemporary life, involved in relationships, exploring new ways of walking the spiritual path, and committed to sacred activism. Father Bede goes on to describe these monastic orders in the world:

> Some communities may remain very loose, some may become very close. Each one has to evolve as the Spirit moves it. . . . We

must keep that freedom of the Spirit by learning from one another, coming together day by day and discerning . . . all in a growth process. . . . It is so easy to get into rules and organization and so to narrow the freedom of the Spirit. . . . It is by learning really to trust the Spirit, in our prayers and meditation, and to share this trust with one another that a new language will gradually form . . . Social action should flow from our contemplation. It should not be a sideline or something inherently different, but should be integrated in our prayer and meditation . . . unless meditation is fed by concern with people's problems and the world's problems it loses its depth. There is no rivalry between contemplation and action.[6]

Father Bede compares these communities to those of the Sufis, practitioners of the mystical branch of Islam, who are often married, have families, and are deeply engaged in the world, organized in communities which help them to live from the depth of their commitment to contemplative life.

Our book is a rallying call for these new types of spiritual life and community, lives that are dedicated to building a sacred world through commitment to one's spiritual maturity, to the growth of community life, and to living out these values while fully engaged in the world. As we will find throughout our book, "in the world" can be many different things, but at its heart lies a passionate embrace for the transformation of our societal, political, and religious structures. This book is meant to help build a foundation for this movement, offering the beginnings of a theological, philosophical, and contemplative understanding to its underpinnings while at the same time providing concrete methodologies and injunctions for its praxis. It hopes to distinguish itself from many New Age spiritualities corrupted with shallow and narcissistic tendencies, humbly placing itself in partnership and collaborative discernment with our time-honored religious traditions.

It also stands as an authentic expression of our own experience of the path, opening up a vision which cuts across humanity's wisdom and religious traditions, bringing us into the midst of something new, a revelatory impulse of the Spirit that as of yet has no home. While embedded within our wisdom and religious traditions, it is beholden to none, and encompasses modern scientific and psychological truths, sociological and cultural insights, and political and economic realities. We have named this movement *new monasticism*.

By monasticism, we mean simply to denote a level of commitment to one's spiritual life. What does it mean to be a monastic, after all? It is not necessarily one's particular beliefs that make one a monastic. For instance, differing religious traditions have varying beliefs on the nature of reality. Nor is it one's lifestyle. Hindu monks often are committed to solitude without an emphasis on cultivating community, while Christian monks most often practice and live in communities. Even celibacy is not a defining feature. Sufis, Hasidim, and some Zen monks and Tibetan Buddhist lamas marry and have families, while Christian and Hindu monks remain celibate. What does link all monastics, however, is a total life commitment to the development and maturation of one's spiritual life. We will explore this in detail in the upcoming Manifesto as the archetype of the monk.

Monastic, then, represents for us a complete commitment to the transformative journey, and we use the term with that specified meaning. This is a journey which takes us into the fullness of our humanity, allowing divinity to flower within us in increasing degrees of love, compassion, joy, sorrow, and wisdom. The monastic is the one who devotes his or her life to this ideal, and allows all life decisions to flow out of this commitment. The root of the word *monk* is *monachos*, which means "set apart." For us, this is not so much a physical separation as a setting oneself apart from our cultural conditioning—from an unquestioning, and *un-questing*, view of life, one that drives us to adulate material success, seduces us into participating in the devastation of our planet, hardens our hearts to the plight of the poor and oppressed, and divorces us from our innate capacity for spiritual growth and maturity.

By new, we refer to the phenomenon of living out this spiritual vocation in the world. This means that one's spiritual journey is inextricably linked to the day-to-day reality of most people's lives—and in an evolutionary sense, to moving our human family into greater depth and maturity. We have found that many people today are feeling the same deep calling as the monks of old, a calling of complete commitment to the transformative journey, yet without the urge to act out this calling in the traditional way. They do not find themselves necessarily drawn to a monastery, or to celibacy, or to disengagement and liberation *from* the world. They instead feel a radical urge to live out this calling *in* the world—to be embedded in the world, with the hardship of financial realities, the ups and downs of political unrest, the blessings and difficulties of relationships—all in the midst of a contemporary society that does not support such a calling. It adds a level of complexity to the monastic vocation, perhaps many levels. Yet those of us who feel this calling could never do otherwise, for deep in our souls we know that our journey to wholeness lies in bringing the radical profundity and divine, transformative energy of our paths firmly into the world.

Raimon Panikkar, one of the greatest intermystical theologians of the twentieth century, from whom we will be hearing much in the pages ahead, has called this a movement from simplicity through renunciation to simplicity through integration.[7] Rather than renouncing the world, the new monastic wishes to transform it. The world is no longer something that can be used merely as a stepping-stone to one's own enlightenment; instead, the transformation of the world itself is given an equal ontological status to one's own. In other words, this new way sees one's spiritual path inextricably linked with the transformation of our global community into a connected, mature, and harmonious whole.

Perhaps even more radically, the new monastic may or may not be drawn permanently into a particular religious tradition. While certainly open to embracing a single religious tradition, this new way also allows for the emergence of untrodden paths, where the boundaries among the traditions become porous, yet not without meaning. Our traditions are seen as a common inheritance for humanity, each with its own integrity, yet also belonging to a universal heritage of human wisdom. They offer us guidance and skill sets with which we may look into our own interiors, and revelations as to what those interiors hold. At their best, they are a storehouse of wisdom for the human family, cartographers of the individual and collective souls of humanity. The wisdom traditions that have been passed down through millennia are now intermingling with one another, as well as with modern science, psychology, sociology, and more. Within the play of tensions and synergies born through mutual interaction, new movements and complexified forms of religious consciousness are emerging.[8]

New monastics may find themselves using tools and techniques from varying religious traditions, not in a haphazard, idiosyncratic way, but in a way that emerges through inner guidance, led by the Spirit and in discernment with their mentors and community. They may find that they no longer belong to one tradition but have become an inner experiment of the merging of various streams of wisdom and emergent, revelatory understandings. These then become intimately related to their vocation in the world. In all of this, their commitment to the transformative journey remains as firm as the commitment that has driven the traditional monk for millennia.

Finally, a note on the word *interspiritual*, of which we will hear much more of in our section on "Interspirituality" in Movement 2. The term was first introduced by Brother Wayne Teasdale, a lay Catholic monk who was also ordained as a Christian sannyasi (an ascetical monk in the Hindu tradition),[9] and refers to a new spiritual movement that has been made possible by the incipient emergence of a connected, global cultural milieu. Interspirituality plants us firmly outside of a fundamentalist adherence to our own particular religious tradition or spiritual path, demanding that we take seriously the revelations, realizations, and contemplative gifts of all authentic wisdom and religious traditions, as well as insights from science, ecology, art, culture, and sociology. It recognizes the potential for human spiritual growth and maturity, and allows for the diverse ways that human beings, at their best, have cultivated tools to accelerate that growth process. It acknowledges unique transmissions of wisdom and divine attributes among the traditions, and opens up the possibility for us to make use of these collective streams in new and unforeseen ways. It puts a premium on a reciprocal sharing of these gifts in ways that change those who participate in the process. As such, it can lead to renewals and transformations of the religious traditions themselves.

We believe interspirituality also offers a framework that can be embraced by a new generation of spiritual seekers who have grown estranged from traditional religious frameworks, while also allowing for the wisdom of our spiritual traditions to be passed on. As we will see, interspirituality allows for a diversity of spiritual paths and religious understandings and for intimate communities to be built within, and embodied by, that diversity. Rather than separating ourselves according to our religious beliefs, traditions, or particular spiritual practices, we can build communities that center around this reciprocal sharing of gifts and support for one another's vocations in the world.

All of this will be further developed extensively as we continue our journey into new monasticism.

NEW MONASTICS' RELATIONSHIP WITH TRADITIONAL MONASTICISM

There is a tremendous value in traditional monastic life, and new monasticism is not meant to supplant it. These communities, made up of those called to lives of retreat, silence, and solitude, incarnate sacred space for all of us. As we look at those monasteries that offer retreat space for outsiders, such as St. Benedict's Monastery in Snowmass, Colorado (where Father Thomas Keating resides), Sky Farm Hermitage of Peace in Sonoma, California, or New Camaldoli Hermitage in Big Sur, California, one is struck by their popularity. In many cases one may have to reserve a year in advance in order to find retreat space. These sacred spaces are sought out because of the great purpose they serve in furthering the transformative journey for people, offering others a chance to imbue the quiet, peace, and energetic support manifested by the prayerful lives of traditional monks. Brother Francis Ali and Sister Michaela Terrio, hermits of Sky Farm Hermitage, follow the Hesychastic tradition and see their vocation as protecting the silence so others may come and drink from its well. They often quote St. Isaac of Syria, a seventh-century hermit monk, who said, "If you love truth, be a lover of silence. Silence, like the sunlight, will illuminate you in God."

Father Thomas Keating recently remarked during a visit to his monastery on the importance of a community of people who are living the life of retreat, essentially a traditional monastic life, at these places in order to nurture the sacred space for those who come. Without a community of monks, the container for silence, solitude, deep inner longing, and transformative experience is in danger of being lost, and these places could cease to serve the important need we all have for them. Anyone who is seriously engaged in the transformative journey knows the fundamental importance of spending time in retreat.

Therefore, the "new" part of new monasticism does not refer to a rejection of traditional monasticism. It emphasizes rather the existential fact that one's own spiritual journey is caught up with "the completing of the world," Pierre Teilhard de Chardin's powerful expression:

> By our fidelity we must *build*—starting with the most natural territory of our own self—a work, an *opus*, into which something enters from all the elements of the earth. *We make our own soul* throughout all our earthly days; and at the same time we collaborate in another work, in another *opus*, which infinitely transcends, while at the same time it narrowly determines, the perspectives of our individual achievement: the completing of the world.[10]

We are called to serve this completing of the world in various ways; for some monastics this is in a monastery, for others it is in the world. Teilhard tells us it is this completing of the world, that infinitely transcending greater opus, which "narrowly determines" our vocation.

This completing of the world requires the sacred spaces created by traditional monastic life, spaces that can offer those of us called to more direct engagement with the world "renewing baptismal waters." In any new monastic formation deep retreats are essential to one's journey. It follows that a traditional monastic life can be, and will be, an authentic calling that a new monastic may also embrace.

In other words, as one undergoes formation in new monastic life it may be discerned that one has a vocation for the life of a traditional monastic, that is, a full life of retreat, prayer, and solitude dedicated to the transformative journey. In addition, one may discern a particular calling to become a Catholic monk, or a Buddhist monk, or a Hindu monk, etc. In all of these cases this vocation, when discerned in clarity and faith, is to be wholeheartedly embraced, acknowledged, supported, and encouraged by one's new monastic formation. From our perspective, there will always be a need for the vocation of traditional monasticism, for a life of retreat, solitude, and prayer, often in community. For some this may be a calling for a period of years, for others it can be a lifetime commitment.

New monastics aim to support and create sustainability for traditional monasticism, engendering a reciprocal partnership between those called to traditional monastic life and those called to a new monastic life lived out in the world. Recall that by monastic we mean a complete commitment to the transformative journey. In fact, we feel that new monastic formation can actually help to create viable and strong candidates for traditional monasticism. A close friendship and dialogue between traditional monasticism and new monasticism is important and can help to authenticate and transform both vocations so that they may serve as coequal partners in this greater opus.

We also envision the formation of nontraditional monastic communities, such as an interspiritual monastic community composed of Catholic, Buddhist, and Hindu monks, or a community of those walking more nontraditional paths (we will hear of one such path in the pages ahead, an interspiritual path) who are called to lives of retreat, solitude, and prayer. Likely as well are communities composed of those walking traditional paths together with those walking more nontraditional ways. In all of these cases there are substantial difficulties to overcome, including tensions from the lack of a shared theological view and differences in spiritual practice. However, they also hold out tremendous potential for synergistic breakthroughs (as creative tension always provides), and serve to diminish an over-identification with one's particular theological framework or spiritual practice. These interspiritual monasteries could also serve as incarnate manifestations of a unity that underlies all religious, theological, and spiritual perspectives, without diminishing the diversity of praxis and spiritual realization that exists. As such, they become beacons, symbols, and signifiers of that unity.

Hence, we strive for a seamlessness between traditional monastic life and new monastic life, not a separation. They are interdependent and reciprocal, both founded on a dedication to the transformative journey and to how that journey may best serve the whole. In this vision there is no spiritually speaking higher calling, where traditional monastic life is the one which truly embodies a dedication to the transformative journey. Rather, there is only uniqueness, partnership, a universal sisterhood and brotherhood, working in mutual reciprocity and support of one another and united in the same goal, the completing of the world.

THE HEART OF NEW MONASTIC LIFE:
SPIRITUAL PRAXIS

New monasticism is not just a theoretical concept. It is an orientation in life, a commitment that asks us to bring every aspect of our lives into a living relationship with God, with the Spirit, with the Buddha Nature-Mind, with one's deepest self. It is a life lived with That Which Is, Ultimate Reality, consciously at the center of everything one does. "Who is a monk?" asks Brother David Steindl-Rast, answering, "If the first thing you think of when you wake up in the morning is God, you are a monk!"

New monasticism is also a discipline, a certain ascetical way of being that allows us to reorient ourselves by making all that we are available to the Divine, so the work of transformation can happen. We look to become the hands of God doing the work of healing in this world, where the Spirit takes hold of us and lives through us.

This kind of life requires structure and commitment to spiritual practice. It is for this reason that many Fathers and Mothers of the fourth century left the world and embraced a disciplined life of being with God. It is for this reason Prince Siddhartha Gautama left his privileged life and family and subjected himself to stringent disciplines in his search for truth. It is for this reason that monasteries have specific schedules that allow monastics to flow through the day making the transformative journey the centerpiece of their lives. And it is for this reason that people called to new monasticism have to adopt specific disciplines of prayer and service. Without this kind of a commitment our highest calling remains stubbornly theoretical and imaginary. With it we can allow our deeper nature to emerge, within which profound change can take place. We move from a self-centered way of being to other-centered life.

Rather than wait until the end of our book to put forth specific suggestions for daily practice, we wish to emphasize the importance of a disciplined life at the beginning, so that what is found here can and should be kept in mind throughout the book. Without the disciplined structure that a mature spiritual life demands, new monasticism remains but an ephemeral dream—beautiful, soaring, and inspiring, but ultimately fleeting. With an embodiment of disciplined spiritual praxis, described here as the heart of new monastic life, it becomes incarnational.

If we accept the definition of praxis as the process by which a theory, lesson, or skill is enacted, embodied, or realized, what is a new monastic's spiritual praxis? How does one live in a way that makes new monastic life a reality? What are some of the specific disciplines that one needs to commit to?

Before discussing particular disciplines, it is important to note what we outline here is an entry point to new monastic life. Practices change as one becomes more attuned to the Divine. The goal of these practices is to create a structure and container within which maturity can unfold and grace can descend. Once that begins to happen, the practice, the schedule, and the commitment can evolve. These practices are meant to prepare us for an experience of being in the depths of who we are. When we can recognize the presence of Ultimate Reality in our lives, our practices become modified. They change to accommodate the uniqueness of our relationship with the Divine so that we may live as a direct response to the guidance revealed in our hearts. Just as there are many stages that one passes through in one's spiritual life, so also are there many stages that one grows into in one's practice.

What then, does the spiritual praxis of a new monastic look like?

Daily Practice

A new monastic may start her day with a morning prayer and silent, meditative practice. These are usually modified based on one's vocation, commitments in the world, and availability. Nonetheless, one always starts with prayer. For people who live in communities, it may start as a group activity. Others may follow their unique way of centering and recommitting to a life of surrender and trust, consciously bringing that intention into activities such as a morning walk (preferably in nature), spiritual reading, or absorbing the morning with silent reflection. Some new monastics may start with a ritual of body prayer, bringing integration and wholeness into their practice after the night's sleep. Yogic asanas, tai chi, breath work, conscious weightlifting, prostrations can allow all aspects of one's being, heart, feelings, thoughts, breath, and body to come together. This is done so that whatever follows can be approached and experienced with openness on all levels, preparing us for the infusion of grace to penetrate not just our mind and heart, but our body as well.

After these types of integrating practice, a new monastic moves into silent practice. As a precursor to silent practice, a new monastic first engages the heart. This happens uniquely based on one's spiritual orientation. It may be a practice of talking to God and feeling God present in the room, opening every aspect of one's heart and sharing it as if God was there, ready to embrace us as a best friend would. It may be a practice of formal prayer. Some may choose to say the prayer of Saint Francis. Others may choose the process of centering and opening by saying the prayer of abandonment by Charles de Foucauld. Many choose to start with a traditional practice of *lectio divina,* or divine reading, where they read holy verses not for information but for inspiration, allowing their hearts to be touched by the spirit of the text and opened to grace. Some may start with a chant. Others may generate compassion for all sentient beings, seeing each as precious pearls caught in the cycle of suffering. Or perhaps one may simply hold one's heart, feeling it in the hollow of God's hand, holding the world with tenderness, mercy, and love. Each soul may have a different way of moving into this silence, surrender, and trust.

What follows then is a silent practice. Different traditions and contemplative orders have developed varying techniques to help people move into, and through, the silence. While their methodologies differ, most agree that silent contemplative practice is foundational to spiritual transformation. In general, silent practices can be divided into two different kinds: concentrative practices and receptive practices. Concentrative practices require us to concentrate on one specific thing. It could be breath or a short prayer, such as a mantra or the Jesus Prayer, or even the nature of reality. These methods often require a certain amount of training and direction from a teacher. Receptive methods have as a goal to put us in a state of openness, where we are simply in a state of receptivity, listening, and consent to God's presence and action in us and among us. For aspiring new monastics, we recommend starting with a receptive method, and then finding a spiritual director who can help one discern a proper silent practice. One powerful receptive method is Centering Prayer, as developed by Thomas Keating, William Meninger, and Basil Pennington.

In order to build a solid foundation for new monastic life, one should practice in a formal way twice a day. It's good to start with twenty minutes of silence twice a day and slowly over time expand the practice to up to an hour or more for each session. It is helpful to set a timer so that one doesn't need to worry about keeping track of time (many smart phones have apps for this, such as a Centering Prayer app or a mindfulness meditation app). As our overall practice evolves, silent practice often tends to grow in conjunction with this. It is important to remember the words of many meditation masters, such as Father Thomas Keating, to the effect that it is none of your business what happens during meditation. It is God's business. These words help us to put in perspective what prayer life is all about. *It is not about accomplishing anything,* but it is about slowly growing and maturing into who we truly are. Particularly in receptive practices, we are not here to become technicians and masters of a specific technique. We are here to make ourselves available to the work of healing, transformation, and divinization—to consent to the process.

In concluding silent practice, one may again choose to end with a prayer or intention, offering one's practice as a blessing to all beings or reflecting on one's new monastic orientation in life. Some people may also choose to finish their morning meditation with a reading or a recitation of their vows. We will talk about specific new monastic vows toward the end of this chapter. Again, this silent routine, allowing for some variation, should be repeated twice a day.

What other practices should a new monastic incorporate into the day? As we mentioned before, to be a new monastic is to have a very specific orientation in life. It is to live and walk in the presence of God, in the reality of the perfectly manifesting mind of the Buddha. It is to be mindful and pay attention to the sacredness of now. To do that, we all need practices that can help us to live in that awareness of Presence. We started with two periods of formal prayer, but we need more than that. We need additional practices until we become naturally and spontaneously "in" our practice at every moment of our day. Then we are given the grace to live as an expression of yes to God at all times. Only then does our practice disappear and Wisdom manifest as not other than our life. To do this, while we recommend silent practice to everyone, we also recommend additional daily practices based on one's temperament and spiritual style, and including a mix of intellectual stimulation and bodily integration.

The first such additional practice is *lectio divina*. It is an ancient practice, first established formally as a monastic practice in the sixth century by St. Benedict. Lectio is a prayerful way of reading a sacred text or the words of a spiritual master for inspiration, not information. We can always carry with us short sacred passages that we like to revisit during the day. Whenever we have a moment of time between our daily tasks, we can approach them with the heart and be present to them. In the process, we will be recentered and reoriented toward our new monastic commitments. The soul of the text can touch the deepest core of who we are and open our daily experience to the Spirit. [11]

Another practice is the "prayer of the name," or a mantra practice. This has been used by many contemplative orders of all traditions. In the Hindu tradition it is said that this practice is the most effective practice for our present times. It consists of consistently repeating a name of the Divine or a *mantra*, and helps us to remain in an awareness of the Divine at all times. This practice grows over time in depth and power. As one Sufi teacher has described it: "It is said that remembrance of God begins with the repetition of God's Names by the tongue. Then, the repetition of the tongue descends and becomes the remembrance of the heart. Finally, the remembrance of the heart deepens and becomes the remembrance of the soul. At first, you chant the Divine Names, then they chant themselves, and then God chants through you."[12]

Another simple but powerful daily practice is taking breaks from one's day, perhaps stopping by a personal sanctuary, to share moments in silence with God or in silent meditation. One new monastic formed by the Catholic tradition enjoys stopping to pray in front of the Blessed Sacrament, others may stop by a mosque and engage in traditional prayers that re-center them in Allah five times a day, Buddhists may program the mindfulness clock on their smart phone, following the formula of Thích Nhat Hanh, to stop for a few breaths of mindfulness every hour of the day. Many will just take moments to stare consciously up at the sky, to relate to a tree or nearby flower, to take in the stars at night, or simply to watch in a heartfelt, reflective way the vast movements of human beings on the streets of the city. Consistency and repetition are the keys with these practices. They create moments which remind us and connect us to the much greater task we are immersed in, beyond the daily concerns, frustrations, sorrows and joys of life, that of our spiritual transformation and the mysterious completing of the world.

Weekly, Monthly, and Yearly Practices

In addition to these daily practices, it is also good to have a few weekly rituals and practices. If a new monastic is part of a faith community, this can often happen in gathering with the community once a week for communal prayer. It is also highly encouraged to participate in dialogical dialogue, a methodology which will be explained more fully in our section on "Dialogical Dialogue" in Movement 2. Many new monastics are also part of self-organizing small groups that gather once a week for prayerful silence and heartfelt conversation, at times followed by the sharing of a meal or a ritual celebration. These practices create space where friends and companions on the journey can be present to one another, reaffirming their vocations, path, and commitment.

New monastics are also encouraged to incorporate an extended day of practice once a week. This could be an extended meditation day, a day of mostly silence spent in nature, spiritual reading and reflection, or perhaps a day of fasting and prayer. This is in the tradition of a "Sabbath" day, a day to deepen our practice, to take a break from the worries and hectic pace of daily life, and to keep our daily commitment to practice strong while enhancing our lives with contemplative grace for the week. For those with children this can be a particularly difficult practice to undertake. If there are two parents, then one can take a day with the children while the other has their "Sabbath" day, and the next week they can switch, or each could take half a day. Being creative and overcoming obstacles to our practice is part of the work of deepening our discipline and commitment.

Following daily and weekly practices, there are also monthly and yearly practices that new monastics need to adopt. We recommend that each month, one develop what some contemplatives call a desert day or a desert weekend. It is a day or weekend when one completely lets go of everything, enters silence, at times fasts, and dedicates one's energies to the practice of contemplative prayer and reflection. One could spend a weekend each month in the silence of a monastery. Others might do a home retreat. Still others like to do a directed retreat. They enter into silence and perhaps once a day can have a session with a spiritual guide, often via Skype, for prayerful conversation.

Finally, it is highly recommended that each year a new monastic go on an extended retreat. The length and nature of these retreats should be determined through prayer and discernment, often done with one's spiritual director and contemplative community. The goal of these yearly retreats is to immerse ourselves in our practice, following the maxims of early desert Fathers and Mothers who said, "Enter your hermitage. Your hermitage will teach you everything." Whether we are literally entering a hermitage for a period of extended silence or simply cultivating the hermitage within our hearts, an extended retreat each year makes it possible for us to go deeper in our life of prayer and service. It is also a wonderful time to learn or develop certain practices that we have felt called to in the *praxis* of our spiritual lives.

In addition to these foundational practices, we also recommend an integration of the following: Sacred Activism: The Spiritual Practice of Vocation; Formal Study; Shadow Work; Spiritual Direction; Spiritual Friendship and Community; and a Commitment to Vows. Here we offer an introduction to each of these, and all will be developed more fully throughout the course of our book.

Sacred Activism: The Spiritual Practice of Vocation

Archbishop Desmond Tutu once said, "Just as we are all meant to be contemplatives and to hear the voice of God in our lives, we are all meant to answer God's call to be His partners in transfiguring the world. This calling, this encounter with God, is always to send us into the midst of human suffering."[13]

Every new monastic is here to bridge the dichotomy of contemplation and action in what Andrew Harvey calls *Sacred Activism*. Harvey tells us, "I've always loved that quotation by French Jesuit Teilhard de Chardin: 'Someday, after mastering the winds, the waves, the tides, and gravity, we shall harness for God the energies of love, and then, for a second time in the history of the world, man will have discovered fire.' Sacred activism is the fusion of the mystic's passion for God with the activist's passion for justice, creating a third fire, which is the burning sacred heart that longs to help, preserve, and nurture every living thing."[14]

Following this mandate to be both a contemplative and an activist, a new monastic seeks to discover one's calling, or one's *vocation*, and to develop talents and put them to use in service of compassion and justice. He or she understands that one's vocation is a unique way of touching Ultimate Reality and bringing divine life into the world. Together, we can fulfill humanity's calling within a greater Kosmic community (we will follow Ken Wilber's use of the holistic term, *Kosmos*, defined in note 15, throughout this book).[15]

In this grand sense, the new monastic is always an activist and an agent for social change. He or she is always engaged in vocation, in building of the Kingdom of Heaven, in completing the world one friendship and one institution at a time.

Formal Study

Especially in these times, when most spiritual seekers learn about spirituality through a series of disconnected workshops, clichéd phrases, and personal tastes, it is important for each new monastic to commit to formal study. Simply said, there is no mature new monasticism without proper formation and training. Traditionally, study took place in the form of individualized study and mentorship with a teacher. We highly recommend the continuation of this practice with a spiritual guide. For many, study happens through a formal commitment under the guidance of a mentor, who helps to develop what the course of study should be. In time, as one grows to recognize the impulse of the Spirit within, he or she may graduate to more inner-directed forms of study. However, in the beginning a program of study under the direction of an authentic mentor is highly recommended.

As such, many new monastics may choose to follow a more traditional form of study by either entering a seminary or a contemplative order such as the Sufi International Order and their training program, Suluk, or by committing to a new monastic training program through the Foundation for New Monasticism. These programs help formalize the process, yet also individualize training, maintaining flexibility and discernment of one's vocation and what that requires. The Foundation for New Monasticism offers individual mentorship, yearly retreats, help with new monastic formation and interspiritual study, and vocational discernment and support, all in partnership with traditional contemplative orders and wisdom traditions.

Shadow Work

As we will stress in earnest in Movement 4, all new monastics must take into account the insights and revelations of modern Western psychology, and in particular an understanding of the *shadow*. The shadow will be explained more fully in its own section in Movement 4, but suffice it to say that it consists of the dark parts of our personality that have been repressed and which formed through an unhealthy integration of various levels of emotional, cognitive, and spiritual development. It is one of the main culprits in sabotaging an integrated and mature spirituality, and therefore an understanding of and working with one's shadow is a primary practice for the new monastic. There are many techniques developed to work with one's shadow, particularly dream work (the interpretation of one's dreams) and psychotherapy.

Without shadow work many practitioners become victims of what John Wellwood calls "spiritual bypass," where we use spiritual ideas and practices to avoid facing unresolved emotional issues, psychological wounds, and unfinished developmental tasks. Speaking of this need for an integration of authentic psychological insights with contemplative practice, Wellwood says that "we need a larger perspective that can recognize and include two different tracks of human development—which we might call growing up and waking up, healing and awakening, or becoming a genuine human person and going beyond the person altogether." He concludes that "We are not just humans learning to become Buddhas, but also Buddhas waking up in human form, learning to become fully human. And these two tracks of development can mutually enrich each other."[16]

Spiritual Direction

Since many new monastics follow a fairly individualized path, spiritual direction becomes crucial, a sine qua non of this orientation in life. We recommend contact with a spiritual director at least once a month, and at certain times much more than that. Nowadays, these relationships can also be cultivated via Skype.

Meetings with one's spiritual director are prayerful in nature, with the director being present to what is alive in her or his mentee's spiritual life, naming movements of Spirit within, and helping the mentee to become open and sensitive to different textures of guidance. A spiritual director is not primarily a teacher or a guru per se. Rather, he or she is primarily a spiritual companion, a *kalyanamitra, anam cara* or soul friend on the path of the heart. Spiritual directors help to locate mentees in the truth of their life and give them a dangerous permission to follow it with dedication. Spiritual directors also help to develop the gift of discernment and can give much-needed encouragement during dark times, encouragement that only one who has passed down a similar road before can offer. One should always keep in mind the words of Father Thomas Keating: "The best direction aims at enabling or empowering the directee to graduate to the more refined and delicate guidance of the Spirit in all matters. The director becomes a fellow traveler and friend on the journey, and the directee and director speak the truth to each other in love. Speaking just the truth can be too harsh. Speaking the truth in love is mutually sustaining."[17]

There are many roads into spiritual direction. Some relationships are more formal, with structured contemplative prayer, conversation, and guidance. Other relationships are less formal, perhaps even unspoken, yet there is a mutual recognition of guidance and spiritual direction. At times there may be only a premonition, a faint attraction of our being to another, a whispering in our hearts. The new monastic commits to following up on these auspicious encounters, to pay attention to the synchronistic happenings of life, and to cultivating discerning relationships with those who may in time become our spiritual directors. The new monastic recognizes the deeper order and auguries of life, graciously welcoming its gratuitous signs and working in synergy with its continual unfoldment.

Spiritual Friendship and Community

One final formal practice, but perhaps the most important, is the practice of spiritual friendship. There is an apocryphal story to be recounted again in the upcoming Manifesto. Ananda asks the Buddha, "Dear Buddha, is spiritual friendship half of the journey to enlightenment?" The Buddha replies, "No, Ananda, it is the *whole* of the journey."

For the new monastic, the interdependent relationship between spiritual friendship and one's personal practice creates the container for one's spiritual growth. It is the basis of our relationship with mentors and fellow wayfarers on the path. New monastics create community. In some cases they choose to live in communities. New monastic communities are like organisms where friends on the journey meet to share their lives with each other. They share in contemplative prayer, sacred reading, heartfelt reflection, discernment of authenticity, friendship, and celebration. In the process, they begin to discover a divine loving presence and action in their lives. Their task is to offer each other support and spiritual friendship so we can have the courage to say yes to what is emerging in us, so that our lives can become an expression of our new monastic commitment in the world. We will hear much more about spiritual friendship, particularly in the context of mentorship, and new monastic communities throughout the book.

A Commitment of Vows

It takes practice and commitment for the new monastic to incarnate a space of grace in his or her life, a space to follow the guidance of the Spirit, build relationships with mentors, and form community. Vows can be powerful tools for our remembrance of that space of grace. In addition to formalizing our commitment to a new monastic life, vows tap into a yet-unmentioned dimension of our Kosmos, a powerful dimension of dynamic energies which express themselves in ceremonial and ritualistic fashion.

New monastic vows represent our deepest intentions for life, named and formalized so that we may remember them. While not all new monastics take formal vows, our recommendation for those we mentor is that one works toward taking vows, in increasing gradations and sobriety, as one's ability to commit to the longings in the heart matures. Similar to traditional monastic training, these vows emerge in stages, with each subsequent commitment marking a turning point on one's journey. The road to a final, solemn profession of vows may last five years or more, while one may take novitiate vows fairly early in one's formation. The set of vows we recommend for new monastic life are ones inspired by the words and commitment of our mentor Brother Wayne Teasdale. These simple yet profound professions capture the essence of the new monastic way of life. For those who are moved to take these vows, one may choose to repeat them each day during the morning period of contemplative prayer, or perhaps revisit them on a weekly basis. We also encourage new monastics to devote a monthly "desert day" or a yearly retreat to deep reflection on what these vows are asking of us at this particular stage of our journey and in the details of our lives.

These new monastic vows are the following: [18]

1. I vow to actualize and live according to my full moral and ethical capacity.

2. I vow to live in solidarity with the cosmos and all living beings.

3. I vow to live in deep nonviolence.

4. I vow to live in humility and to remember the many teachers and guides who assisted me on my spiritual path.

5. I vow to embrace a daily spiritual practice.

6. I vow to cultivate mature self-knowledge.

7. I vow to live a life of simplicity.

8. I vow to live a life of selfless service and compassionate action.

9. I vow to be a prophetic voice as I work for justice, compassion, and world transformation.

The essence of each vow above will be explored more fully in our section "The Nine Elements of Spiritual Maturity" in Movement 4.

THE BOOK AND THE MANIFESTO

The short manifesto, by a similar name to this book, "New Monasticism: An Interspiritual Manifesto for Contemplative Life in the 21st Century" (previously and henceforth known as the *Manifesto*), was written in the summer of 2012. It was originally commissioned as a guiding document for a weeklong dialogue with Father Thomas Keating and others on new monasticism that took place at St. Benedict's Monastery in Snowmass, Colorado, that year. Since then, we have continued to hold dialogues with Father Keating on a yearly basis, exploring the themes of this emerging movement.

The guiding document quickly began to morph into something more than a small outline for discussion, and became the beginnings of our collaborative articulation of an emergent vision for spiritual life in the twenty-first century. Much of what the two of us had been discussing over the course of the previous two years poured forth. These discussions were inherently dialogical, where we felt that our interactions actually began to evoke the Divine in our midst, clarified the resonance between our own individual paths, and brought to light differences in our orientations to—and expressions of—the Path. This led to further synergistic emergences that fed off each other's insights, complementing and in many ways completing our individual expressions. We began not only to talk about dialogical emergences, unique gifts, and unity in diversity, but to live their realities in our own emerging spiritual friendship. As we surveyed the contemporary spiritual milieu, we felt the need for a new expression of spiritual life, one that we were beginning to understand in a more universal context through our shared interaction. What first emerged out of this process was the Manifesto, which is reprinted in this book in whole in Movement 1.

The Manifesto was then posted online by Sufi teacher Llewellyn Vaughan-Lee, who subsequently informed us that after only one day there had been over a thousand downloads of the document. It continued to go viral, and we began to receive emails from monks, nuns, hermits, academics, and young people who felt that it named something for them— something they had been living and that was emerging in their hearts, yet needed to be named in order to be acknowledged. Several spiritual elders from different traditions offered us help and support as we continued to work on structures that could assist young people on their transformative journey. Jamie Manson at *National Catholic Reporter* did a three-part series on it, a Catholic monastery in Berkeley, California, featured it in one of their newsletters, and we were asked to speak on it at numerous conferences and churches.

We realized that there was a deep resonance with the spirit of the Manifesto. We received many questions regarding the specifics and practicality of the vision, as well as how an actual spiritual path based on the vision might look. This book is in many ways an efflorescence of those questions and insights, instrumental in helping us to clarify the vision. It represents a significant development of the impulse from which the Manifesto was born, an organic emergence in dialogue with those who sometimes asked difficult questions. One of the most extensive dialogues it began was with traditional wisdom paths and religious traditions, revolving around the question of how—or even if—one can walk a mature spiritual path without being embedded in a religious tradition.

A dialogue of particular interest was begun by Pir Zia Inayat-Khan (whose father, Pir Villayat Inayat Khan, was a well-known Sufi teacher, and whose grandfather, Hazrat Inayat Khan, was the articulator of a universal Sufism that explicitly included other religious traditions). Pir Zia sent a letter to Adam Bucko and Zachary Markwith, an Islamic and Sufi scholar and author of the book *One God, Many Prophets: the Universal Wisdom of Islam*. In it, Pir Zia offered a series of questions, and suggested the Manifesto as a starting point for dialogue. We thought we might listen in to that dialogue here, as an excellent entrance into a wider conversation. The full dialogue can be found at the Seven Pillars House of Wisdom website.[19] In his initial letter to Adam and Zachary, Pir Zia writes:

> We live today in a world in which almost all of the great spiritual traditions of the world are within reach of the modern seeker in some form.

This plethora of choices creates new questions. Should the seeker remain committed to the traditions and institutions of her ancestors? Should she, instead, study the various available traditions, and choose the one that speaks most meaningfully to her? Should she try to ascertain commonalities between the various traditions, and follow the principles and practices of more than one faith? Or should she abandon traditional forms and institutions altogether, and create her own worldview and practice? These, I believe, are questions that many young people are grappling with today. . . .

You clearly have in common a deep sense of the sacred, but it seems to me that you have quite different approaches to religion and tradition. I feel that a conversation between you could be very fruitful. It could help, I think, bring into focus the questions, problems, and opportunities that confront the modern seeker. . . .

Key questions in the discussion might include:

Tradition and change: How is "tradition" defined? What kinds of adaptations are legitimate? Who decides?

Esotericism and exotericism: Is orthodox exoteric observance a requirement for authentic access to the esoteric dimensions of a tradition? Is it possible to successfully practice multiple exoteric and/or esoteric traditions simultaneously? What is the relationship between the inner and outer layers of a faith?

And, individuality and community: Is an authentic sense of community, shared vision, and responsibility possible without tradition? Does tradition impose unacceptable limits on individual experience and discovery?

We will continue with Adam and Zachary's responses later in the book, at the beginning of Movement 2, following the Manifesto.

The book itself is composed of four movements, following our "Beginnings" here. Movement 1, in addition to reprinting the whole Manifesto, opens with an intimate portrait of one of our foundational elders and guides Brother Wayne Teasdale.

Movement 2 takes a more clear-eyed view at the underlying impulse of the Manifesto. It will open with a vista of our contemporary milieu, "A Global Mythos," then sections on "Interspirituality" and an emerging spiritual path that we have dubbed "An Interspiritual Path." We then offer sections on foundational methodologies for new monastic life:

"Dialogical Dialogue," "Dialogical Sophiology" (or how one builds an intellectual framework in dialogical relationship with the other), "Meditations on Vocation," and "New Monastic Communities."

Movement 3 is an extended dialogue between Rory and Adam that was recorded and edited. We believe it is of immense help in teasing out subtleties, giving context and texture for our narrative, and, perhaps most importantly, offers a sapiential taste of the dialogical methodologies we articulate, unveiling their evocative, creative, and emergent dimensions. In it, we discuss the thirty-year experiment originally convened by Father Thomas Keating known as the Snowmass Conference (or the Snowmass Interreligious Conference) and its subsequent evolution into the Snowmass Interspiritual Dialogue Fellowship. We then explore the dialogical nature of spiritual direction and mentorship, superpersonalization and the spiritual orientation of a new generation of seekers.

In Movement 4 we present a short overview of the spiritual path itself, following the work of Father Thomas Keating, Ken Wilber, and St. John of the Cross. In our development we pay particular attention to the unique challenges and potential graces of new monastic life, and offer a novel hypothesis on the importance of the "dark nights." We use insights of modern psychology and sociology to outline a spiritual path that concentrates on stages of development as opposed to the attainment of states of consciousness, while acknowledging the importance of the latter but focusing on the primacy of the former for new monastic life. We also look at the nine elements of spiritual maturity, which parallel the nine new monastic vows, and conclude with the consequences of an evolutionary perspective for one's spiritual path.

As for the collaborative nature of this book, it is a synergy of various gifts, friendship, and love. The formal process began with a series of dialogues between Rory and Adam recorded in Steamboat Springs, Colorado, in 2014. We then transcribed those dialogues and used the insights as guidelines, thereby embodying the evocative and dialogical nature of the process from the beginning. Rory wrote the sections "Remembrance," "A Global Mythos," "Interspirituality," "An Interspiritual Path," "Dialogical Dialogue," "Dialogical Sophiology," and Movement 4, with input and editing from Adam. The other sections are a collaboration of both Rory and Adam. "Meditations on Vocation" includes writing from both Adam and Rory as well numerous quotations from many sources. Rory collected these writings, edited them, and put them into their present form.

We believe it is the united voice which is so powerful, and in which we find a common resonance with so many others. Among us there lives something greater, more tender, and wiser, a higher (and deeper) power that situates us in our unique truth while uniting us in a grander and more grounded work, that greater opus of which we spoke. When we tap into that collaboratively, we just might find that it is Life that speaks.

MOVEMENT 1

The Manifesto

REMEMBRANCE: BROTHER WAYNE TEASDALE
AS NEW MONASTIC GUIDE AND ELDER

In the coming Manifesto, we offer a passionate vision for the spiritual impulse we see arising in our contemporary age, particularly among the younger generation. In it we make heavy use of inspirations and guides such as Raimon Panikkar, Pierre Teilhard de Chardin, Brother Wayne Teasdale, and others to articulate our vision. The fertile ground beneath this evolutionary emergence has been tilled by many who have come before us, in all walks of life, both known and unknown, and to them we offer deep, heartfelt gratitude.

The vision is born first and foremost out of the praxis of many lives, including our own, and is but an expression of these journeys. As a prelude to the *Manifesto*, we offer a remembrance of one of our elders, Brother Wayne Teasdale. It will, we hope, personalize some of the real-world experiences that lie behind the vision, bypassing in subtle ways the conscious mind and connecting us to the transformative energy by which we have been touched.

Adam corresponded with Brother Wayne for about three years before his passing in 2004, and Rory acknowledges Brother Wayne as his first real spiritual mentor and teacher. Brother Wayne's role in the envisioning and articulation of new monastic life was crucial to its development. It is Brother Wayne who envisioned that the Indian institution of sannyasa should be open to all people, not just celibates or those in a religious tradition, and that this emerging "universal order of sannyasa" could serve as a primary institution to help transition us into what he called an inter-spiritual age. We will hear much more on Brother Wayne's thought, but below Rory offers an intimate portrayal of Brother Wayne's inner life through his daily practice and major life transitions. These are meant to ground us in the praxis of Brother Wayne's life as we explore later many of his soaring ideas and synthetic articulations of new monastic life.

RORY:

"By their fruits you will know them," taught the famous carpenter from Nazareth. By any measure, it seems to me the late Brother Wayne Teasdale has been one of the more fruitful personalities of our time. His legacy is alive and well in those who knew him, as well as in countless others involved in the various movements his writing foreshadowed and inspired. A true spiritual outlier, Brother Wayne was not always understood or appreciated in his lifetime.

When I first met him in 1999, Brother Wayne was just beginning to speak more openly in a public fashion. His voice was small, hard to hear, and he was quite shy. He was a bit scared to come out of his shell, worried about his ego taking the reins and getting in the way. He struggled with how to allow his realization to come forth. As a result, he could be too easily dismissed as a nice, friendly—if perhaps a little socially awkward—genuinely likable man who lived on his own as a monk. Even today you can hear people say, "What's the big deal about Brother Wayne Teasdale? I met him, I knew him, I found him very nice, but not of much significance."

As the years roll by since his passing in 2004, we are beginning to see some of the significant fruits of Brother Wayne's life, not the least of which is the bourgeoning and maturing interspiritual movement Brother Wayne helped to inspire, as well as other projects such as Pir Zia Ilnayat-Khan's Seven Pillars House of Wisdom, Eboo Patel's Interfaith Youth Core, and the lives of many individuals whose spiritual journeys he deeply influenced.

Brother Wayne's coining of the word *interspiritual* in his classic book *The Mystic Heart: Discovering a Universal Spirituality in the World's Religions* has brought his work into the forefront of spirituality in recent years, as people search for new language to describe the emergent spiritual longings they are experiencing. Interspiritual has been defined in numerous ways: as a spirituality of the heart, the phenomenon of wisdom traditions sharing resources with each other, even as a new religious path. As the twenty-first century unfolds and Brother Wayne's vision is coming to light, his work is being recognized for its prophetic insight. In truth, however, Brother Wayne's greatest legacy was simply the example of his life.

Brother Wayne was born in Connecticut in 1945, and suffered a difficult childhood. His mother remarried when Brother Wayne was still a young child, and her new husband forced her to choose between him and her son. She chose her new husband; Brother Wayne was taken to an orphanage, and eventually raised by his uncle, John Cosgrove. I do not believe he ever knew his real father, nor did he ever see his mother again. The shining beacon in his life was his Uncle John, whom he always spoke of as a godsend, perhaps even a saint, who helped form Brother Wayne's early mystical view of the world. From a very early age, Brother Wayne always felt he was meant to be a priest or a monk.

At seventeen, after suffering a "dark night" experience during his teen years, Brother Wayne discovered Father Thomas Keating while visiting St. Joseph's Abbey, a Cistercian monastery near Spencer, Massachusetts, where Father Keating was then abbot. Father Keating was a founder of the centering prayer movement and widely considered a spiritual master. Brother Wayne came under his spiritual direction and ever since considered him his spiritual father. He eventually received a master's degree in philosophy and later, in 1986, a PhD in theology from Fordham University, where he studied under Ewert Cousins. His dissertation was on the theology of the Benedictine monk Bede Griffiths, who had lived much of his life at a Christian ashram, he guided in southern India, Shantivanam. After his dissertation, Brother Wayne received an invitation to join Father Bede at his ashram, and in 1989 he was initiated by Father Bede as a Christian sannyasi, and given the orange robes he would often wear on formal occasions. Brother Wayne went on to teach at DePaul University, Columbia College, the Benedictine University, and the Catholic Theological Union in Chicago, where he lived for many years. He was associated with many interreligious dialogue forums and groups, including the Parliament of the World's Religions, the Synthesis Dialogues, Common Ground, the North American Board for East-West Dialogue, the NGO Interspiritual Dialogue, and Monastic Interreligious Dialogue, and was the coordinator of the Bede Griffiths Trust.

I knew Brother Wayne well. During the final four and a half years of his life, we spent much time together traveling to dialogues and conferences, hanging out with many of my friends from college, working together on the Parliament of the World's Religions, visiting with the homeless, and engaging in countless hours of spiritual direction in his one-bedroom hermitage on the South Side of Chicago. He was not only my first formal spiritual teacher, but a close friend. He spent a number of Christmases in my family home, and I accompanied him on his final trip to Dharamsala, India, to visit with His Holiness the Dalai Lama, with whom he was on intimate terms and whom he considered a mentor. I was also with him during his two battles with cancer, the last of which brought him into his final days of earthly life and his transition into a new form.

All of this time spent together left a profound imprint on my being, so much so that I have found it difficult to speak much of my time with him. It seems too close to me, too deeply embedded in my heart, too sacred. My hope is through my writing about him others will discover the wisdom and vision of one of the great mystical pioneers in our modern age, and one of the more loving and transparent souls to have walked this planet.

Our relationship began in earnest at the 1999 Parliament of the World's Religions in Cape Town, South Africa. I was attending the parliament with a group of ten or so from my alma mater, Lake Forest College—mostly college students or recent graduates and our religion professor, Ron Miller. Each night during the weeklong conference we found ourselves closing out the evening over drinks in the hotel bar, discussing the presentations we had seen and engaging in discussion and dialogue around ideas of the spiritual path. Inevitably, Brother Wayne would meander in and join us. He could have been spending time with any one of the much-esteemed presenters and spiritual teachers there, literally hundreds of them, but he chose to spend this time with us, a small coterie of young spiritual neophytes. His quirky jokes added much laughter to our conversations, and his warm presence grew on us all. Clearly, for me, these nights were of a unique significance, for upon returning to the States following the Parliament, Brother Wayne had successfully and playfully captured my soul, and subsequently guided my feet firmly onto my spiritual path.

For me, it was a twist of fate that only the Divine could have orchestrated. Having Brother Wayne guide my initial forays into that deeper dimension of existence was both prophetic and formative. At the time, I remember thinking what a funny little word interspiritual was, with little inkling that it would gain such wide acceptance as a catchphrase for what I was *living*. My own spiritual journey has been "interspiritual" in ways that have exceeded perhaps even Brother Wayne's vision for the term. While Brother Wayne himself was deeply formed within Christianity, and from that standpoint reached out and experimented with the wisdom of other traditions, my path has developed squarely outside of any one tradition, yet has been informed deeply by many of them. Yet, at its basis and root, I cannot say it is different from the path Brother Wayne walked. Our paths both stem from a fidelity to the guidance of the Holy Spirit, and to follow its breath wherever it may blow. Brother Wayne never asked or encouraged me to choose a specific wisdom path, neither Christianity nor any other. Rather, he was open to the movements of the Spirit as they occurred among and between us, and he was willing to allow the uncertainty and freedom of movement for me to follow my path, even if did not look like one that could be easily recognized or even named.

In a recent posthumously published article, "Swami Abhishiktananda: Christian Sannyasi and Advaitin," Brother Wayne shows his openness and deep reflection on these new emergences of the Spirit. In it, he recounts the life of Henri Le Saux, a French Benedictine monk who preceded Bede Griffiths at Shantivanam and eventually became known by his Indian sannyasi name, Abhishiktananda. Abhishiktananda struggled for much of his life to come to terms with the Indian advaitic, or nondual, experience, one he had cultivated in solitude, and the Christian understanding of the trinitarian godhead. In the end, Brother Wayne tells us, "He [Abhishiktananda] came to a place of consciousness that brings together Hindu and Christian mysticism to a new species of contemplative understanding that is both and beyond both."

In his 2002 book *A Monk in the World: Cultivating a Spiritual Life*, Brother Wayne shared an intimate view of how he lived his life. He wrote it during the years we were often together, and I can testify to the fact that the book accurately reflects the vibrancy of his day-to-day life, authentically capturing his spirit and demeanor which shine throughout. In it, Brother Wayne describes his life as a "committed monastic, yet without a monastery." He felt there was a special need in our age for the monastic ideal to be lived out in the world:

> Without doubt, there is great value in spirituality that empha-
> sizes and supports withdrawal from society. But in our time,
> with its special needs, we require a spirituality of intense involve-
> ment and radical engagement with the world. . . . It is in the real
> world that the wisdom of the monks must be made accessible. It
> is in the real world that their awakening and development need
> to occur, not off in remote solitude. . . . Why do I choose to be a
> monk in the world and not locked away in a remote hermitage?
> Because I want to identify with and be identified with all those
> who suffer alone in the world, who are abandoned, homeless,
> unwanted, unknown, and unloved. I want to know the insecu-
> rity and vulnerability they experience, to forge solidarity with
> them. . . . I wish to be near the least, the forgotten and ignored,
> so I can be a sign of hope and love for them and for all others
> who need me in some way.[1]

Brother Wayne developed the ideal of a monk outside of the context of a particular religious tradition as well, becoming one of the main inspirations for the interspiritual new monastic movement:

> Monasticism has its origin here in the hidden places of the
> heart . . . It is this *heartfelt* monasticism that has inspired so
> many souls to venture to mountain caves, desert huts, and
> remote communities throughout the East and West, whether
> these seekers be Hindu, Jain, Buddhist, or Christian. . . . An
> inner monk doesn't require an overtly religious context. It is an
> innate expression of the mystical quest that everyone can reach
> by virtue of our common humanity.[2]

In the same book, Brother Wayne discussed his spiritual practice and mystical experiences, his visionary role for the Catholic Church (to which he felt an intimate and prophetic responsibility), the importance of spiritual friendship, his personal relationships with homeless people and what they have to teach us, as well as the phenomenon of interspir-ituality and his struggle to bring about change in our cultural, politi-cal, and economic institutions. In a particularly stirring chapter entitled "Tough Grace," Brother Wayne spoke about humility and the redemptive possibility of suffering through the lens of his first bout with cancer, which resulted in the removal of half of his palate, teeth, gums, and associated bone.

The day before Brother Wayne was diagnosed with cancer he had a powerful dream, one which foretold of an "impending crisis," followed by a unitive experience with the Divine, "in which the Spirit took a hold of my entire being and poured love into me, saturating my being." Brother Wayne interpreted these events as a "harbinger meant to prepare me . . . , to put my mind at ease . . . , [and it] was part of a special grace."[3]

In recounting his suffering during this time, Brother Wayne echoed the Buddha, who taught that suffering was fundamentally part of life, in terms of the suffering of birth, illness, old age, and death. The Buddha also taught that in addition to this fundamental suffering, there is a self-inflicted suffering that comes out of ignorance and our attachment to desire or aversion to emotions and events. Brother Wayne told how, during his illness, he was forced to give up many of his own ideas about happiness. "Suffering forces us to see beyond where we might be stuck. It helps us to transcend our attachments, our hidden agendas, our elaborate attempts to have it our own way . . . It throws us into utter simplicity; we understand precisely what we really need."[4]

Brother Wayne also let us in on the intimate discussions he had with Father Thomas Keating, to whom *A Monk in the World* is dedicated. Father Keating was convinced that Brother Wayne's illness was a "dark night of the soul, an inner purification preceding a permanent union with the Divine. He [Father Keating] told me that my illness was a step forward, a sign of real progress."[5]

It is here that Brother Wayne opens up for us a deeper understanding of suffering, not just as an intrinsic part of life or a misguided choice, but as disposing us "more readily to divine union." He understood suffering as something that arrives when we're ready for it, after years of being strengthened and sturdied through dedicated spiritual practice and searching. Brother Wayne related this type of suffering to the redemptive power of Christ's suffering, which "performed a kind of divine composting. He took our sin, negativity, and inhumanity and transformed them by his sacrificial love, just as compost is slowly converted to rich earth. . . . Through that act a cosmic, mystical transformation occurred."[6]

Going even further, Brother Wayne hinted that this redemptive understanding of suffering may hold the key for our future progress as a human race. "We require a mature approach to this part of our lives, an approach that will allow us to understand the gift in the challenge, the jewel in the pain, the light in the darkness beyond the suffering. The progress of each one of us, as that of the human race itself, depends on a more adequate understanding of this mysterious reality in our lives. . . . Suffering manifests an ultimately beneficial, salvific power that transforms all of human negativity into something beautiful, powerful, life-giving, and productive of positive results for everyone, at least potentially."[7]

When Brother Wayne wrote that chapter, he was unaware that in only a few more years he would once again be diagnosed with cancer, and this second battle would be much more terrible than the first. It was a full immersion into his "dark night of the soul." In the weeks before the second surgery those of us who were with him could literally feel the divine darkness that was encompassing him. When he came out of surgery, he found himself cut off from the world. His palate had been completely removed. He couldn't speak and was in extreme pain—both physical and emotional. A man who had lived mostly as a hermit monk throughout his adult life could no longer live on his own and had to be taken care of by friends. For a number of months following surgery this was his state, as he endured an aggressive chemotherapy campaign. The day after finishing his final chemo treatment, as many of us were preparing for his healthy return, a blood vessel in his brain popped while he slept, and Brother Wayne transitioned into a new life.

Recalling his first bout with cancer, Brother Wayne had written, "The inner darkness of my spirit was inviting me to subtler levels of surrender. I found myself wanting to radiate the intense love of the Divine Presence, and that became my purpose during recuperation."[8] In those waning months of his life, as his body was ravaged by cancer and chemotherapy, many of us who were with him experienced a transfiguration of his body. He seemed to shine with radiance and peace, intermixed with pain and suffering. I remembered then something he had once remarked to me, in a particularly transparent, vulnerable, and moving moment in his apartment. I had asked him if there was anything he desired, and he replied he had a strong desire to be a saint. He seemed almost childishly innocent in that moment. As I watched him navigate the trials of cancer it seemed to me that his desire had been granted.

Although I lost a dear friend when Brother Wayne died, his words and my memories of him remain fresh and always with me. I remember vividly the day I first met Brother Wayne in 1999 at a talk in Chicago called "The Mystic Heart" just a few months before the parliament was to begin. During the talk, I made a comment related to the idea of humility. Brother Wayne looked down at me and grew quite serious. As the crowd looked on he asked me, "What is humility?"

I responded, "Humility is always being open to the possibility of being wrong. . . ."

Brother Wayne paused for a time, "Yes, but see, humility is more than that—it is truth."

Humility is truth. I had wondered what this might mean. We so often associate humility with a feeling of being small, of not thinking much of ourselves, especially where others hold us in high esteem. Humility is Truth? Fourteen years later I continue to reflect on that day and the wisdom of what Brother Wayne said.

Brother Wayne's struggle for humility was, in some sense, one of becoming less humble in the way that we most often understand it in order to bring forth his truth and power. Brother Wayne was one of the few individuals I have met whose spiritual development, in my opinion, exceeded his own realization. In other words, he was further along than even he knew. His was a journey of trusting inner guidance, a willingness to go slowly, to let things emerge, to recognize mistakes and grow from them. When Brother Wayne relaxed into this trust his transmission began to shine. In the many times we spent together, his spiritual magnificence would come forth, and at times I felt I was in the presence of a spiritual giant. But it was a struggle for him. He spoke to me of it on more than one occasion—yet he was committed to what the Spirit was calling him to do. Even if mistakes were to be made, they would be in service to the ripening fruit of his body, for his intentions were pure. This seems to me to be the only true road to humility.

I'd like to close this remembrance with one of my favorite stories of Brother Wayne, one that reveals his depth and innocence and the esteem he was held in by others. During his final visit to His Holiness the Dalai Lama, at His Holiness's private residence in Dharamsala, India, in 2002, Brother Wayne was sharing a number of ideas he had been envisioning, such as convening a council of sages, or a peace walk through the Middle East from Jerusalem to Medina. He then tentatively and a bit bashfully inquired what His Holiness thought about these projects, and if he might be interested in participating. His Holiness paused for a moment, and then slowly leaned over and took Brother Wayne's hand. A deep sense of poignancy filled the air. Looking deeply into Brother Wayne's eyes, he said, "I would be supportive of and interested in any and all of your projects." Then he paused for moment, continuing, "Because of who you *are.*"

A palpable feeling of warmth and love saturated the room. Brother Wayne melted into his chair, displaying the smile of a child who knows just how deeply he is loved and supported. His Holiness saw in Brother Wayne what I was blessed to see and be part of, a humble saint with a mystic heart deeply in love with God and all of humanity.

THE MANIFESTO

New Monasticism: An Interspiritual Manifesto for Contemplaltive Life In the Twenty-First Century

Prologue

> What we seek is an experience that transforms our lives and incorporates us into the destiny of the universe. We are looking for an intuition capable of giving us an orientation in life, even if for the time being, for our being in time.
>
> —*Raimon Panikkar, The Rhythm of Being*

As we look out at the world today we take inspiration from what is happening around the globe, from young people who started a global movement for solidarity and justice through camping out on Wall Street, in Cairo, Istanbul, San Paulo, and Barcelona in nonviolent occupations, often risking their lives by standing up for a dream that is emerging in their hearts. We look also to the new monastic movement among evangelical Christians dedicated to prayer and radical service to the poor, to the conversation of an "emerging church" ("not a new religion, but a new way of being religious"), to small groups of Muslims who are gathering together, allowing women to lead worship, and reinventing what it means to answer God's call, to "engaged Buddhism," blending the sublime practices and compassion of the Buddhist path with social activism, to the "spiritual but not religious" youth who are beginning to take responsibility for their own spiritual lives outside the walls of our traditional religious institutions.

We see these movements as spiritual impulses, moving us away from an era of fixed dogmatic religious formulations and embedded power structures. These impulses are awakening a whole new generation of people across the globe. These are people who are not interested in imposing a new and fixed rule, but rather want to commit to a daily practice of putting aside their egos and exploring what it means to create a world that works for all, a world that is rooted in the principles of direct democracy, mutual aid, trust in our original goodness, and a radical acceptance of each individual and the unique gifts each has to offer.

These movements need the deep contemplative wisdom of our human race to ultimately be successful; without this, the movements risk playing a diminished role in the ultimate triumph of the human family. It is the triumph of the human soul, in totality, that we all await, and our lives are longing, consciously or not, to serve that birth. It is only through a contemplative path, a path leading to spiritual maturity, that this service is ultimately achieved.

New monasticism aims to take on this responsibility, cutting across traditions, across academic disciplines, across vocational differences, across the secular and the holy, breaking boundaries and building bridges to a contemplative life for the twenty-first century. Traditional monasticism has long held this space for the human race. Yet traditional monasticism has increasingly diminished in our contemporary milieu, particularly in Western society.

New monasticism looks to embody this role in a substantive way, not through moral laws, dogmas, or new creeds, but through supporting the unique and indispensable flowering of every individual and community on Earth. This support comes through dedication to a deep and disciplined contemplative life and a life of service to all.

New monasticism is an intratraditional manifestation of the Bodhisattva, an incarnate symbol of our basic humanness, our basic goodness, and above all of our unity as one being. It is a manifestation of the mystical body of Christ, the revelation of the one Being among us, in which "we live and move and have our being."[9] It is to this audacious goal that new monasticism dares to foresee—more than dares—*sees only it*—and pledges our lives to becoming an ordinary, disciplined, loving expression of its attainment.

> Let us be in harmony in our intention,
> in harmony in our hearts
> in harmony in our minds
> that we may live in concord.   —*Rig Veda X*

Prelude

> Let us establish ourselves in the divine milieu. There we shall find ourselves where the soul is most deep and where matter is most dense. There we shall discover, where all its beauties flow together, the ultra-vital, the ultra-sensitive, the ultra-active point of the universe. And, at the same time, we shall feel the plenitude of our powers of action and adoration effortlessly ordered within our deepest selves.
>
> —*Pierre Teilhard de Chardin, The Divine Milieu*

The arc of our discussion will follow the way of creation. . . . We will begin at the beginning, which is to say with the beginningless, the primordial Idea of the human being, the purusha, the archetype of the monk. We then follow its distillation through the course of time, weaving its way into our contemporary milieu, transmuting itself into ever-new forms, yet always in fidelity to the original impulse. We heighten our awareness as it seeps into the practical grist of our present-day lives, and open our hearts as it disappears once again beyond the horizon of time. We allow that bright, burning sun to stream down its warmth, love, and wisdom, on us, within us, and among us, as we give birth to the varied beauty of new monasticism . . .

For this we pray and in this we delight.

The Beginningless: The Archetype of the Monk

> I speak of an aspiration and an urge. It is not because one wills it that one becomes a monk. The monk is compelled, as it were, by an experience that can only articulate itself in the praxis of one's life. It is an experience of the presence of the goal of life, on the one hand, and of its absence (of not having reached it) on the other.   —*Raimon Panikkar, Blessed Simplicity*

We begin our discussion with what makes a monk a monk, looking through the window of traditional forms into the interior dimension within the human being that gives birth to the monk. We then turn to the evolution of these traditional forms into what we call new monasticism. By *evolution* "we imply both change and continuity; something which is not just an unfolding of the past, but which also makes use of an underlying identity."[10]

Throughout our discussion, and particularly in its early stages, we will make generous use of Raimon Panikkar's *Blessed Simplicity: The Monk as Universal Archetype*. Panikkar was a man of remarkable cross-cultural understanding, which makes him particularly pertinent for our discussion here. He was a Catholic priest who also became a Hindu and a Buddhist, and once famously remarked, "I 'left' as a Christian, 'found' myself a Hindu and 'return' a Buddhist, without having ceased to be a Christian."[11] In addition to his cross-religious exploration, Panikkar held doctorates in philosophy, chemistry, and theology, spoke eleven languages, and wrote in six of them. It is hard to find another person who was able to immerse himself so completely in such diverse cultural milieus.

Blessed Simplicity, the outgrowth of a symposium between monastics from both Eastern and Western traditions and new monastic contemplatives, is a seminal work on the emergence of new monasticism from traditional forms. It reads like a symphony from the depths, and as one yearns to share rather than improve upon Mozart, we will quote from it extensively. Panikkar's book puts forward the thesis that the monk represents a constitutive dimension of the human being, which he dubs the archetype of the monk: "an archetype [is] a product of human life itself [and is therefore] mutable and dynamic. . . . To speak of *the archetype of the monk* . . . assumes that there is a *human* archetype which the monk works out with greater or lesser success. Traditional monks may have reenacted in their own way 'something' that we too may be called upon to realize, but in a different manner."[12]

So what is this constitutive dimension of the human being, this archetype of the monk? "We may have no other entrance into the *archetype* than to study or come to know the *monk* as archetype."[13] It is the monk who has most often represented this ideal among the human family. When we look at the monk and peer deeply into "those aspects of the human being that are most rooted in his nature . . . [we find that] the monk ultimately becomes a monk as the result of an urge, the fruit of an experience that eventually leads him to change and, in the final analysis, break something in his life for the sake of that 'thing' which encompasses or transcends everything."[14]

"By monk," Panikkar writes, "*monachos,* I understand the person who aspires to reach the ultimate goal of life with all his being by renouncing all that is not necessary to it, i.e., by concentrating on this one single and unique goal. Precisely this single-mindedness, or rather exclusivity of the goal that shuns all subordinate though legitimate goals, distinguishes the monastic way from other spiritual endeavors toward perfection or salvation."[15]

Yet the monk is also a personal affair, "An indefinite number of people can realize, each uniquely, their own perfection. Humanity is manifold. In this sense *the* perfect human nature does not exist."[16] The transition occurs when we see the traditional monk as

> only one way of realizing [this] universal archetype. . . . If the monastic dimension exists at least potentially in everybody, the institution of monasticism should be equally open to everybody. . . . The monastery, then, would not be the 'establishment' of the monks, but the *schola Domini*, the school where that human dimension is cultivated and transmitted. . . . Here appears the consequence of our distinction between the *monk* as archetype, i.e., the monk as a paradigm of religious life, against the *archetype* of the monk, i.e., the human archetype lived out by the monks, but which may also be experienced and lived today in different ways.[17]

All of us, at some time or another, have felt stirrings of what the monk aspires to, whether we are religious, atheist, or agnostic. We have all had moments of transcendence, moments of deep passion for justice and truth, outpourings of compassion for others in suffering, or a perfect feeling of love toward our partner or children. These moments are part and parcel of our human experience. They touch a hidden dimension inside of us. The monk is, in some sense, the person who recognizes the legitimacy and the *primacy* of these moments. She resolves within herself to get to the heart of the matter, as it were, and to explore whence these moments arise, to peek through the doorway into which they point. This peering eventually moves beyond mere curiosity and becomes the all-consuming goal of one's life. Many people today, and in particular young people, may have had such immanent and yet transcendent experiences and may be feeling deep within the enchantment of this calling, yet without the desire or need to enter into a monastery or even to follow a particular religious tradition.

New Monastics: Monks in the World

> May the time come when men [and women], having been awakened to a sense of the close bond linking all the movements of this world in the single, all-embracing work of the Incarnation, shall be unable to give themslves to any one of their tasks without illuminating it with the clear vision that their work—however elementary it may be—is received and put to good use by a Center of the universe.
>
> When that time comes to pass, there will be little to separate life in the cloister from the life of the world.
>
> —*Pierre Teilhard de Chardin, The Divine Milieu*

"The new monk is an ideal, an aspiration that lives in the minds and hearts of our contemporary generation."[18] The model of traditional monasticism was one of turning away from the world, of simplifying one's life, and of renouncing many of the comforts and impulses of life in the world. Traditional monks were usually celibate, often lived apart from others and in isolation, and aimed for the blessed simplicity that would bring them into the fullness of their being. However, "The whole challenge of *modern* monkhood," Panikkar asserts, "consists in the impossible attempt—at first sight—to acquire by its simplicity the *fullness* of human life."[19]

This is what Panikkar calls "simplicity through *integration*. . . . The modern monk does not want to *renounce,* except what is plainly sinful or negative; rather he wishes to *transform* all things. . . . He is not interested in stripping himself of everything but in assimilating it all."[20] As for our use of the name "new monk," Panikkar confronts the issue head on:

"It could be that in the last analysis we would prefer to do away with the word 'monk' altogether and find another less overburdened one, but this would not prove that what the contemporary monk intends does not correspond to what the ancients were trying to do."[21]

We assert that new monasticism names an impulse that is trying to incarnate itself in the new generation. It is beyond the borders of any particular religious institution, yet drinks deeply from the wells of our wisdom traditions. It is an urge which speaks to a profoundly contemplative life, to the formation of small communities of friends, to sacred activism, and to discovering together the unique calling of every person and every community.

Perhaps we should pause here for a moment to elaborate on what is meant by contemplative. Thomas Merton beautifully describes the state of contemplation in *New Seeds of Contemplation*. Contemplation is

> Life itself, fully awake, fully active, and fully aware that it is alive. It is spiritual wonder. It is spontaneous awe at the sacredness of life, of being. It is gratitude for life, for awareness, and for being. It is a vivid realization of the fact that life and being in us proceed from an invisible, transcendent, and infinitely abundant Source. Contemplation is, above all, awareness of the reality of that Source. It knows the Source, obscurely, inexplicably, but with a certitude that goes beyond reason and beyond simple faith. . . . It is a more profound depth of faith; a knowledge too deep to be grasped in mere images, in words, or even in clear concepts. It can be suggested by words, by symbols, but in the very moment of trying to indicate what it knows the contemplative mind takes back what it has said, and denies what it has affirmed. . . .

> Contemplation is also the response to a call: a call from Him Who has no voice, and yet Who speaks in everything that is, and Who, most of all, speaks in the depths of our own being; for we ourselves are words of His. But we are words that are meant to respond to Him, to answer to Him, to echo Him, and even in some way to contain Him and signify Him. Contemplation is this echo. It is a deep resonance in the inmost center of our spirit in which our very life loses its separate voice and resounds with the majesty and the mercy of the Hidden and Living One. . . . It is awakening, enlightenment, and the amazing intuitive grasp by which love gains certitude of God's creative and dynamic intervention in our daily life. Hence contemplation does not simply "find" a clear idea of God and confine Him within the limits

of that idea, and hold Him there as a prisoner to Whom it can always return. On the contrary, contemplation is carried away by Him into His own realm, His own mystery, and His own freedom.[22]

In Panikkar's words, "Contemplation is that activity which situates us in an open space from which we can observe and contribute to the course of the universe . . . that activity that delights in the well-being of all being. The contemplative life is simply life; life in its fullest sense. . . . The central point is the development of the core of the human person to its fullest—in whatever sense this core or this fullness may be interpreted."[23]

Traditionally this dedication to a contemplative life stressed the primacy of being *over* doing, while the new monk "stresses the unity of being and doing. . . . True action is contemplative and authentic contemplation acts."[24] The goal and struggle, or perhaps it is the play, of the new monk is to incarnate the fact that the spiritual and contemplative life includes action, and that action does not have to be in opposition to contemplation. In fact, action can become contemplation. The new monk works toward a new way of being in the world where one becomes an expression of Spirit, a form through which God can live and work in the world, an empty vessel through which the Buddha Mind manifests.

Through contemplative prayer and practice one comes upon a deep state of receptivity and listening, openness and spaciousness, and from here one senses an inner impulse and then moves in accordance with this action. One becomes aware of a perfectly functioning field which fits everything together into a seamless whole with the utmost sensitivity, love, wisdom, and compassion. This awareness is not opposed to action. In fact, without this integrated action, contemplation cannot be said to be complete. St. Teresa of Avila captures this need for action within contemplation in Christian terms:

> Christ has no body but yours
> No hands, no feet on earth but yours,
> Yours are the eyes with which he looks with Compassion
>   on this world,
> Yours are the feet with which he walks to do good,
> Yours are the hands, with which he blesses all the world.
> Yours are the hands, yours are the feet,
> Yours are the eyes, you are his body.[25]

The new monk hears the pains and moans of a new creation taking place all around him and cannot turn away from the suffering. He feels "that the shaping of this world is a religious and even a contemplative concern not alien to or at odds with the monastic vocation. . . . [and finds that] the demons and asuras of the cold and lonely regions have been converted into the shouts and cries of the human milieu . . ., the daily papers with their news have been converted into spiritual reading."[26] The modern monk feels at the root of his soul a calling to the contemplative life, but "cannot renounce the secular world because he does not believe it to be secondary; cannot renounce activity in the world because he believes this to be indispensable."[27]

This leads the new monk into a radical intuition of the "holiness of the secular." This is one area where the evolution we spoke of in the beginning may be seen more clearly. By *secular*, we refer not only to a peculiar independence from any particular religious institution, but also, in a mysterious sense, to an independence from a purely eternal and immutable "nature of things." In other words, by the holiness of the secular, we mean the holiness of all that exists in *this* world. Panikkar describes the secular as the "temporal character of things," and goes on to describe this intuition: "This temporality is now being taken not only as something that matters, but as something definitive. Instead of being just fleeting, passing, ephemeral, the temporal structure of the world now represents a coefficient of reality that cannot be eliminated. . . . It is no longer considered something you can dispense with, or even utilize in order to reach something more important."[28] Therefore, the modern monk

> tends toward the secular, without thereby diminishing his pursuit of holiness. . . . Secularity represents the affirmation that the body, history, the material world and all temporal values in general are definitive and insuperable. . . . That it is legitimate to be involved in temporal affairs, that time has a positive value, and that the religious person must occupy himself with reforming the very socio-political-historical structures of reality. . . . It means the incorporation of the divine in the human and its impregnation of all the structures of the material world. . . . If this represents a mutation in the conception of the holy, it equally signifies a parallel revolution in the experience of the secular. The secular is no longer that which is fleeting, provisional, perishable, contingent, and so forth, but is rather the very clothing of the permanent, the eternal, the immutable.[29]

This intuition naturally leads the new monk into all areas of the human arena, notably into the areas of embodiment, intimate relationships, environmental concerns, community building, and politics. The new monk sees the body as a holy incarnation and part of her spiritual work is in maintaining a healthy, nurturing and transformative relationship with it. New monasticism also encourages intimate relationships, both deep and meaningful friendships and committed and loving sexual relationships. New monasticism is concerned with discovering the divine nature and proper place of *all* relationships. It is not opposed to celibacy; rather it recognizes it as a profound and genuine calling, albeit a rare one. However, it equally recognizes that celibacy is not a necessity for the working out of the archetype of the monk.

New monastics acknowledge the gap between idealized intimate relationships and the reality that is most often lived out, and call on each other to help heal these wounds and to build true intimate relationships based on integrity, trust, spiritual friendship, and love. They want to see the spirit enter into all arenas of human life, and because of this "seek a spirituality that is not exclusively spiritual. . . . Not only will [they] not scorn any human value, but [they] actually attempt to cultivate them all. . . . The monk loves everything that exists and is even passionate about everything human, without excluding the material and the temporal."[30]

It may be said that the new monks hear the words of Jesus not only as "The Kingdom of Heaven is within you," but equally and perhaps more substantively as "The Kingdom of Heaven is *among* you." They find the need to work out their salvation through relationships: with each other, with the Kosmos, with their work in the world, and with Ultimate Reality, however they may conceive of or be initiated into it. As such, no human endeavor remains beyond their reach, and it is in their struggle to uplift all they see as valuable in the human condition that they find their unity with one another. They feel themselves participating in the ultimate act of creation, the incarnational act of bringing spirit into form and transmuting form into spirit.

Another point of departure from the traditional role of the monk comes in the area of spiritual direction. More often than not, the new monastic is not drawn to the traditional ideas of obedience to a superior or complete dedication to a guru. While respecting traditional roles and many of the successes they have borne, the new monastic finds spiritual direction most often in the depths of spiritual friendship and dialogical relationships. A story that illustrates this new inclination comes from a time when Adam approached a quite popular spiritual teacher to ask him if he would be his spiritual director. The teacher replied, "Under one condition; that you will be *my* spiritual director as well."

The new monastic recognizes beyond any doubt the necessity of elders, the need for spiritual direction and mentors, and the great gift afforded to her by those who have advanced further along than she. She struggles to develop her sense of discernment, and her spiritual mentors are indispensable to her as a means to reflect back her own decision-making process and with whom to check her insights. She sees this spiritual direction as the most profound blossoming of friendship. Friendship becomes the keynote of the new relationship between mentor and mentee, between teacher and student. One is reminded of the apocryphal story of the Buddha and his attendant, Ananda. Ananda asks, "Dear Buddha, is spiritual friendship half of the journey to enlightenment?"

The Buddha replies, with a grand smile, "No, Ananda, it is the *whole* of the journey."

This notion of spiritual friendship helps the new monk to recognize the importance of human communities, which is how one might define politics in its pure sense. She is interested in building communities that are sustainable, infused with a sense of the sacred, and support their members to discover and live out their sacred vocation in the world. The efforts to build sustainable and enriching communities extend beyond a mere comfortable existence for one's self. The new monastic sees it as part of her mission to help all of creation, to show how human beings can live in supportive, sustainable, and nurturing environments. Her care extends not only to others, but to the natural world around her and to all living creatures.

The new monastics may be artists, scientists, spiritual teachers, elementary teachers, social workers, waiters. It is not so much the job that matters, as the place from which they approach their work. Their work cannot be separated from their spiritual path. They endeavor to bring a heightened awareness, intimacy, and authenticity to their work, whether this be washing dishes or feeding the poor. Obviously, there are some professions that the new monk could not participate in, such as ones involved in the building of weapons, open degradation of the environment, or the exploitation of others for profit. Most professions, however, are not only open to new monastics, but are in desperate need of the mindfulness, kindness, and infusion of grace that they endeavor to bring into their lives.

Monetary considerations matter not to the new monk, yet she is not naïve in these matters. She understands the way the modern world works, and is pledged to work intelligently within it, but she cares not for the convenient notions of success in our modern age, too many of which are but thinly veiled aggrandizements of the ego, excuses for the exploitation of our environment and other human beings. Our modern productive society is but a sad and ephemeral notion at best for the new monk, and at worst an insidious, demoralizing, and demeaning way of life for the human spirit. To the modern monk, a truly productive society would allow ample time for leisurely retreat, prayer, meditation, and reflection of the soul.

The key point may be summarized as this: new monastics do not see a split between their inner and outer lives. The new monk is "in the world but not of it," as Jesus taught us to be. He "playfully plays the game [of life in the world] . . . but does not abide by the rules . . ., and in playing changes some of the rules—at the risk of his life, obviously. For by changing the rules he will eventually change the game."[31]

For the new monastic, there is only his or her life and how that life may best serve the greater whole. This is an intensely personal movement for each individual, and the question of vocation becomes an important one for the new monastic. The new monk must struggle with this question of his or her calling, for it is as unique as everyone's own individuality.

This discovery of one's calling and gifts is once again about the unity of contemplation and action. Contemplative action arises from receptivity and listening; some may say that the action arises from a consenting to God's action in us, or from a clear and subtle perception of the primordial working of the Buddha Mind. This action may take an infinite number of distinctive forms; however, it is essentially action as an expression of healing, wisdom, compassion, and love. The action is unique to who we are and to the situation we are in, and utilizes all of our life experiences and gifts. It is an action through which we truly become who we were born to be.

Once it arises out of the contemplative space we have created in our lives, our crucial responsibility is to say yes to it. This requires not only willingness, but also patience and discernment. In doing this, we begin to answer the universal call to incarnate the fullness of our being. True contemplation is not really contemplation in its fullest sense until it includes this yes, and within this yes also arises a no. This is a no to all the elements of this world that violate our love, compassion, and sense of justice. Through this process arises the prophetic voice of the new monk, the "sacred activism" of Andrew Harvey, the prophet as a "mystic in action" in the case of Matthew Fox, and the "conscientization" of Brother Wayne Teasdale, "the awakening of a deeper awareness of problems that require of us some kind of response, especially where people are suffering."[32]

This requires the new monk to think deeply and intelligently about her actions, and about how those actions affect the well-being of all. The new monk recognizes that all of her actions have universal consequences, whether arising from a contemplative space or not, and her goal is to allow all of her actions to arise from her "contemplative reservoir." She endeavors to discover her true calling, how she may best serve the Kosmos, and trusts in the inner action of her spirit. This is not an individual project, but proceeds in discernment with her mentors and sangha, or community of spiritual friends.

In the end, it is the dedication to an engaged, contemplative life and a life of intelligent service to all beings that makes one a new monastic. The new monk seems to be tasked with the impossible: to build nothing less than the Kingdom of Heaven on Earth. She cannot just tear down the old society. She is pledged to build it not just for herself, but for everyone, especially for those who find themselves on the bottom rung of our society, the poor and oppressed, the mentally afflicted and sexually abused—"the salt of the earth."

Yet her compassion does not stop there. With her keen eye the new monk sees the desperation in the faces of Wall Street and the loneliness and despair of soul of so many of the rich and privileged, and she works for them as well. The religious fanatics, who have so twisted the spirit and message of love of their founders, also fall within the breadth of her compassion. The new monk is to build this new world not by violence, but through the force of her compassion, her prophetic voice, her wisdom and love—and through the mobilization of all those who will stand with her. That is the work of the new monastic, to incarnate a new world that will allow for the unique flowering of the Spirit in every individual and community on Earth.

Building Bridges: Contemplative Life in the Twenty-First Century

> Time is not an accident to life, or to Being . . . Each existence is tempiternal . . . ever old and ever new.

> Our task and our responsibility are to assimilate the wisdom of bygone traditions and, having made it our own, to allow it to grow. Life is neither repetition nor continuation. It is growth, which implies at once rupture and continuity. Life is creation.

> If creation is an act of contemplation, as Plotinus says, real growth would be to reenact in a contemplative way our partnership in the very creative activity of reality.

> —*Raimon Panikkar, The Rhythm of Being*

In the beginning we spoke of an evolution, implying "both change and continuity; something which is not just an unfolding of the past, but which also makes use of an underlying identity."[33] As we speak of contemplative life in the twenty-first century, we now turn our sights to a fundamental element of success for the new monastic movement, the relationship between our living spiritual elders and the new monk. By our "elders," we refer to those precious souls who have gone before us in their journey to spiritual maturity, the vast majority of whom have done so mainly within the structures of established wisdom traditions. Father Thomas Keating poses a question of great importance to the new monk:

> The most precious value that the world religions have in common is their accumulated experience of the spiritual journey. Centuries of Seekers have discovered and lived its conditions, temptations, trials, development and final integration. This wealth of personal experience of the transcendent bears witness to the historical grounding of our contemporary search. It is not just a passing fad. At the same time, this vast reservoir of practical wisdom inherited from the past raises an important question for Seekers. Can one transcend the empirical ego and false self without plugging into the spiritual tradition of one of the world religions?[34]

The new monk recognizes that the world's contemplative traditions contain within them the wisdom, transmissions, and lineages she aspires to assimilate within her and give birth to in the modern world. Much of this wisdom is contained not only in our elders' words, writings and presence, but also in the structures that have grown up around their attempts to pass on the wisdom of the tradition. These structures themselves help to curtail certain dangers along the path, and have built-in mechanisms to help seize and guide those moments when the spiritual path reaches one of its many climax points. Like a cat at the mouse hole, spiritual directors and the methods they develop help us to recognize these moments and to remain alert and ready for them. They also subtly direct our efforts and orient us so that our struggles may bear fruit. Perhaps most important, they serve as a trusted cultural background and testing board for us to hone our own powers of discernment and discover our own unique truth. It would seem that they are indispensible fountains of knowledge for the spiritual aspirant, which the new monk certainly is.

Yet we must recognize that we are living in many ways in a postreligious and interspiritual world. Many young people no longer connect in such a profound way with our wisdom traditions. In recent surveys, around 30 percent of the American population declared themselves "spiritual but not religious,"[35] and in some surveys this number ballooned to 75 percent of Americans between the ages of eighteen and twenty-nine![36] The world's wisdom traditions are struggling mightily to recruit young monastic vocations. The language of our religious institutions is no longer speaking to young hearts and souls as it did in the past.

Can the answer to our contemporary situation really be to tell young people they have to connect with a religious institution in the traditional way in order to come to spiritual maturity? We ask: Is it possible that the impulse driving people beyond the walls of established traditions is itself being orchestrated by the Holy Spirit?

We believe that here we are seeing the need for a new movement, a movement that can respond to the needs of today's changing world while preserving the deepest truths and insights of our wisdom traditions. We, as a generation that is still in touch with our elders, have a solemn obligation to assimilate and pass on this wisdom to the younger generation. However, in doing so, we cannot just pass on traditional forms, for those no longer speak to so many of our youth. Instead, we are being asked to translate those truths in a way that they can be relevant to some of today's most pressing questions and younger minds. We need a movement that can articulate a new universal framework, a framework for a contemplative life in the twenty-first century. This framework must be able to inspire a new contemplative life and new contemplative communities, ones that will change hearts, transfigure lives and relationships, and help us to birth a new world. In this endeavor we need the wisdom and guidance our elders can provide. Hence we see the importance of this intergenerational dialogue and a mutual desire and need: the need for our elders to pass on their wisdom, and the need of the new monk to receive, assimilate, and translate it for a new generation.

This synergistic relationship between the keepers of the collective spiritual wisdom of our planet and the path to be incarnated by new monastics is of prime importance—bridges must be built. In light of this, and in consultation with some of our most respected elders and mentors, we call into life the Foundation for New Monasticism. This nonprofit foundation is an intergenerational alliance that is dedicated to reaching and inspiring the younger generation to commit to a contemplative life and help them with the resources to build their lives around that. It will endeavor to birth a universal network of contemplatives that brings together some of our most esteemed elders and young contemplatives. We feel that if properly nurtured, it can provide an opportunity for contemplatives, young and old, from various traditions, to be present with each other in a way that these new inspirations are calling us to, a way that is intimate, democratic, and reciprocal. We envision a model advocated by the founder of the Quakers, George Fox, one of being present with each other in a way that can enable the wisdom of the Holy Spirit to come through everyone participating. This, we trust, will inspire friendships, communities, and new frameworks for living contemplative life in the twenty-first century.

We envision this new framework as a highly decentralized and yet interconnected way of incarnating unity in diversity. It will embody a new type of leadership, a new way of building spiritual communities, and a new way for elders and youth to collaborate with one another. This new leadership becomes more about being able to relate to others in a way in which transmission becomes possible, allowing all to discover their gifts and offer them to the whole, and share them in a way that is free and nonhierarchical. At times it may not even be clear who the leader is, for leadership just happens as all discover their gifts and engage them in service of compassion and justice.

We envision all communities subscribing to some general principles, but being free to actualize new monasticism in a way that feels true to their vocation, as individuals and as communities. Some communities may reflect a more formal monastic life, with vows and robes, while others may be very much embedded in the world, yet deeply centered in the contemplative way of life. Each one could create a path that is integrated, that does not see contemplation and activism as opposing factors in life, and that is committed to transfiguring all domains of life, be they personal, institutional, religious, economic, or political.

Individuals within a community could embody different vocations as well. These communities become a way for those who aspire to a contemplative life to come together and begin to build the Kingdom of Heaven one friendship at a time. This can be true of small networks of friends as well as larger intentional communities. Each community will have a unique expression and each may have a slightly different spirituality. Some could be Christian, some Hindu, some Muslim, some Buddhist, some Jewish, some a mix of two or more traditions, and some more purely interspiritual—yet all would have a resonance with basic principles.

What are these basic principles? His Holiness the Dalai Lama articulates them well in his book *Beyond Religion: Ethics for a Whole World*. His Holiness argues that "the time has come to find a way of thinking about spirituality and ethics that is beyond religion,"[37] and he attempts to create a basis of shared values through what he calls "inner values." "By inner values I mean the qualities that we all appreciate in others. . . . We all appreciate the inner qualities of kindness, patience, tolerance, forgiveness, and generosity, and in the same way we are all averse to displays of greed, malice, hatred, and bigotry. So actively promoting the positive inner qualities of the human heart that arise from our core disposition toward compassion, and learning to combat our more destructive propensities, will be appreciated by all."[38]

An Interspiritual Path

> The essential marvel of the divine milieu is the ease with which it assembles and harmonizes within itself qualities which appear to us to be contradictory. . . .
>
> In the divine milieu all the elements of the universe touch each other by that which is most inward and ultimate in them. There they concentrate, little by little, all that is purest and most attractive in them without loss and without danger ofubsequent corruption . . .
>
> At the heart of the divine milieu . . . things are transfigured, but from within. They bathe inwardly in light, but, in this incandescence, they retain—this is not strong enough, they exalt—all that is most specific in their attributes.
> —*Pierre Teilhard de Chardin, The Divine Milieu*

The word *interspiritual* was first coined by Brother Wayne Teasdale in 1999 in his book *The Mystic Heart*. In the last decade, the interspiritual movement has exploded onto the scene, now registering over five thousand hits when searched on Google. The word was used to denote the phenomenon of the world's wisdom traditions moving beyond interfaith dialogue into a more intimate and symbiotic relationship. Interfaith dialogue was seen as a first step, allowing the traditions to learn about one another and even engender deep respect and trust with one another through dialogue. Interspirituality, however, built upon those initial forays and deepened the sharing among traditions, moving them to begin sharing actual "spiritual technologies" and mystical realizations with each other on an experiential level. It also connoted a dawning recognition that the world's wisdom traditions, far from being at odds with each other, could be viewed as a common heritage of humankind's spiritual wisdom: "varied insights scattered like so many precious seeds among the religions are viewed as belonging to the inclusive domain of the mystical."[39]

Brother Wayne intuited the "spiritual but not religious" movement, and predicted that interspirituality would embody the future direction of humanity. "The real religion of humankind can be said to be spirituality itself, because mystical spirituality is the origin of all the world religions. If this is so, and I believe it is, we might also say that interspirituality—the sharing of ultimate experiences across traditions—is the religion of the third millennium."[40]

Kurt Johnson and Robert Ord, in their book *The Coming Interspiritual Age*, make a powerful argument for seeing the interspiritual movement in the context of humankind's evolutionary process. Johnson and Ord describe interspirituality as "the natural discussion among human beings about what we are experiencing . . . about who we are, why we are here, and where we are going. . . ."[41] Johnson and Ord go on to expand upon Brother Wayne's vision:

> The primary vector of our species' spiritual and ethical development wasn't any one of the world's countless spiritual paths, but the shared direction of all of them . . . their historical development has been a single experience on behalf of humankind—an unfolding existential convergence continuing to this day and defining an aspect of the maturation of our species. . . .
>
> Interspirituality, then, starts from a different understanding of religion. Even as a teaching, it begins with the view that the entire religious experience of our species has been a *single experience* that has been unfolding through many lines and branches, together empowering our species for ever higher evolution. In other words, interspirituality recognizes a common *experience* within all spirituality. It acknowledges a shared origin, shared process, and shared maturing.[42]

Interspirituality in this context is concerned with the human family as a whole. This leads one to an intuition of what might be called *the* tradition, the human tradition. The human tradition sees all of humanity in the evolutionary process of maturation. Here humanity finds itself responsible not only for all of its constituent parts, fellow human beings, but also for all creatures on our planet and the well-being of our Mother Earth, Gaia. The human tradition recognizes that to shoulder our responsibility we must strive for spiritual maturity and find ways to assimilate and pass on the collective wisdom of our race. This tradition knows no bounds except those of the human race itself. In this blossoming, we are all integral parts, yet we each contain the whole. The microcosm is a reflection of the macrocosm.

So how is the new monk to approach this understanding in terms of his or her own spiritual path? There are different ways to be sure; some new monks are and will be called to incarnate their path within a particular established wisdom tradition. Yet they must also be willing to view paths other than their own as wholly legitimate—as ones leading also to spiritual maturity. The Vedanta Society, the monastic order based around the spiritual genius of Ramakrishna, an Indian saint, embodies this philosophy. Within the Vedanta Society itself four main paths are articulated: *bhakti* yoga, the path of devotional love; *karma* yoga, the path of selfless service; *jnana* yoga, the path of knowledge through nondual realization; and *raja* yoga, the royal path of meditation. However, practitioners are asked to choose only one path and concentrate on that. Even very advanced practitioners are discouraged from engaging in more than two. Yet all paths are recognized as wholly legitimate and fruitful.

Many new monks will also be called to follow the path that has been carved out by the majority of our elders. This consists of growing strong roots in one tradition, and from that vantage point branching out to drink deeply of the wisdom of varying traditions. This can be seen in the example of Christian monks becoming Zen roshis or cultivating the advaitic experience (nondual realization) found in the Hindu Vedas and Upanishads. There are many examples of this path, including those of Thomas Merton, Father Thomas Keating, Ramakrishna, Brother David Steindl-Rast, Father Bede Griffiths, Brother Wayne Teasdale, and many others. This path has been so popular that it has become somewhat of a clarion call among many of our elders that one should become firmly established in a particular tradition before experimenting with others.

However, the new monk may not always find one of these more traditional paths resonating in his soul, and there are other roads the new monk may travel. There is the way of multiple religious belonging, discussed eloquently by Matthew Wright, a young Episcopal priest, in *Reshaping Religion: Interspirituality and Multiple Religious Belonging*. This path includes visionaries such as Lex Hixon and Father Henri Le Saux, also known by his Hindu name, Abhishiktananda. This path consists of fully embedding oneself in multiple religious traditions. As Wright explains:

> Such a person does all she can to truly understand the new tradition from the inside out—taking initiation and involving herself in the community, worship, study, and prayer of the second tradition, while also maintaining the similar requirements of her original tradition. As is obvious, this requires hard work, and it is not for everyone. Because of this, I place multiple belonging in the special category of vocation. It is essentially an act of faith, and one must be so called. . . .

> Different religious traditions, on the level of doctrine and historical formulation, are often contradictory, and the multiple-belonger must confront this reality head on, if they are to maintain honesty and integrity. They stand fully in both worlds, allowing the apparent contradictions, and often historic wounds inflicted by one tradition on the other, into their souls. Out of this tension,

one waits for something creative and healing to emerge—which requires deep trust in the calling.[43]

There is also a more wholly nontraditional path, which has been the one traversed by the authors. It is perhaps the least articulated one to date. We name it here as an interspiritual path, though we note that all of the ways mentioned above may be considered interspiritual. This interspiritual path may not include being fully embedded in any of the existing wisdom traditions. It stems from a universal recognition of the potential of the human being for spiritual maturity as the basis of one's path, and cognizes clearly the interspiritual vision of the wisdom traditions as a common heritage for humanity. It also hints at a more radical understanding of our spiritual traditions. Not only are they all paths to spiritual maturity, but in a mysterious sense one feels they may complete one another.

Each wisdom tradition may hold a puzzle piece as to the ultimate flowering of humanity. This view recognizes that each tradition has explored and emphasized subtle differences of the human experience, thereby becoming experts on differing aspects of our human potential, as well as discovering potential pitfalls and ways to navigate these as we journey along the way. Each tradition contains pure gold nuggets of human understanding, but none has a complete picture. In this understanding of interspirituality, each tradition is both teacher and student, having both something to offer and to learn. In *The Mystic Heart*, Brother Wayne proclaimed, "In the end, I am convinced that the religions complete one another's understanding of ultimate reality."[44]

If the new monk finds himself on this path, it will be out of a sense of being guided into it. However, there are dangers that one should be aware of when embarking on this path. It should not be undertaken simply out of a sense of curiosity or exploration. While those traits are encouraged, they are not sufficient. This path requires the guidance of elders on traditional paths and a high level of integrity and responsibility. The new monk must be keen to dig one deep well rather than many shallow ones, to choose his spiritual mentors wisely, and to remain vigilant of the confrontation with his own ego.

One must avoid the New Age pitfalls of walking a shallow spiritual path that comforts rather than transforms the ego. One thing the new monk can be sure of: that she will encounter parts of the journey in which she will shrink from the true transformative process of the contemplative life, as have all who have gone before her. Demanding as it does, perhaps many times over, an uncompromising death process, the new monk on this path must soberly assess whether without the framework of a traditional wisdom tradition she will really be able to see herself through? It is here that the guidance of an established spiritual mentor who has walked the territory before her becomes essential.

One might ask, why even mention a new path? Is not the spiritual path already fraught with such difficulty that we may be only adding burdens to an already herculean task? And who cannot doubt these pitfalls as one surveys the deadened spiritual milieu of the new age, with its shallow "feel-good" and "positive thinking" spiritual paths, too afraid to confront their shadow and deal with the dark cocoon of spiritual alchemy? Why part from the tried and traditional ways? This is a difficult question to answer. Perhaps it will suffice to say that the new monk on this path has a deeply felt sense that it would be a rejection of her true path to do otherwise.

She feels at the root of her soul that her relationship with God, her identity with the Buddha Mind, life itself, has guided her into it—and continues to guide her through it. Her fidelity is to this impulse in the depths of her own being, to this inspiration and guidance of Spirit, and she could no more rid herself of it than she could her own heartbeat. She seeks and needs the guidance and discernment of her elders and of traditional paths, but her spiritual maturity, her path, is ultimately her own responsibility, and it belongs to her and her alone. The fruits of her path belong to all.

We have found that an invaluable aspect of this path, in addition to a disciplined, daily spiritual practice such as meditation, is building relationships and receiving spiritual direction from our elders. When this is done with integrity, respect, humility, surrender, and deep spiritual yearning, one may receive from these elders a true and authentic spiritual transmission. Yet this transmission is not based on one's complete acceptance of the elder's tradition. It includes elements of the tradition, but in its essence is the elder's experience of Ultimate Reality as he or she has experienced it within his or her tradition. The elders are passing on their lived experience of this human life and its relationship with Ultimate Reality.

This infusion process requires a certain humble disposition, one which is not naturally cultivated in our Western societies. It requires the ability to bow in deep gratitude to another. The venerable Chogyam Trungpa captured it well when he once said words to the effect that, transmission is like pouring tea into a cup. The cup must be lower than the teapot. This is just a statement of fact. It does not contain any hierarchy. If the cup is not below the teapot, the tea will not end up in the cup.

This path is perhaps a great bridge of incarnate understanding for a new generation. It is a path that may be able to assimilate many of our spiritual lineages without becoming fully embedded in, or beholden to, the religious frameworks that surround them. It is particularly those on this path who are tasked with bringing into existence an understanding for the youthful generation who aspires to the great ideals of humanity, but needs the deep wisdom of our collective spiritual paths, elders, and transmissions to embody those ideals. It is not a theoretical path, but one that has grown out of the praxis of our own lives.

All paths of an interspiritual nature are revolutionary. While they may not lead to a complete understanding of Ultimate Reality, they certainly increase our understanding of humanity within Ultimate Reality. They require us to reevaluate our traditions in the light of personal contemplative experience, in light of the revelations of other traditions, and in light of what we have learned about the world through science, psychology, and sociology. They also ask us to take seriously the impulse that is incarnating in the new generation, and to be open as to how we might pass on the wisdom of our human family.

We end this section with another gem from Brother Wayne, this time from his book *A Monk in the World*, capturing some of the pitfalls and pearls of these interspiritual paths:

> In a sense, to pursue an intermystical spiritual life is to be a real pioneer of the Spirit. It is not an easy path to travel, because not many maps exist yet, and many people fear losing their way, but it yields rich deposits of wisdom along the way. If we trust, keep moving on, and share our experience with others, while seeking their advice, we will be fine. In fact, uncertainty can lead to even greater spiritual realizations. Without the familiar rituals and beliefs of our tradition to fall back on, we sometimes come closer to realizing the true goals of religion.[45]

Epilogue: Touching the Horizon

> "There is no word impossible for God." And this is precisely the task, to achieve what at first glance seems quite impossible: to unite Heaven and Earth, Flesh and Spirit, the World and God, Masculine and Feminine, Secular and Sacred. "The Buddha Way is unattainable. I vow to attain it!"
>
> —*Raimon Panikkar, Blessed Simplicity*

We situate new monasticism in terms of a *movement*, an organic arising of a deep desire to live a meaningful life and serve the world through our work and our compassion. It grows out of the desire to incarnate a contemporary spirituality, one that drinks deeply from the wells of human wisdom that have been dug throughout our ages, but one that also speaks to our modern sensibilities, to the unique occurrence of the coming together of the human race in one globally connected world, and that addresses the multiple and complex needs of a humanity in the throes of transition into a new era;

an era where our differences are understood within the context of our unity as human beings, and where our diversity is celebrated, encouraged, and supported; an era where what we do is worth much less than who we are, and what we produce is judged in terms of its sustainability and its contribution to the betterment of human relationships and the easing of suffering on our planet. New monasticism may well be the beginnings of a physical manifestation of what is already true in spiritual realms, where a connected and collaborative effort of spiritual energies and truths work together and in harmony for the good of all life on our planet. This can be seen in the new monk's ability to move seamlessly between wisdom traditions, art, music, solitude, hard work, community, and friendship.

New monasticism is a search for the deepest humanity in us all. It is in this search that we are all united, not only to our fellow monks, but to all who long to birth a new world that lives and breathes of the Spirit, to all who desire to come to the utter depths of their being, and then to enter the world through that doorway. A new monastic is one who feels the calling to her own evolution, her own depth of Spirit, her own transformational path, and responds. She embarks on this path in order to better serve all of Life, not knowing where this journey will take her, but knowing that she can no longer view anything in her life as separate from this journey. She is motivated by her ideals of love and compassion for others, as well as an unshakable belief in the truth and reality of human spiritual maturation, of its transformative power, grace, and sustaining ground. She is committed to serving the world in growing degrees of sacrificial love, skillful wisdom, and joy. Any such person may rightly be called a new monastic.

MOVEMENT 2
Unpacking the Manifesto

QUESTIONS KINDLED BY THE MANIFESTO:
A DIALOGUE WITH TRADITION

If we stand now at a unique moment in history, when the great religions of the world are converging, then new and bold modes of thought are called for. . . . The convergence of religions is pressuring us to penetrate to new levels of our inner world and to explore its richness. To make this exploration, we must develop new structures of thought and relatedness; we must be ready to take new steps. Our venture calls for us to be both creative and critical—to propose ideas imaginatively, but also . . . tentatively. As we proceed, we will have to test our proposals in the multi-dimensional context that is emerging. In our new complex spiritual environment, we must learn to think in a multi-dimensional way: to test our ideas for the future against the present and the past and against the religious experience of all of humankind.[1]

—*Ewert H. Cousins*

Let us now return to our dialogue between Adam Bucko and Zachary Markwith, an entrance into some of the thoughts and concerns spurred by the Manifesto and a catalyst for what we hope to be an ever-growing and deeper relationship between new monastics and the long-established wisdom paths of our religious traditions. If you missed our initial introduction to this dialogue, please return to briefly read of its origin and the questions posed by Pir Zia Inayat-Khan which sparked the following conversation found toward the end of the section "The Book and the Manifesto."

Zachary is the first to respond to Pir Zia's invitation, using the Manifesto as an initial basis for the dialogue:[2]

Dear Adam,

I share your inclusive vision of the revealed religions, humanity and the world. It seems to me that we can and in some cases must take cognizance of and learn from all of the great traditions, East and West, and those who embody their highest ideals in the past and present. You have mapped out some of the different paths a spiritual seeker might take, including adopting a single religion, creating a synthesis between two, and even forging one's own path not bound by any one. It seems to me that each revealed religion is a unique path that leads to the same Summit. . . .

What is most important to me is what works and the evidence suggests that the surest way to enlightenment or sanctity is through one of the great living traditions. . . . It is true that inspired syntheses exist and continue to create men and women of virtue and even sanctity. . . . However, I wonder how helpful it is for most people to explore these possibilities when spiritual disciplines and guidance remain accessible in Buddhism, Orthodox Christianity, and Islamic Sufism, for example? . . .

There are many who find doctrinal and aesthetic supports from other religions—their sacred texts, saints, and art—but in my view it is most helpful to be rooted in the practical aspects (i.e. rites, spiritual disciplines, etc.) of a single tradition. . . . While I firmly believe that all of these paths lead to Self-realization, it seems to me that it is sufficient and in most cases necessary to focus on the Divine through one. . . . I think we have a challenge to preserve religious diversity precisely so that we can perceive our spiritual unity with all that is. The revealed religions remain so many pathways to that realization.

Responding to Zachary's letter, Adam writes:

Dear Zachary,

Thank you for your thoughts. . . .

I would like to open my response by saying that I too think that following one single path is often the best way to pursue the journey into God. In my own life, I often desired that kind of straight path and guidance. However, as my life unfolded, I realized that . . . much of my path was directed and inspired by mentors from traditions other than Christianity. . . . Reconciliation of those experiences with mentors has not always been easy. It is because of that that I looked for guidance in people like Br. Wayne Teasdale, Andrew Harvey, Matthew Fox, and Father Bede Griffiths. . . .

In addition to my own "interspiritual path," which through difficulty and praxis has shown itself to me to be an authentic contemplative path to God, I have also worked with young people for over a decade, and have learned that most young people these days don't start or end their search in a single tradition. . . . Many of us feel that the rise of "spiritual but not religious" is not a sign of spiritual decline but can be a new kind of spiritual awakening if it can be shepherded in a mature way.

For me, the burning question then becomes, what does it mean to have a deep spiritual and contemplative life in this new framework? How does one enter and commit in a mature way to this path? Is it possible for this interspiritual path to deliver the type of transformation that all of the more traditional paths promise? ... Like Rilke's advice to the young poet, however, the answer to those questions lies less in trying to find articulations that satisfy the mind than in the wholehearted living out of them in the praxis of one's life and in proper discernment of the results. ...

[Rory's and my] perspective has been informed by our experiences of the contemplative journey and by our wonderful teachers and mentors from varying traditions. ... We feel that the Manifesto is an expression of a specific lineage that has been lived by people like Raimon Panikkar, Swami Abishiktananda, Fr. Bede Griffiths, and most recently Brother Wayne Teasdale, who was a close, personal friend and mentor for Rory. In it we are attempting to name an impulse that we feel arising in our world and to articulate a framework that can begin to guide young seekers into a genuine contemplative path. ... This all, of course, has to be done in a very careful, patient, and mature way that is led by and infused at all stages by the Spirit of God.

As you mentioned in your letter, in the Manifesto we talk about three different ways of being interspiritual:

(1) When one has a solid grounding in one tradition, and from this foundational point reaches out to experience and understand the wisdom of other traditions. This has been the way of many of the founders of the Interspiritual movement, such as Father Bede Griffiths and Brother Wayne Teasdale.

(2) When one goes the way of "multiple belonging" by fully immersing oneself in multiple traditions, such as Lex Hixon, also known as Shaykh Nur al-Jerrahi, did.

(3) When one follows one's inner guidance, what George Fox, founder of the Quakers, called one's "inner teacher," and what Christians have often referred to as the "guidance of the Holy Spirit" as a primary methodology for one's spiritual path. [This is what we call an interspiritual path.]

In your letter you refer to this third path as "forging one's own path not bound by any [tradition]." When people talk about this third way of being interspiritual, they often assume that one is creating their own path by following "whatever one wants" (relying on self with a small "s" vs. the guidance of the tradition). I would like, however, to distinguish following "whatever one wants" from "following the guidance of the Holy Spirit." Especially in my own experience of the Christian tradition, there is a tradition of saints whose primary way into God was following the guidance of the Holy Spirit. . . . In our age this way may not lead to being embedded in a particular tradition (without eliminating this possibility). . . .

It is this distinction between self and Holy Spirit that I believe allows us to really explore what it means to have an authentic spirituality that can serve young people, many of whom don't necessarily feel called to start or end their journey in one specific tradition. It is also important to recognize that we make pains to assert that this journey doesn't occur on one's own, but requires the discernment of a "sangha," one's spiritual community, as well as deep and intimate relationships with elders. It is how our journeys have unfolded. . . . While there are many examples of people who simply "shop around" and use their quest and lack of commitment as a way to bypass important issues of the path, it is important to make a distinction between that and what we are talking about here . . .

In my experience, most young people (especially those who call themselves "spiritual but not religious") start with this third way of being interspiritual. The longing of their hearts and the guidance of the Holy Spirit brings them into contact with a set of principles and practices (like yoga or meditation). While this leads to some insight and in some cases helps people to fully commit themselves to a spiritual path, it rarely gives them a framework and guidance that can produce spiritual maturity. . . . As a result, one can spend years taking workshops and never really get a sense of depth and direction. The guidance of the Holy Spirit also becomes very difficult to recognize, unless one can work with a seasoned spiritual director or guide who can help one recognize the unfolding of God in one's heart.

It is for this reason that Rory and I feel that it is not so much whether young people will choose a specific tradition, but rather will have access to proper training and formation that can speak to their hearts and teach them to humbly empty themselves so they can welcome the "whisperings and light of the Holy Spirit." To this end, we are currently collaborating with elders . . . [on] a formation process that will include personal guidance with a spiritual director, a theoretical framework, deep contemplative practice, small group work, silent solitary retreats, immersive dialogical dialogue and forms of heart-filled celebration and community. . . .

If spiritual training is what will determine the depth of spirituality of the new generation, how does one offer training in an interspiritual context? In few words, it is our view that training may start with a universal framework like the one articulated by Br. Wayne Teasdale. Once some work is done in gaining an understanding of the framework, and once one works with a spiritual director for an extended period of time (focusing on learning how to recognize God's unfolding and guidance in one's heart), one can be encouraged to train within a tradition (in some cases more than one if the spirit demands that) and receive extended training within that tradition, working with a guide from the tradition and fully respecting the integrity of that practice and tradition. So, naturally one may move from a type 3 of interspirituality to a type 1 or 2. This brings us closely to what you suggested in your letter, namely that there are benefits to being faithful to a specific set of teachings and guidance. In the end, one may still go back to type 3 of interspirituality. . . . [I]t remains to be seen, but we do feel that those who are called to [an *interspiritual path*] can serve in such a way that their insights may benefit the building of new frameworks, ones that may be necessary for our future.

In our final installment, Zachary responds to Adam's letter:

Dear Adam,

It seems to me that you are indeed speaking to a particular impulse and serving many spiritual seekers, which I can only commend. The Prophet Muhammad is reported to have said, "There are as many paths to God as there are children of Adam." The human response to the Divine is characterized by diversity. . . .

I don't make a sharp distinction between religion and spirituality, even if there are many who practice religion more or less without spirituality and others spirituality without religion. The Traditionalists or Perennialists maintain that spirituality is in fact the inner or esoteric dimension of religion that awakens or actualizes the inner aspect of the human being, eventually leading to the alchemical wedding of the Spirit with both the soul and the body. . . .

It seems to me that being rooted in a particular tradition has many advantages for a spiritual seeker. . . . I am not entirely against borrowing certain elements from other traditions and learning as much as we can from them, but the central rites and spiritual dimensions of each religion seem to have certain conditions that require regular and even exclusive observance to be fully efficacious. . . .

While recognizing that flashes of inspiration illuminate all souls and societies, including our increasingly secular ones, it seems to me that many spiritual seekers are looking for more stable and lasting nourishment from the Spirit. . . . Given the potential failings of human nature inside or outside of religion, one has to search for authentic teachers and rely on one's own discernment.

I would suggest that the millennial religions remain our best options because what directly descends from Heaven can best ensure a felicitous return. Manmade experiments have been going on for some time, but they rarely produce a Saint Francis of Assisi, Rumi, or Sri Ramana Maharshi, as well as great works of art such as Chartres Cathedral, the Dome of the Rock, or the Taj Mahal. It is precisely our loss of tradition as something living . . . that has created so much confusion and disequilibrium in the modern world, including alienation, the loss of meaning and spiritual orientation, destructive forms of technology, the environmental crisis, as well as religious and secular fundamentalism. . . .

My advice for the person who is spiritual but not religious is that one can find tried and tested methods or spiritual paths in the living religions. Authentic teachers may be more rare today, but the path of the Buddha, Bodhisattva, and enlightenment remains accessible through Buddhist teachers; the way of Christ, the Virgin, and deification through Christian teachers; and the way of the Quran, the Prophet, and Sufi through Muslim teachers. One simply has to have the discernment and courage to dismiss those who use religion for their own questionable motives. Then one can truly benefit from what a Thomas Merton, Thich Nhat Hanh, or Seyyed Hossein Nasr have to teach us about religion and spirituality, not to mention those who have dedicated themselves specifically to the path of service, such as Mother Teresa, Mahatma Gandhi, and Ahmadu Bamba.

Some blessed souls have taken from more than one tradition. A few even traverse the path in a somewhat solitary manner, although generally within the matrix of a revealed form. I recognize and honor these possibilities. However, I am not sure how far a path entirely outside of a given religion can lead. Some of these specific questions and possibilities seem rather nuanced, complex, and contextual. . . .

No one should be compelled to accept a given faith, which is against the spirit and very letter of the Quran, which reminds us that, "There is no compulsion in religion" (2:256). While it is now imperative to recognize all revealed religions as authentic paths to God and Divine realization here on earth—and the freedom of religion in general—the practical commitment to a single religion and spiritual path offer us sustained contact with the Spirit and That which is beyond all limitations, secular, religious and even spiritual. Some will no doubt get there through a more circuitous route, even though we maintain that the way of a given Prophet, Avatar, the Buddha or Christ is most direct. And God knows best.

Zachary is not alone in his concerns, as we share them as well. However, while new ways are not necessarily for everyone, and many are still called to walk traditional paths, there are nevertheless many as well for whom returning exclusively to a traditional path no longer feels like an option. We have to respect that. Furthermore, we feel compelled to name and affirm the validity of this emergence as a genuine movement of the Holy Spirit, as revelatory, and as a movement to be nurtured with care and in dialogue with traditional paths.

Which leaves us with Adam's "burning questions": What does it mean to have a deep spiritual and contemplative life in this new framework? How does one enter and commit in a mature way to this path? Is it possible for this interspiritual path to deliver the type of transformation that all of the more traditional paths promise? How does one offer training in an interspiritual context?

We offer the remainder of this book as a prayer, a song of exploration, a copious journey—into the heart of these questions.

A GLOBAL MYTHOS

You cannot look directly at the source of light; you turn your back to it so that you may see—not the light, but the illuminated things. Light is invisible, so too with the myth. . . . Myth is that which we take for granted, that which we do not question... The myth is transparent like the light, and the mythical story— mythologumenon—is only the form, the garment in which the myth happens to be expressed, enwrapped, illumined.[3]
—*Raimon Panikkar*

Through the centuries, a general plan appears truly to be in course of realization around us. Something is afoot in the universe, a result is working out which can best be compared to a gestation and birth: the birth of a spiritual reality formed by souls and the matter they draw after them.[4]
—*Pierre Teilhard de Chardin*

Thus, the failure to communicate with a new generation drives the creative flow. . . . The tragedy of the "communication-gap" turns out to be but the birth pangs of a new paradigm, the catalyst for a spiritual revolution. . . . At that moment, a ferment of syncretistic-creation suddenly arises, guided by a teleological pull toward a new paradigm. It is a period of radical experimentation and rich cross-fertilization. . . . The once rigid forms become fluid again. . . . The memory of the "old" is re-interpreted and elaborated to suit the needs of a new age, a new spiritual landscape. And in this way, another reality map is born![5]
—*Rabbi Zalman Schachter-Shalomi*
and Netanel Miles-Yépez

In the Midst of Epochal Change

The Manifesto is birthed out of our contemporary milieu, one in a state of transition. The signs of this are legion. You can hear and read about this transition in nearly every field: religion, sociology, politics, environmental science, economics, spirituality; even what it means to be secular is undergoing a deep re-visioning. In each of these fields there are those who feel the world they have known is being torn apart, degraded and splintered, who are living in fear of an unknown future. There are also those who find themselves on the edge of this transition, experimenting with new ways of horizontal leadership, solidarity, economic systems, "natural hierarchy," pluralism that goes beyond mere tolerance, and of course spirituality, this last often outside traditional religious structures. The fear of those who feel their old world collapsing around them is well founded. The world they know is coming to an end.

The Polish sociologist Zygmunt Bauman speaks of us living in "liquid times . . . an age of uncertainty." Raimon Panikkar talks about a world where we have lost our mythos, standing in between the death of the old and among the birth pangs of a new *mythos*. In short, we are in the midst of an epochal change.

In the book God Hidden, Whereabouts Unknown by the late Rabbi Zalman Schachter-Shalomi and Netanel Miles-Yépez (on the kabbalistic concept of tzimtzum, or the contraction of God), we find an excellent description of life during such a time. They describe the emergence of an epoch as a "new beginning, a fluid period of transition, establishing 'new gods' for a new era. . . . In such liquid moments . . . a discontent seeded through an entire generation awakes. It is a slow process, as the new 'light' filters down and is absorbed and intuited by those sensitive to it, leading to dissatisfaction with the answers and understandings of the past epoch. People discover a 'taste' for something they have never before experienced."[6]

As people discover this "taste" they are compelled, as it were, to begin questioning old answers and ways of living. They become disillusioned with past structures, and intent on building new ones.

> [The] system of shared religious and cultural beliefs by which we orient ourselves in all situations—begins to break down, initiating a process of shifting from one paradigm to another. . . . It is a tool for reshaping the landscape of our collective mental and spiritual frontiers, creating a new reality-map to replace the one that preceded it. . . . What was once responsive, and even innovative, is now clumsy, struggling even to understand the questions being asked of it. . . . The situation is untenable, and the utter frustration of it is what eventually gives rise to the dynamic period of conception between paradigms.[7]

"The dynamic period of conception between paradigms"—that is where we find ourselves today. It is for us to remain forward-looking, trusting the evolutionary thrust of Spirit.

Complexity, Consciousness, and Convergence: An Evolutionary Story

A major element of this new emerging paradigm, the mythos of our time, is an understanding of our place *in* time—that is, a historical understanding of how we have gotten to where we are. This entails an evolutionary story, and includes over 13.8 billion years of evolutionary development which we understand today as never before. It is a story from a Big Bang to stardust to galaxies to solar systems to planets to amoebas, plant life, fish, reptiles, mammals, and finally, yes, the human being. Simply understanding the evolutionary development of the last link in the chain, that of the human being, is a long tale in and of itself.

Understanding how we got here gives us clues as to where we are going and which direction we should head to get there. Perhaps the best book written about humanity's development is Ken Wilber's *Sex, Ecology, Spirituality* (the first of a supposed three-part *Kosmos Trilogy*), a beautiful, grace-filled book that weaves a marvelous story for us to understand our place in history and to situate our various realms of knowledge so that we may integrate them into a synthetic whole. Another option is *A Brief History of Everything*, Wilber's highly readable popular version of the story told in *Sex, Ecology, Spirituality*.

The beginning of *our* story was contemporary life within an epochal change. It continues here with the work of Pierre Teilhard de Chardin, a Catholic priest and highly regarded paleontologist, who wedded his scientific insight into the mechanisms of evolution with a stunning view of future human development. Teilhard saw evolution proceeding not haphazardly through "survival of the fittest," but rather through "the organic relationships linking *consciousness* and *complexity* within the Universe," with a specific teleological pull toward greater unity and consciousness.[8] Teilhard introduced a novel notion into the evolutionary picture, that of the development of complexity, unification, and increasing consciousness. Through this Teilhard brought together the realms of material reality with interiority and consciousness, and saw both of them operating within the realm of evolution and accordingly by the same mechanisms—mainly, increasingly complex unions leading to greater consciousness. In Teilhard's words:

> The fact of evolution comes to remind us that the principal movement of reality is a synthesis, in the course of which plurality manifests itself in increasingly complex and organic forms, each further degree of unification being accompanied by a growth of inner consciousness and freedom.[9]

In other words, the higher the degree of complexity in a living creature, the higher its consciousness; and vice versa.[10]

The phenomenon of growing consciousness on earth, in short, is directly due to the increasingly advanced organization of more and more complicated elements, successively created by the working of chemistry and of Life. . . . Life moves toward unification.[11]

This process is fairly easy to see when we look at the development of single-celled organisms to more complex systems. At each step, we see an increasingly complex arrangement of individual parts, and an expanse of "consciousness," or interiority and freedom. Consider the unification of the various molecules into cells, cells into organs, on up to cellular organisms and finally the amazing complexity of the human brain, the apex of evolution in the physical landscape. Each step can be classified as representing an increase in consciousness, in interiority and freedom. According to Teilhard, at each step the organization of the increasingly complex elements occurs through "center-to-center" unions of the individual elements. Ewert Cousins describes these unions as "touching each other at the creative core of their being, [where] they release new energy which leads to more complex units. Greater complexity leads to greater interiority which, in turn, leads to more creative unions."[12]

As Teilhard saw it, life on our planet has continued to fan out since its first conception, creating innumerable living beings, plants, animals, microbes, with an almost inexhaustible creativity, yet always in the direction of more complex unions and increasing consciousness, seemingly searching for something. Then, with the emergence of the human being, a shift in the evolutionary impulse occurred. No longer did it fan out in the direction of creating new life forms.[13]

Henceforth, it would be concerned with *humanity*.

Teilhard envisaged "a world whose evolutionary capacity is *concentrated upon* and *confined to the human soul*. The question of whether the Universe is still developing then becomes a matter of deciding whether the *human spirit* is still in process of evolution. . . . We shall then see that a vast evolutionary process is in ceaseless operation around us, but that it is situated within the *sphere of consciousness* (and collective consciousness)."[14]

The uniqueness of the human species lay in its ability for reflection. The human being represents, in the evolutionary process, a fundamental break from what had come before. In the human being, evolution, in a sense, found the form it was looking for. Through this novel phenomenon of reflection, an exponential deepening of interiority and consciousness occurred. As a consequence, a much greater relatedness within the species was born, the result of which would be more complex forms of communion and unity, and hence consciousness. In fact, Teilhard saw the phenomenon of reflection not so much as an individual deepening, but primarily as a social phenomenon:

> Man not only knows; he knows that he knows. He reflects. But this power of reflection, when restricted to the individual, is only partial and rudimentary. . . . It is only when opposed to other men that he can discover his own depth and wholeness. However personal and incommunicable it may be at its root and origin, Reflection can only be developed in communion with others. It is essentially a *social* phenomenon.[15]

Being primarily a social phenomenon, this had profound consequences for the future direction of our species. The same evolutionary forces that had magically and painstakingly led to the emergence of the human being from nothing less than stardust over the course of nearly fourteen billion years were now inexorably bringing humanity closer and closer together. Rather than fanning out, or diverging, as evolution had done for millions of years, it suddenly crossed a new threshold and became convergent.

> At the human level a radical change, seemingly due to the spiritual phenomenon of Reflection, overtook this [divergent] law of development. . . . [Human beings] become capable (indeed are under an irresistible compulsion) of drawing close to one another, of communicating, and finally of uniting . . . with the result that the entire system . . . which in the ordinary course would have culminated in a knot and a fanning out of new divergent lines, now tends to fold in upon itself.[16]

> What can this mean except that its eventual completion and wholeness must exactly coincide (in full accord with the Law of Complexity) with what we have called the *planetization* of Mankind. ... In due course . . . it must supercenter itself in the bosom of a Mankind *totally reflexive upon itself.*[17]

For Teilhard then, an increasingly connected humanity, as seen today in virtually every field of human endeavor, was an evolutionary necessity, and marks a tremendous potential leap forward for humanity. It has brought serious problems, no doubt, including cultural, religious and ethnic clashes, as well as the horrendous degradation of our environment. However, if Teilhard is right, then we are also caught up in much greater currents than we can imagine, ones which dwarf the destructive tendencies we see all around us. For the tremendous opportunities being brought about in new synergistic emergences, arising out of the creative tensions being thrust upon us, are being sought by the very currents of evolution.

And for Teilhard, evolution *is* incarnation. "Incarnation does not take place *in* evolution. . . . Rather, the whole evolutionary process is incarnational."[18]

Unification

Evolution proceeds through increasingly complex forms of unity, where each in turn leads to an expansion of consciousness. Teilhard saw this process throughout the entire evolutionary strata, which thus endowed all forms of matter with at least a minimal form of consciousness. In this, Teilhard parallels the great mystical insights in all the world's religious traditions. Interestingly, his insight into these depths of matter, being imbued with consciousness as they were, seems to stem from mystical experiences he had in his childhood, recounted in his autobiographical essay, "The Heart of Matter." Teilhard did not pick up these ideas from other religious traditions or even from his own—they seemed to develop in a unique way within his own personal experience of life.[19] It's as if from his earliest days, Teilhard was being prepared for the development of his evolutionary philosophy, synthesizing the insights of both science and religion, weaving together the disparate elements of matter and consciousness in order to apply them to human spiritual growth.

Returning to our narrative, we find ourselves where humanity is being drawn closer and closer together by the phenomenon of reflection, "the forces of collectivization . . . the constant tightening of economic bonds; the spread of financial and intellectual associations; the totalization of political regimes; the closer physical contact of individuals as well as of nations; the increasing impossibility of being or acting or thinking *alone*—in short, the rise, in every form, of the *Other* around us."[20]

Teilhard's prophetic realization of a world coming into closer and closer contact, where we find ourselves continually face to face with the other, will play an important role as we unpack the Manifesto. What are the consequences of this for a contemporary spiritual path? How do we deal with this reality in a spiritually mature, and spiritually maturing, way? These questions are of major concern for all new monastics.

But first, we finish this section with how Teilhard understood this further coming together of our human family, driven so inexorably by the forces of evolution: "the human particles do not merely multiply in numbers every day at an increasing rate, but through contact with one another automatically develop around themselves an ever denser tangle of economic and social relationships. . . . [U]nder the pressure of these relentless factors—relentless because they are a part of the deepest and most generalized conditions of the planetary structure—there is only one way in which the tide can flow: the way of ever-increasing unification."[21]

Recall that evolution always proceeds by increasing complexity and consciousness, which involves the unification of increasingly complex elements. In the human sphere, this unification differs notably from the more mechanistic unities of the geosphere and biosphere. For example, the specialization of cells which unify by performing various individualized, mechanistic functions, such as white blood cells attacking foreign materials, while red blood cells deliver oxygen to the body. Among our human family, the unity is not functional per se, but first and foremost social. "We see Nature combining molecules and cells in the living body to construct separate individuals, and the same Nature, stubbornly pursuing the same course but on a higher level, combining individuals in social organisms to obtain a higher order of psychic results. The processes of chemistry and biology [rightly understood as processes of increasing complexity and consciousness] are continued without a break in the social sphere."[22]

In the human sphere, therefore, the unification sought cannot be brought about in a monolithic way, e.g., through a totalitarian state or through the adoption by every human being of a similar belief system (which would correspond to a functional unity, not a social unity). In fact, it has to occur in exactly the opposite direction. We are being drawn together in order to effectuate a more complex unity than has previously been, in order that an ever-greater consciousness can be born. Consequently, the unity of the human family can only be brought about as all individual human beings cultivate within themselves their own uniqueness to the highest degree, hence increasing the complexity of the unity to be brought about in the human family. This uniqueness Teilhard refers to as "personality."

What is being formed then, is

a more synthetic organization of the human world. . . . And this new order, the thought of which is in all our minds, what form can it take other than a . . . Mankind become at once more complex and more centered upon itself?[23]

The tightening network of economic and social bonds in which we live and from which we suffer, the growing compulsion to act, to produce, to think collectively which so disquiets us— what do they become, seen in this way, except the [preparation] . . . not to mechanize and submerge us, but to raise us, by way of increasing complexity, to a higher awareness of our own personality?[24]

True union, the union of heart and spirit, does not enslave, nor does it neutralize the individuals which it brings together. It *superpersonalizes* them.[25]

This union of highly individualized units come into being, as with all evolutionary unification, through center-to-center meetings. For the human being this means through love, *caritas*. "If the synthesis of the Spirit is to be brought about in its entirety . . . it can only be done, in the last resort, through the meeting, *center to center,* of human units, such as can only be realized in a universal, mutual love."[26]

Teilhard was not ignorant of the many problems that this process would entail (he served as a stretcher-bearer in World War I)—not the least of which is humanity's extreme difficulty in coming into contact with the other. It is telling though how Teilhard saw so much of the negative tendencies in humanity, such as totalitarian regimes, world wars, a predatory global economic system—even the current ecological crisis Teilhard would surely see in the same light—as essentially enforced mechanisms to bring humanity closer together. Behind them was the evolutionary impulse. Teilhard saw up ahead a great change approaching humanity, where rather than being forced to converge, we would learn to live and move in the world in such a way as to willingly cooperate with this teleological pull, so intrinsic to the Kosmos itself, a collaborative effort destined to bring about the creation of a higher consciousness.

Although individualistic instincts may rebel against this drive toward the collective, they do so in vain and wrongly. . . . The real nature of this impulse that is sweeping us toward a state of super-organization is such as to make us more completely personalized and human. . . . [We need] to pass beyond the *enforced* phase, where it is now, into the *free* phase: that in which . . . a natural union of affinity and sympathy will supersede the forces of compulsion.[27]

The new monastic movement attempts to bring people together in just such a union of affinity and sympathy, in love, united behind a passion to bring a new world into being, a global civilization of the heart, and dedicated to the cultivation of each person's uniqueness within a process of spiritual maturation. We will look much more closely at Teilhard's development of personality, as well as his insight that "unification differentiates," in our upcoming section on dialogical sophiology.

A Second Axial Age

While Teilhard extrapolated the processes of the evolutionary impulse and applied them to humanity's trajectory, Ewert Cousins, one of the great theologians of the twentieth century, articulated some of the specific emergences within the evolutionary process itself. He dubbed these emergences the dawning of a "Second Axial Age." We will follow Cousins's development of a Second Axial Age from his timely book *Christ of the 21st Century*.

The notion of a First Axial Age was put forward by Karl Jaspers in his book, *The Origin and Goal of History*. It referred to roughly the period from 800–200 BCE. What Jaspers saw during this time was a revolution in human consciousness, which gave birth to the mindset within which all of our present-day religious traditions were formed. It was during this time that Lao-Tzu and Confucius lived in China, the Upanishads were revolutionizing religion in India, along with the Buddha and Mahavira (the founder of Jainism), Zoroaster founded a religion in Persia, the Jewish prophets (particularly Jeremiah) brought forth a new understanding of justice and righteousness, and Socrates, Plato, and Aristotle gave their gifts that became the foundation of the Western world, forming a basis for subsequent Christian theology and philosophy.[28]

What was this revolution in consciousness? It was the emergence of an individualized consciousness, one which allowed human beings for the first time to think apart from "the tribe," apart from the collective; to question the worldview they had been given, essentially to think for themselves. It is here, in the First Axial period that a monastic spirituality develops for the first time, and it is here that the basis of science develops as people for the first time could stand apart from nature and look upon it as an object.[29] Monastic spirituality wasn't possible before this time, because primal people's "consciousness could not sustain it. Primal consciousness did not contain the distinct center of individuality necessary to produce the monk as a religious type."[30] It is also here that one is able for the first time to criticize social structures and injustices, as seen among the Jewish prophets who emerge in this period.[31] "With the awakening of reflective subjectivity, the individual could take a stand against the collectivity, become a distinct moral and spiritual self, and embark on an individual spiritual journey."[32]

Pre-Axial consciousness was not individualistic; it was tribal, seamlessly connected to the cosmos, nature, and the collective. It had no perspective of itself as separate from nature or from the tribe. It was inherently mythic and ritualistic, "embedded in the cosmos and in the fertility cycles of nature. Thus there was established a rich and creative harmony between primal peoples and the world of nature, a harmony which was explored, expressed, and celebrated in myth and ritual. Just as they felt themselves as part of nature, so they experienced themselves as part of the tribe. They had no sense of independent identity apart from the tribe."[33]

Today, according to Cousins, we are now entering a Second Axial Age. We discuss his thesis here because we believe that his expression of what is happening within the Second Axial Age, and what is needed in order to bring it to fruition, is fruitful ground for a new monastic spirituality to be understood. Too many people today wish for either a return to a pre-Axial consciousness—where we are unable to differentiate between ourselves and nature, between ourselves and the collective, and in this project an unrealistic utopian dream onto our future—while others wish for no more than a continuation of a First Axial consciousness, a propagation of individualism complete with selfish economic theories and the protection of entrenched interests. Neither of these are the basis for a new monastic spirituality and the world we strive to build.

The Second Axial Age is an age of integration, and through this, new and creative syntheses. In particular, it involves an integration of both pre-Axial and First Axial Age consciousness. We need both our individuality, the development of our uniqueness in higher and higher degrees, *and* an understanding of our intrinsic belonging within a vast Kosmos. We "must recapture the unity of tribal consciousness by seeing humanity as a single tribe. And we must see this single tribe related organically to the total cosmos."[34]

To return to Teilhard's thought, the synthesis the evolutionary impulse is driving us toward is a unification of the human family, a social unification which in the end can only be effected through the development of that which is most unique and incommunicable in us, our personalities. The true fulfillment of First Axial consciousness (individual consciousness) can only come about with a renewal and integration of the best of pre-Axial consciousness (our unity as one people organically related to the cosmos), and this higher synthesis is spurred forward by the convergent, and emergent, evolutionary factors at work. This is at the heart of a Second Axial Age.

Religious Traditions in a Second Axial Age

As a result of the impulse toward unity, a Second Axial age must be truly global in consciousness, and Cousins uses Teilhard's thought to understand and analyze the convergences happening today in this light. In particular, Cousins was interested in what this meant for our religious traditions. "Now that the forces of divergence have shifted to convergence, the religions must meet each other in center to center unions, discovering what is most authentic in each other, releasing creative energy toward a more complexified form of religious consciousness."

He calls such a creative encounter the "dialogic dialogue." We will be looking more closely at this particular methodology in a later chapter, as it holds substantial importance for the new monastic. If such encounters are successful, then Cousins believes the religions can renew themselves in the light of a Second Axial Age consciousness. "This will be complexified global consciousness, not a mere universal, undifferentiated, abstract consciousness. It will be global through the global convergence of cultures and religions and complexified by the dynamics of dialogic dialogue."[35]

However, in order for this dialogic dialogue to be successful, it will require the rediscovery of some of the gifts of pre-Axial times, mainly the shamanistic gift of passing over into different "worldspaces" or states of consciousness and then returning to the tribe with gifts and wisdom to share. Cousins refers to a "shamanistic faculty" where "we can leave, as it were, our distinctive forms of consciousness and enter by way of empathy into the consciousness of others. In so doing we enter into their value world and experience this from the inside. Then we return enriched, bringing into our own world these values and a larger horizon of awareness."[36]

Cousins called this a "shamanistic epistemology," "a faculty whereby we can pass over into the consciousness of another religion, gather new insight and return enriched to our own." This faculty has lain largely dormant since pre-Axial times, as it has not been needed, but Cousins now feels it should be a fundamental component of any religious—or even simply human—education.[37]

There are other ways in which Second Axial Age consciousness is global as well. One is "in rediscovering our roots in the earth."[38] We must face up to and address our ecological crisis. However, this must not be done in a merely mechanistic, scientific, First Axial Age way, but, more important, through rediscovering the wisdom of primal peoples, and through experiencing our relationship with the organic unity of which we are all a part. It is only with the knowing of ancient peoples that we will be able to solve our ecological crisis, for Earth needs our hearts and beingness more than it needs our minds.

As seen in the Manifesto, and more clearly laid out in the chapters ahead, new monastics are a product of a Second Axial Age consciousness. Their path is experiential, mystical, and spiritually active. In this they find themselves personally united in the depths of their being with all of humankind, with the earth and all of its creatures, and integrated into a larger Kosmic family. It is evolutionary, taking seriously our movement forward as a human family, and interested in the dynamics of how to reflect this impulse, unity, and uniqueness within our lives. It is religiously interdependent, participating in the construction within each one of us of a complexified religious consciousness. Finally, it partakes of the holiness of the secular, and cannot see its path as separate from any of the socio-economic structures needed for the establishment of a global civilization with a heart.

A New Generation

There can be little doubt that traditional religious frameworks are no longer speaking to new generations as they have in the past, especially in the West. In a op-ed piece in the *Los Angeles Times*, Philip Clayton, former dean of faculty at Claremont School of Theology, writes that the fastest growing religious group in the United States is "spiritual but not religious," in some surveys a shocking 75 percent of Americans between the ages of 18 and 29.[39] *Time Magazine* declares "The Rise of the Nones" one of the top ten trends changing American life, "nones" being those who do not declare a religious affiliation.[40] Clayton argues that young people are not necessarily rejecting a sense of God, but rather they feel "that religious organizations are too concerned with money and power, too focused on rules and too involved in the structures of the political status quo."[41] In fact, surveys show that many of the spiritual but not religious actually pray and engage in spiritual practice *more* than those who declare themselves religious.

Diane Butler Bass, in her insightful study on religious trends in the West, *Christianity After Religion,* finds similar results. Only around 20 percent of the population of the United States has a "great deal of confidence" in organized religion, yet only a paltry 1.6 percent consider themselves atheist. [42] Further, nearly 48 percent claim to have had a mystical encounter with the divine.[43] This leads Bass to conclude that "many of them are traveling new paths of meaning, exploring new ways to live their lives, experiencing a new sense of authenticity and wonder, and practicing new forms of community that address global concerns of human flourishing."[44]

This speaks to a vast number of people in the West who are exploring nontraditional spiritual and religious paths outside of traditional boundaries. Bass believes that

> the United States (and not only the United States) is caught up in the throes of a spiritual awakening, a period of sustained religious and political transformation during which our ways of seeing the world, understanding ourselves, and expressing faith

are being, to borrow a phrase, "born again." . . . This transformation is what some hope will be a "Great Turning" toward a global community based on shared human connection, dedicated to the care of our planet, committed to justice and equality, that seeks to raise hundreds of millions from poverty, violence, and oppression.[45]

Scholars and theologians Ilia Delio, OSF, and William D. Dinges describe in similar terms the arising of a "new spirituality":

a hybridization of traditions of the past, beliefs and practices of the present, and innovative ideas surrounding a new scientific synthesis and cosmology, . . . the widening cultural democratization of the sacred . . . [and] a quest for the sacred *within* the secular.[46]

The new spirituality is profoundly this-worldly . . . in its post-millennial, progressive-looking agenda for the transformation of individuals and societies. . . . [It] reveres the grandeur of nature in an unfolding universe. It celebrates embodied spirituality . . . ; reflects the subjective turn of modernity and postmodernity; emphasizes feelings, experience and the quest for human authenticity; accentuates human fulfillment in this world; reveres and affirms the cosmos and our belonging to it; finds the sacred in the secular; promotes a recomposed and embodied spirituality; and recognizes the infusion of nature and matter with spirit, consciousness, or life force.[47]

The resonance with what we described as the consciousness of a Second Axial Age is profound. The truth is there is a quiet revolution happening. People are beginning to reevaluate what matters and to rediscover spiritual life outside of traditional forms, in stark contrast to Western society's empty vision of a consumer-driven world. This is happening not only in religious life, but throughout society. Recent movements for solidarity and justice such as the Occupy movement, the Arab Spring, protests over the treatment of women, racism and police brutality—all of these are manifestations of this deeper Spirit. Despite their failings or successes, they are but an early efflorescence of something deeper emerging in our collective soul. In particular, young people are no longer interested in living in a world that doesn't feel like their soul's home, and they are willing to question the way things have been done in the past. It is to this questioning, this questing, that we speak here.

Too often these trends have been described as selfish (the "me generation"), ineffective (Occupy), syncretic (nontraditional paths), or simply failures (the Arab Spring). But the truth is they are merely the beginnings, the early footsteps of a newborn humanity, still struggling to emerge from the power structures of old. The Mother, spiritual partner to the great Indian sage Sri Aurobindo and a revered spiritual teacher, captures the essence of these struggles:

> We are in a very special situation, extremely special, without precedent. We are now witnessing the birth of a new world; it is very young, very weak—not in its essence but in its outer manifestation—not yet recognized, not even felt, denied by the majority. But it is here. It is here, making an effort to grow, absolutely *sure* of the result. But the road to it is a completely new road which has never before been traced out. . . . It is a beginning, a *universal beginning*. So, it is an absolutely unexpected and unpredictable adventure.
>
> There are people who love adventure. It is these I call and I tell them this: "I invite you to the great adventure."
>
> It is not a question of repeating spiritually what others have done before us, for our adventure begins beyond that. It is a question of a new creation, entirely new, with all the unforeseen events, the risks, the hazards it entails—a *real adventure*, whose goal is certain victory, but the road to which is unknown and must be traced out step by step in the unexplored. Something that has never been in this present universe and that will *never* be again in the same way. If that interests you . . . well, let us embark.[48]

As two people who have walked nontraditional spiritual paths, we are wary of the transition we are in and the tensions it causes. We are also awake to the emergent possibilities it calls forth. We know that this will take more than an ephemeral and self-glorifying declaration of having the new paradigm or being what we are looking for. We understand that our inner light can be clouded over, overlaid with years of cultural conditioning, trauma, and fear. We also know that in order for these new paths to be fruitful they must cultivate a partnership with traditional wisdom paths, and need the mentorship and guidance that holy souls, most often found within our religious traditions, can provide. Yet we also know that many people are no longer returning to traditional paths; they have branched out on their own, not out of a sense of selfishness, but through following that which is most alive in them. They need and demand the help and guidance of those who have walked paths to spiritual maturity before them. They are in want of new structures, ways of mentorship, and articulations to understand their journey and to help them walk it fruitfully.

Being under forty, both of us still feel connected to the younger generation, yet recognize that we are part of a linking generation. We both grew up within a religious tradition (Catholic), yet did not feel a need to be dependent on it or for it to be our sole guide into God. We have both been graced with deep mentorship from within numerous traditions (Hindu, Sufi, Buddhist, Christian, Jewish, indigenous wisdom). We are familiar with traditional religious symbolism and have also cultivated a respect for our religious traditions, particularly for the mystical streams and lineages they embody. Yet we also have no sympathy for repressive hierarchical structures, misogynistic tendencies, patriarchal domination, or dogmatic language and formulations that do not touch our lives personally. Additionally, as is clear in the Manifesto and throughout this book, we have grown considerably beyond the boundaries of any one tradition, and embrace the spirituality of a new generation. As such, we believe we find ourselves in the unique place of being both connected in deep ways to our religious traditions as well as in touch with a younger generation that is growing only more estranged from these traditions. Our hope for this new monastic vision, lifestyle, and practice is for it to serve the much-needed work of bringing into symbiosis these divergent memes.[49]

> Religious traditions and elders must come to recognize this impulse not as selfish, but rather as the movement of the Holy Spirit—opening up possibilities for new structures, new understandings, and even new spiritual paths to arise. They need to see that what is happening can lead for many people to a real commitment to the transformative journey, to taking responsibility for the inner impulse that arises and finding the courage to commit to it with all of one's being. This new spirituality demands a certain freedom of movement to be able to follow the guidance of the Spirit that one receives, moving us away from a reliance on religious doctrines, gurus, and institutions.

Toward the culmination of Brother Wayne Teasdale's classic book *The Mystic Heart,* he offers a prophetic "Message to the Young." It speaks to the spirit of this new spirituality.

I offer the following to the younger generation:

You must stand up on your own two feet in the spiritual life. You are responsible for this process; it cannot be shifted to your parents, your friends, or your teachers. . . . Don't concern yourself with what others are doing. . . . You must find your own way, and you must be faithful to the truth you know or discover.

As you look to your parents or friends for guidance, ask yourself: "Are they good examples of the spiritual life? Are they serious about their own development and transformation, or are they wasting time on activities that distract them from the work of life?" . . . Learn what you can from them. . . . But if it doesn't include authentic spirituality, and it isn't open to other traditions, then discover your own path and find your own spirituality.

Look to all the traditions of the spiritual life and adopt an attitude of interspirituality. Claim the wisdom dimension of all the traditions for yourself, and let wisdom guide you. . . . Bracket the negative influence of your culture. . . . It allows our inner values, voice, and vision to emerge into clarity.

Don't give in to the temptation of cynicism and despair. . . . Always leave the door of hope wide open. Cast off skepticism, and be a radiant presence of depth, compassion, love, and kindness to others. Dare to be different! Dare to be yourself! . . . Be who you know yourself to be in your moments of greatest clarity; don't allow others to determine your identity for you. Don't give away your power of self-determination.

Cultivate a love of quiet; learn to appreciate it. Gravitate toward silence; rest in the stillness. . . . It's restorative and revelatory . . . It will awaken the capacity for contemplation in you. . . . Let your spiritual practice revolve around it by adopting some form of meditation practice. Watch what will happen; it *will* transform you![50]

We call Brother Wayne's message, written in 1999, prophetic. In our experience, the younger generation is only coming to resonate more strongly with his message. In these pages we name an impulse that many people are already feeling and practicing in their daily lives. In doing so we hope to make it explicit, to bring it more fully into the light, so that those who are enlivened by this impulse can more fully embrace it, understand it, and grow roots within it. In the sections ahead we lay out some of the most important components we believe are necessary to build within this impulse a fuller structure and support for one's spiritual journey.

INTERSPIRITUALITY

The mystical life of the next thousand years and beyond will . . . be contemplative, interspiritual, socially engaged, environmentally responsible, holistic, engaging of other media, and cosmically open. . . .

It will be an enhanced understanding of the inner life through assimilating the psychological, moral, aesthetic, spiritual, and literary treasures of the world's religions. Each tradition will define itself in relation to every other viable tradition of the inner life; each will take into account the totality of the spiritual journey. . . .

It is deeply concerned with the plight of all those who suffer, wherever they are. . . .

It follows a strict adherence to ecological justice. . . .

It doesn't just depend on books or spiritual reading, but looks to art, music, and movies, . . . universal languages of vast sacred potential, . . . to nourish contemplative life. . . .

It recognizes that we are part of a much larger community . . . the human, the earth, the solar system, our galaxy, and the universe itself. . . .

Intermysticism is the deepest expression of the religious dimension of human life. It is the actual religion of each one of us when we arrive at the point of spiritual maturity.[51]

— Brother Wayne Teasdale

No single religion—not even all traditional religions taken together—has a monopoly on religion.[52]   —Raimon Panikkar

I use the term "global spirituality" or "global theology" to emphasize the emergence of a new planetary consciousness, breaking through traditional religious categories and disciplinary boundaries, that is affecting all life studies and systems. Global consciousness is revealing a new type of religious experience—what we might call multi-religion or interspiritual—that is giving rise to novel forms of spiritual practice, and new ways of living and approaching the spiritual journey and God.[53]

—Beverly Lanzetta

Origins

As mentioned previously, interspirituality was a word originally developed by Brother Wayne Teasdale in his 1999 book *The Mystic Heart*.

Interspirituality and intermysticism are the terms I have coined to designate the increasingly familiar phenomenon of cross-religious sharing of interior resources, the spiritual treasures of each tradition. . . .

We need to understand, to really grasp at an elemental level, that the definitive revolution *is* the spiritual awakening of humankind. This revolution will be the task of the Interspiritual Age. The necessary shifts in consciousness require a new approach to spirituality that transcends past religious cultures of fragmentation and isolation. The direct experience of interspirituality paves the way for a universal view of mysticism—that is the common heart of the world. . . .[54]

[Interspirituality is] a foundation that can prepare the way for a planet-wide enlightened culture, and a continuing community among the religions that is substantial, vital, and creative.[55]

For Brother Wayne, then, "interspirituality" was his way of articulating what was happening in this Second Axial Age and how it would proceed. It was about a deep sharing among humanity's wisdom traditions, but it was also about a democratization of the spiritual life. "We don't need to enter monasteries to become mystics or to cultivate our spirituality: We are all mystics! The mystic heart is the deepest part of who or what we really are. We need only to realize and activate that essential part of our being."[56]

Our religious traditions were seen as existing in subtle relationship with one another, with unforeseen connections leading to possibilities for expanded views of our humanity and emergent spiritual paths to be born:[57]

Interspirituality recognizes that many paths lead to the summit, and each one of them is valid. Yet each has its unique perspective on the nature of the summit. Interspirituality is open to growth in perspective; it implies a commitment to always push forward toward a more adequate understanding of the source, the meaning of life, and the best methods of proceeding in our spiritual lives.

The *inter* in interspirituality . . . means that through all the diverse forms of spiritual experience and insight we can evolve a higher view. We need this higher view; its cultivation and attainment are the tasks before us.[58]

In order to find this "higher view," Brother Wayne realized that interspirituality was about more than a new relationship among spiritual traditions. It was also about social, economic, and ecological justice as well. Interspirituality demanded a fuller engagement with the world, and the merger of that engagement with traditional contemplative life. As such, Brother Wayne was foundational to the new monastic movement.

In his book *A Monk in the World*, in essence an autobiographical testament to his life as a contemplative living in the world, he wrote:

> Each one of us is a mystic; a monk dwells in each of our depths, just below our everyday awareness. For me, the mystical path means awakening this monk within and nurturing its development in encountering the world. This path is reinforced by spiritual practice, with its breakthroughs and graces; supported by like-minded friends, with their love and challenges; empowered by thoughtful navigations through the limitations of time, work, and money. It means living with compassion and love in the concreteness of daily encounters, especially with the most vulnerable. It means taking risks for the sake of justice, which requires us to speak the truth boldly, clearly, and firmly to power in all its forms, especially the political, economic, and religious.[59]

For Brother Wayne, "No [spiritual] tradition is exempt from the necessity of social engagement where justice is at stake; indeed, the work of justice is itself a spiritual practice."[60]

Brother Wayne also spoke explicitly of the importance of our relationship with nature, and the organic qualities of the spiritual traditions themselves:

> All forms of spirituality must incorporate the dimension of the natural world and the openness to the cosmic community. They must guide us into a harmonious relationship with the earth and the universe itself. . . .

> Each form of spirituality is a living social organism capable of infinite growth as it acquires new insights, methods, and ways of formulating the goal of the mystical journey. We need to trust the experience of other traditions so that we can make it our own. In the long run, each tradition of the spiritual life will come to the service of the whole of humanity.[61]

Brother Wayne envisioned an interspiritual age and an interspiritual paradigm "that permits people from various traditions, or from no tradition, to explore the spiritual dimensions of any religion,"[62] and felt that "we often walk the interspiritual or intermystical path in an intuitive attempt to reach a more complete truth."[63]

In the following chapters we will water this embryonic seed that Brother Wayne has planted, that of an interspiritual path. We believe the time has come to name it outright—a path that has grown out of the deep intermystical minglings of the religious traditions. It has its own methodologies to offer those who walk its ways, its own inner heartbeat and sense of integrity, its own unique way of bringing forth spiritual maturation. It is a path that aims to incarnationally respect the uniqueness of each individual, with "superpersonalization" woven into the fabric of its ground. It is a path that cultivates the complexified religious consciousness of the Second Axial Age by being fundamentally religiously interdependent, and embodies a passionate drive to change the secular structures of the world in order that they may embody what is in our hearts. As such, it has a unique vocational emphasis and dialogical methodology. In all of this, it holds a humble prayer in its heart for bridges, partnerships, and guidance to be brought from traditional religious and wisdom paths. We know that we are not alone in being called to this path, as Spirit continues to weave further emergent possibilities.

In a foreshadowing of the new monastic movement, Brother Wayne also spoke of new structures that would be needed to help birth the interspiritual age. The one closest to his heart—and closest as well to new monastic life—was the universal order of sannyasa. Sannyasa, as Brother Wayne explains, has always been understood in the Hindu tradition as making "possible something beyond the comprehension of religion, something that transcends religion, because it is infinite and ineffable. It eludes the capacity of any concept or doctrine to express it."[64]

Brother Wayne had a beautiful vision of this order that enfolds its spirit within both the interspiritual and new monastic movements. This universal order would welcome

> as members individuals from all the world's religions and even from no tradition at all. . . . [It would] provide a forum for the further exploration of the mystical journey in all traditions, and in the emerging universal tradition as well. . . . It would also democratize the spiritual life as a state in which people could help one another, sharing their insights and spiritual resources . . . [as] an existential place of encounter.[65]

The movement's goal would be to provide a universal forum of diversity, bringing about openness to change by becoming agents of spiritual and intellectual ferment. Simply by being spiritual in a more spacious way—in an interspiritual way—it would broaden the horizon of our experience and knowledge. Its goal would be to enlarge our wisdom and our scope of action, to constantly radiate attitudes of charity, kindness, love, and compassion. The more this spirit spreads, the more it will awaken human consciousness to something greater than what we've known.[66]

The Present-Day Movement

Interspirituality has grown into a full-blown movement since Brother Wayne's passing in 2004. It is a broad movement, consisting of a wide variety of various constituencies and multiple meanings in our present day. It is important to mention that the impulse itself did not start with Brother Wayne; he was standing on the shoulders of those who came before him, and there were many who inspired him. One of the most crucial inspirations was his close relationship with Father Bede Griffiths and other Christian sannyasis. Many of the ideas that Brother Wayne articulated can be found in seed form in Father Bede's writings, and these seeds have continued to grow in other streams which parallel Teasdale's thought.

In speaking of some of these parallel movements, two worth mentioning are the work of theologian Matthew Fox and the scholar Andrew Harvey. Both of them had close contact with Father Bede. In the case of Matthew Fox, he developed the term "deep ecumenism" in 1988 in his book *The Coming of the Cosmic Christ* and today he uses "deep ecumenism" and "interspirituality" interchangeably. Fox's theology was often read at Father Bede's ashram, and Father Bede called Fox's theology of creation spirituality "the spirituality of the future."

Another transmission of Bedean spirit could be said to be present in Andrew Harvey. A teacher and mystic scholar extraordinaire, Harvey points to Bede Griffiths as one of his main inspirations and refers to him as his spiritual father. He could be said to be holding a distinct part of the Bedean lineage that specifically focuses on combining deep contemplative spirituality with prophetic work for social justice. We incorporate in new monasticism both the monastic articulation of Brother Wayne's vision and Andrew Harvey's "sacred activism."

Also of great importance is the scholarly, contemplative, and mystical work of Beverly Lanzetta who has produced some of the most extraordinary treatises on the new emerging spirituality, including *Emerging Heart: Global Spirituality and the Sacred* and *Radical Wisdom: A Feminist Mystical Theology*. Lanzetta has produced a dense mystical text as well, *Path of the Heart*. She is a contemporary of Brother Wayne, with both of them doing their doctorate work under Ewert Cousins at Fordham University, and she also spent time with Raimon Panikkar. Lanzetta's work runs parallel in many ways to Brother Wayne's insights.

However, it is especially influenced by a much-needed feminist theological perspective. Her development of a *via feminina*, a spiritual path that acknowledges and takes into account woman's perspective and experience of the world, offers tools to integrate the feminine within the context of the mystical path for both men and women.

Ken Wilber's "integral" work has also dovetailed wonderfully with the work of Brother Wayne, and there are inspired recorded dialogues and a video of the two of them discussing interspirituality just before Brother Teasdale's passing. Against the wishes of his doctors, Brother Wayne traveled to make these recordings. It was one of the final public appearances he made.

After Brother Wayne's passing, Kurt Johnson, a close associate of Brother Wayne, played a special role in bringing together a wide variety of constituencies and helping to organize them into a broad movement that is now known as the interspiritual movement. His book *The Coming Interspiritual Age,* cowritten with Robert Ord, offers a broad vision of the interspiritual legacy. Johnson was uniquely positioned to play the role of a convener for the movement. His diverse background would seem to require several lifetimes, combining the experience of a former Christian monastic for over a decade; a PhD in evolutionary science, scientific work in the field that led to him naming over 200 butterfly species, becoming a world authority on Vladimir Nabakov, producing a few hundred scientific publications (including a recent publication with scientists from Harvard on DNA sequencing), and being ordained in three distinct religious traditions. All of this positioned Johnson as a person who is able to bring together people from diverse backgrounds and experiences and create frames of reference for people to collaborate. Currently, Johnson is working with the United Nations, which recently adopted the "Interspiritual Declaration" alongside the "Earth Charter" and the "Charter for Compassion" as guiding documents in the process of globalization.

The present-day movement also has many other wonderful voices, such as teacher and scholar Mirabai Starr, who is known for her beautiful contemporary translations of Spanish mystics, and whose interspiritual work includes the recent book *God of Love,* which is used by many in the movement as a devotional text combining the three great monotheistic religions. Ed Bastian, who after close contact with the Dalai Lama in the early 1970s was directed by him to study and be trained as a Buddhist teacher with esteemed Tibetan lamas, now dedicates much of his time to developing unique tools and publications that help with the spiritual formation of interspiritual practitioners. Reverend Diane Berke, an interfaith educator for over twenty-five years, acknowledged with a prestigious Huston Smith Award, has been at the forefront of the emerging interspiritual movement through her initial work with New Seminary and in the last decade through the One Spirit Learning Alliance interfaith seminary that she founded. Reverend Berke merges the best of interspiritual insights within a deep psychological framework, and together with Ms. Starr, Ms. Lanzetta, and Reverend Cynthia Brix, is a powerful female presence within the movement.

There are also teachers such as Father Michael Holleran, who after spending sixteen years as a Carthusian hermit monk is now both a diocesan Catholic priest and a Zen teacher; he remains a very influential presence and respected elder in the unfolding movement. Another great contribution to the movement is the Reverend Brother Dyron Holmes, an African-American educator, actor, playwright, and activist who founded The People's Monastery, an interfaith organization in New York City that combines artistic expression and ritual with education forums and interspiritual celebrations.

On the culture-changing front, organizations such as the Global Peace Initiative of Women and its offspring, Contemplative Alliance— both convened by Dena Merriam—are doing foundational work in bringing together the wisdom of contemplative traditions and exploring how, in collaboration, they can play a stronger world-changing role. Through their international gathering of spiritual leaders from around the world, including Africa, Afghanistan, Iran, and the United States, Merriam has brought together diverse religious leaders such as Father Thomas Keating, Kabir and Camille Helminski, Lama Palden Dromla, Rabbi Zalman Schachter-Shalomi, and Sister Joan Chittister. Seven Pillars House of Wisdom, an organization founded by the Sufi Teacher Pir Zia Inayat-Khan, is dedicated to bringing together a diverse community of people devoted to cultivating a living wisdom for our time, and was uniquely inspired by Brother Wayne's vision and his conversations with Pir Zia.

There is also the interspiritual work of Forum 21 at the United Nations, which specifically is dedicated to using the interspiritual framework to work with diverse groups within the UN affecting future world decisions. The international gender reconciliation work of Will Keepin and Rev. Cynthia Brix, through their Satyana Institute, also deserves mentioning. The institute collaborates with Desmond Tutu and his foundation to bring equality, reconciliation, and healing to men and women around the globe. Above and beyond this work, Keepin and Brix have been movers and shakers within the interspiritual movement as conveners of the Dawn of Interspirituality international conference in 2013, which brought together an eclectic mix of interspiritual leaders and aspirants from around the globe. They are currently working on plans for a second conference to be held in South America in the near future.

Finally, we should mention a few people who have been supportive of the interspiritual new monastic movement in particular. These include Father Thomas Keating, who has dubbed this later phase of his life, beginning with his move to St. Benedict's Monastery in Snowmass, Colorado, in the early 1980s (and including his founding of Contemplative Outreach and convening of the Snowmass Conference) his "interspiritual phase." Father Keating has graciously invited us up to his monastery on a yearly basis to hold retreats and dialogues with him around new monastic life. Reb Zalman (Rabbi Zalman Schachter-Shalomi), who passed away in 2014, was also very supportive of the development of new monastic life.

Sufi teacher Llewellyn Vaughan-Lee has also been particularly supportive, and had some key insights which found their way into the Manifesto. As mentioned previously, he was instrumental in getting the original Manifesto out to the public. Kurt Johnson and Beverly Lanzetta have also played key roles in supporting this vision. Kate Sheehan Roach, editor of *Contemplative Journal*, has continuously supported, mentored, and encouraged emerging new monastic voices to write for the journal. Netanel Miles-Yépez, a fellow new monastic, scholar, artist, teacher, and close student of Reb Zalman, who blends in his own path the depths of Hasidic wisdom and the Sufism of Hazrat Inayat Khan, has been one of our closest colleagues and friends. Finally, the hermit monks at Sky Farm Hermitage, Sister Michaela Terrio and Brother Francis Ali, have played especially important roles in transmitting the spirit of the Christian Sannyasi into the new monastic vision, and the impetus for the Manifesto was born during a retreat at their hermitage and inspired by dialogues the two of us had with them.

There are many others involved in this work, but alas, the range of our discussion here does not allow us to mention them all. In bringing together such an eclectic range of people and interests, the present-day interspiritual movement has been true to its roots as a uniting force among those dedicated to building a global civilization of the heart. Given the catholic nature of the movement, "interspiritual" itself has resisted any one definition. However, it is always related in some fashion to the ideal of the coming together of the human family in relationship with each other and with the greater Kosmos.

We have already seen in some detail how Brother Wayne originally used the term. In *The Coming Interspiritual Age*, Johnson and Ord relate interspirituality to what they see as a common experience of "unity consciousness" within the religious and mystical traditions the world over. Interspirituality is "centered on the recognition of a common experience within all spiritual traditions—a sense of profound interconnectedness, and what this implies for how humans should behave both individually and collectively."[67] They then extrapolate from this experience of unity consciousness, looking at many modern movements that have the sense of oneness, unity, or "we as opposed to me." They also connect interspirituality to an evolutionary framework that sees our spiritual and religious traditions as one movement in the spiritual maturation of humankind, and "interspirituality as the way authentic spirituality has inherently responded to humankind's advancing sense of unity and the inevitable processes of globalization and multiculturalism."[68]

Ed Bastian's description of interspirituality in his book *Interspiritual Meditation* shares commonalities with Johnson and Ord's work but concentrates more on shared processes and experiences:

> InterSpirituality is a term that we apply to the processes and experiences shared by the world's contemplative traditions that are nested within the world's major religions. It connotes a more nuanced approach than conventional inter-faith or inter-religious dialogues offer that are based on "tolerance," "rapprochement," and "respect." InterSpirituality goes far deeper, indeed, to the very heart of the spiritual experiences that give rise to the major religions. It holds the promise of a genuine sharing of our respective spiritual experiences, and a conscious joining at the deeper levels of our being. InterSpirituality represents the next phase of understanding between people of diverse spiritual traditions.[69]

The popular author and spiritual teacher Rabbi Rami Shapiro has also expressed his notion of interspirituality as related to the meeting and dialogue between and among religious traditions, acknowledging a common unity in the heart while also allowing for differences in theological understandings: "InterSpirituality is a profound way of working toward the goal of global understanding, respect, and peace by elucidating the common themes, methodologies, meanings and truths of the world's religions while respecting the unique gifts and particularities of each tradition."[70]

What We Mean by Interspirituality

We also have our own particularities in our use of the word, and it is important here to make those clear. We don't intend to imply that our way should be the only way to use the word (as should be clear by the examples given above), but it is important as we continue to understand what we mean when we use the word in the context of our development of new monastic life and an interspiritual path. Primarily, we intend to use *interspirituality* to denote an emergent attitude of presence-based exploration among and between wisdom traditions and individual spiritual paths, calling us to dialogical dialogue with one another and leading to new flowerings of spiritual understanding, communities, and even spiritual paths. We believe this understanding of interspirituality, as a reciprocal sharing of realizations and contemplative gifts—in which each person's insights help to affirm, deepen, and direct the other's journey—is in particular a frame of reference that can help support a new generation of spiritually hungry youth as well as allow for intergenerational bridges to be built between elders, wisdom, traditions, and the younger generation.

This dialogical understanding of interspirituality puts a premium on the creation of intimate circles of dialogue and community (and what we mean by "dialogical" will be explored much more fully in upcoming sections). One of the great examples of such a circle has been the Snowmass Interspiritual Dialogue Fellowship, and its precursor, the Snowmass Conference, an ongoing thirty-year experiment, originally convened by Father Thomas Keating in 1984, which brought together people from different religious traditions "that were following a spiritual path, seeking experiential depth. The emphasis was not on finding official or accredited representatives appointed by religious organizations. [Father Keating] wanted authentic seekers who were trained and well grounded in their own traditions but who sought more than outer observance."[71] In the letter sent out to participants, the group describes interspiritual dialogue:

> The emphasis is not on formal theology or religious law or external observances. . . . Inter-spiritual dialog is dialog which proceeds from the depths of spiritual experience among dedicated spiritual practitioners in an atmosphere of trust. It seeks to share the experiential rather than merely the theological, the interior content rather than the external form. "Experience" here doesn't mean that this is dialog for those who have experienced some sort of enlightenment or altered states. It is a sharing of participants' experiences of the spiritual path, whatever those experiences might be at whatever level. Inter-spiritual dialog must, above all else, be authentic.[72]

In creating these intimate contemplative circles that can live and breathe of the Spirit, we allow ourselves to come together in such a way that our gifts are received and nurtured, and where we can speak from the depths of our own authentic experience—with a willingness to be changed in the light of the revelations of our brothers and sisters. We become gardeners of the collective heart of humanity; sowing seeds and watering sprouts, pruning leaves and branches, and in time standing in awe of the amazing beauty that Wisdom bestows in her own gratuitous way. We begin to build our global civilization with a heart.

Interspirituality is something we believe can help unite the human race, not necessarily in a particular spiritual experience per se, for interspirituality cannot be defined by any singular spiritual experience. Nor could any such experience be a requirement for a seat at the interspiritual table. Rather, interspirituality must always leave ample room for the messy complexity, the blood and marrow, which diversity demands. But it must do so by offering a framework that includes humanity's deepest wisdom and revelations about the transformative journey, where each of us can situate our own deepest truths in relation to one another and learn to share and receive those truths in reciprocity.

Interspirituality is about entering into a divine milieu, where "things are transfigured . . . but in this incandescence they retain—this is not strong enough, *they exalt*—all that is most specific in their attributes."[73] It is about the fruition of humanity, and for this to ultimately be discovered in full it needs each of our individual experiences of life in its lived depths and revelations. It is then through the sharing of these gifts that a new fullness, a new understanding, can emerge. What is true for us individually is true for our religious traditions as well. Each religion, we believe, offers a unique way into the Ultimate Mystery and yields unique fruits, as does each individual journey. We are ready to move into a unity that is full, that welcomes all textures, where the Buddha's equanimity complements Christ's radical love in action, and where the Hebrew prophetic outrage can be merged with the incarnate spirituality of the prophet Muhammad, peace be upon him, and the timeless revelations of the Hindu sages.

Interspirituality embodies the universalizing process we call spiritual democracy, putting aside our egos and relating to each other in a way in which we can be surprised by the Divine, through which Wisdom, *Sophia*, can make her entrance through everyone participating, and God emerges as the "between" between friends.

For it is here, *among us*, that the Kingdom of Heaven awaits, where that which Jesus spoke of so intimately lies, waiting to be discovered through our intimacy with one another. This will lead to new structures, narratives, and forms of spiritual life; it will lead to communities connected in bonds of friendship and understanding—cells of a new world. And one day this emerging web of contemplative being and acting will become a center for all of life—not because someone imposes it or lobbies for it, but because Life attracts more life.

AN INTERSPIRITUAL PATH

> The wind bloweth where it chooses, and you hear the sound of it, but you do not know where it comes from or where it goes. So it is with everyone who is born of the Spirit   —*John 3:8*

> This call to religious openness, is initiated not by religions or masters, but by the action of the divine in the souls of people around the globe. It is a direct touching of the inner spark of the soul by Divine Mystery that is calling contemporary pilgrims— many of whom never thought about leaving their traditions—to a deeper experience of the sacred that is related to but may be outside of formal religious community. While individual in the context of life experience, this global spiritual movement shares common spiritual processes and virtues that herald the unfolding of a new revelatory consciousness for humanity.[7]
>
> —*Beverly Lanzetta*

> We must all achieve our identity on the basis of a radical authenticity. It is only in the real world of the person—neither singular nor plural—that the crucial factors influencing the course of the universe are at work.[75]   —*Raimon Panikkar*

> Behold, I make all things new.   —*Revelation 21:5*

We believe that the interspiritual phenomenon has contributed to the emergence of a new path, one that partakes of a globalized and transreligious consciousness. It is born of the Spirit and breathes the complexified religious consciousness articulated by Ewert Cousins. It is also one that allows for spiritual synergies, for new frameworks and understandings of the human predicament to be developed. In the Manifesto, we spoke of different ways of being interspiritual. There was the way of the majority of our founders, where one becomes established in a particular religious tradition and then reaches out to other traditions, even crossing over into them, partaking of their wisdom and knowledge, and returning to one's root tradition with new insights and an expanded view of our humanity. There was the way of multiple belonging, where one takes on fully the depths of religious practice in more than one tradition. Finally there was a third way, one that is emerging more fully in today's intercultural and interreligious globalized world. It is this third way we have dubbed an interspiritual path.

The interspiritual path may or may not include belonging to any specific wisdom tradition, but allows for and even necessitates a deep reciprocal relationship with them. Those who do not ultimately embed themselves within a tradition, will, in all likelihood, undergo mentorship within one or more traditions for specific periods of time.

If one is to walk it, it is a path that one should feel authentically called to. That act, the fact of being called, substantiates the path itself, for at its foundation lies this sense of being called, of being guided, and of one's relationship with Life. Its emphasis lies on the relationship aspect of the Ultimate Mystery. In the Christian tradition this inner heartbeat has been named as the guidance of the Spirit. However, it is a spiritual reality found in all wisdom traditions. The experience of one's life being intertwined with Life has always been ever present.

Therefore it is with this—the guidance and discernment of the Spirit—that the underlying foundation and integrity of this path is found. All paths have their own integrity, their own foundational insights around which their spiritual technologies are built. Tibetan Buddhism has its insight into "no-self," a radical interdependence and humility, and a subsequent arising of *bodhichitta,* the "mind of enlightenment" or perfect compassion; Islam has the experience of the utter transcendence of God, of God's mercy and the need for total submission to Allah; advaitic Hinduism has the search for the Self, the nondual penetration that liberates any notion of difference between the *Atman* and Brahman; Christianity has its personal relationship with Christ, the mysterious depths of his incarnation, and an unsurpassed intuition into Love, that integrating energy of the Kosmos without which one may "comprehend all mysteries and all knowledge" yet "gain nothing."[76] It has also explored in unique ways the movements of the Spirit, that which "searches everything, even the depths of God."[77]

For an interspiritual path the foundation is explicitly this guidance of the Holy Spirit. Though we use words here from the Christian tradition it must be understood that the Spirit is not Christian. The Spirit has many aspects, but primarily it reveals itself in the cultivation of one's relationship with Life.

There has been much talk in widely divergent circles (theological, artistic, sociological) that this Second Axial Age is an age of the Spirit. Perhaps this is true, perhaps not. Nevertheless, an interspiritual path has been birthed within the contemporary age. The guidance and discernment of the Spirit, of course, has always been present, but perhaps not fully recognized as a path unto itself, with the radical freedom that entails. We hope to offer some initial scaffolding and budding methodologies to wayfarers who may now be called to it.

As we now journey into some of the characteristics of this inter-spiritual path, it is important to understand that all which follows—its individualized nature with an emphasis on following the guidance of the Spirit; the importance of dialogical relationships and intellectual forma-tion; mentorship and vocation as a spiritual practice—should be viewed in light of the practices described in the section "The Heart of New Monastic Life: Spiritual Praxis." The unique textures of the path that we describe in this and the following chapters are not there to replace commitment to spiritual practice and prayer but rather to enrich it and change one's relationship with how those practices unfold in one's life. We would do well to listen to the advice of Andrew Harvey, who has lived this multi-traditional path of universal mysticism:

> I think it's so important what you're doing . . . you're offering
> people a permission to listen to their unique hearts. But, there is
> a danger in this offering of permission. And that is that it is very
> difficult often to tell the difference between the authentic guid-
> ance of the heart and your own confused desires. . . . So unless
> you develop deep discernment and have some inner experience
> of the difference between the you that is driven by ego . . . and
> the you that arises in spaciousness and love when you are free
> from ego, it's going to be hard to hear what your true voice is
> saying.

With this admonishment in hand, let us now continue our journey.

This path is a movement beyond the meeting of traditions, a road prepared for us in the deep, dialogical encounters between the mystics and contemplatives of humanity's traditional paths. They left imprints in our collective consciousness, insipient "Kosmic Habits" (à la Ken Wilber), allowing us—perhaps enticing us—to follow in their footsteps under the guidance and organic integration of the Spirit. Rather than grounding ourselves in a tradition and then reaching out to experience others, as many of our elders had done, we began with those who had passed through this process as our mentors and guides.

One must exercise discernment in the calling to this path. Without a heartfelt sense of being called and an authentic sense of guidance, one is in danger of putting together a variety of spiritual practices that result in more harm than help—a hodgepodge of frameworks and techniques that can serve to reinforce one's ego as opposed to uproot it. This is one reason we put such a foundational emphasis on solid mentorship as one becomes established on this path. Mature spiritual mentors can watch over us and safeguard us from many of the dangers on the path. Through mentorship one is able to protect oneself from simply latching on to different spiritual practices that flatter the ego while avoiding those that bring a sense of danger—even death—to its many layers. One must be able to humble oneself and to hold the spiritual accomplishments of our elders in awe, learning to bow to them in the depths of our being. On an interspiritual path one can allow oneself to partake of the sacred elements of various traditions through being guided into them, not necessarily out of one's personal choice, but rather through the infinite Wisdom and discernment of the Spirit.

At the same time, one cannot simply give oneself over to a spiritually accomplished individual, no matter how advanced that person may be. One must always refer back to one's own inner guidance, and base one's decision to accept a mentor on discernment from that guidance. In this way, one maintains the integrity of this path—continuing to strengthen its foundation throughout the course of one's journey. This requires that one take full responsibility for one's own spiritual growth and the decisions one makes along this road, such as the choice of one's mentors.

This also requires that our spiritual traditions and elders take seriously this new way. They must not feel that one has to fully enter into or commit to their tradition in order to receive mentorship. Even the deepest levels of wisdom and transmission they have to offer must be open to those who are ready. If our spiritual elders are willing to open their lives in this type of life-giving dialogical relationship with those called to this path, they will find a new population of spiritually hungry aspirants who are open to—and in need of—their wisdom and experience. In this way they can pass on the lived experience of where their tradition has taken them, rather than focusing on theological or dogmatic formulations. Through their trust in this process with us—in a recognition of their own participation in the emergence of this way—they can pass down their wisdom and traditions in such a way that it allows questions, insights, and revelations from a new generation to be present, creating spaciousness for the synergistic work of the Spirit, allowing new spiritual intuitions to dawn, and facilitating novel articulations of timeless truths. Reciprocally, this necessitates that those on this path allow themselves to be mentored, developing the deep gratitude and humble demeanor necessary for the transmission of wisdom, while at the same time taking responsibility for the continual cultivation of our own inner guidance and integrity.

Ewert Cousins captures the disposition of the new monastic on this interspiritual path toward the traditions:

By this I mean that tradition can be seen as an archetype, or primordial, dynamic structure of consciousness which establishes our roots in history, which links us to the great minds of our past, and which opens a channel for their wisdom to flow into our lives. Seen in this way, the archetype of tradition does not have content itself but is the dynamism through which the content of past wisdom can be retrieved. . . . For tradition to function as an archetype it must be evoked and cultivated by an attitude of reverence and respect; it must be received with humility and gratitude.[78]

As we hold lightly the theological frameworks surrounding the trans- missions of wisdom we receive, we find that the guidance of the Spirit always deepens and softens us, never pumps up our ego. It does not lead us down shallow pathways, but always forward into greater expansions of its beauty and harmony. Through meaningful mentorship one can gain a considerable degree of competency in listening to—and follow- ing—one's inner guidance, and this is reinforced by a strong sangha (or spiritual community) of mutually developed wayfarers. We need other spiritually mature friends on this journey with whom we can share our inner being, deepening our discernment and immersion into Spirit.

Too often this third way has been dismissed as being selfish, flaky, a spiritual Esperanto, or arising out of an inability to commit. Sadly, these are greatly mistaken notions. As we have been strenuous in insisting, this path is founded on commitment. It is about fidelity to the inner impulse that arises within one, and courage to commit to it with all of one's being. It is a shift from reliance on gurus or dogmas or institutions, as helpful (and harmful) as they can be, to the depths of one's own guiding light. Beverly Lanzetta is one of the foremost articulators of the divine authenticity of this emerging spiritual impulse. We have quoted her at beginning of this chapter, as well as throughout our work, and return again to her passionate testament:

> In naming it "revelatory," my intention is to emphasize that this multi-religious spiritual focus . . . emerges as a faith experience of the utmost seriousness that compels each person. . . . [It] is born of prayers and tears. It is not a superficial entertainment or a naïve belief. . . . Thus global spirituality is not a personal construction but an inflow from the divine, a re-vealing of a new way of being religious. It is a faith experience, a call from God, to become more loving, to become more holy.[79]

We ask for our traditions and elders to recognize this impulse as genuine, to help authenticate it as nothing less than the breath of the Holy Spirit blowing once again upon the waters of humankind. They must open their eyes to what is happening. Once they do they can bathe in it, give birth to it, participate in it. If they refuse this grace, closing in upon themselves in fear of that which is new, they may tragically become increasingly isolated from the next generation. While yearning to be a catalyst for the blossoming of our human family, they may instead become an impediment.

For those who feel that a mixing of divergent spiritual practices can only result in confusion, discord, and spiritual abeyance, we not only provide the evidence of our own lives and praxis to the contrary, but emphatically affirm that the "mixing" on this path is woven under a Wisdom greater than ourselves, one which was there when the Divine "drew a circle on the face of the deep,"[80] who knows "what is truly God's,"[81] and whose primary manifestation is of harmony. Let us turn, once again, to Raimon Panikkar:

> My motto would then be *concordia discors,* "discordant concord" . . . as the always paradoxical Heraclitus liked to put it: "The mysterious harmony is stronger than the evident one"; or again, "The unspoken harmony is superior to the verbalized one:"

But we may still quote:

> *Kai ek ton diapheronton*
> *Kallisten harmonian*
> *Kai panta kath erin ginesthai.*

> (And from divergences
> The most beautiful harmony [arises],
> And all happens through struggle.)[82]

This path does not invoke the freedom and guidance of the Spirit for the sake of freedom itself—it has a purpose. It is the newest and yet most ancient way, as it lies at the origin of all our wisdom traditions. It does not depart from revealed spiritual truths or traditional structures and stages of the path. Yet it does facilitate the birthing of new consciousness: not Christian, nor Buddhist, nor Hindu, nor Muslim, nor Jewish, nor indigenous, but in harmonious interaction with elements of all. It modifies itself into varying forms, manifesting differently for different people, but it contains core elements that cannot be compromised. Among these are a commitment to one's spiritual path, awareness and discernment of the guidance from Life, ecological awareness, respect for those who have gone before us, and the cultivation of a dialogical presence in relationship with one's elders, sangha, and humanity's revealed wisdom (including the revealed wisdom of secular sciences). This path also involves as a core component the integration of its varying attributes in service of one's vocation.

Mirabai Starr, the critically acclaimed author, translator of mystical texts, speaker, and retreat leader, has shared intimately some of her own struggles and realizations along this path, highlighting the misunderstandings which arose among her mentors, the depth and authenticity of the calling within her, and its eventual bearing of fruit:

> [In my younger years] I practiced Eastern meditation techniques and Christian contemplative prayer, chanted in Arabic and Hebrew, fasted and vision-quested and studied ancient texts. Well-meaning elders patted me on the head and told me it was very nice that I was sipping from the cups of all these different traditions, but that one day I was going to have to choose one and "go deep" if I ever hoped to have any kind of substantial spiritual experience. Naturally, the underlying message I picked up from this was that I must be a superficial dabbler incapable of showing up for the rigors of a Real Path.
>
> But I was neither lazy nor ambivalent—quite the opposite. I knew what I wanted: nothing less than union with the source of all the love in the universe. And nothing could stop me from getting it, not even a sanctuary in the wilderness promising to hook me up for the small price of exclusive membership to their particular religious club. Everything in me resisted this. Choosing one form in which to worship felt like violating my essential covenant with my Beloved, who could not be held in any single container. Eventually I realized that I already was "going deep" in multiple traditions, and had been all along, not in spite of my pluralistic behavior but *because* of it: by having profound and life-changing encounters with the God of Love wherever I could find him.[83]

Father Matthew Wright, an Episcopal priest and young new monastic, has also written extensively of the experience of walking new ways of spiritual life, and addresses specifically the concerns of traditional elders here:

> This work often grows out of the discovery of a spiritual resonance that doesn't seem as readily available in one's original tradition. Traditional spiritual teachers, however, have often cautioned those who attempt to engage more than one path [or religious tradition]. The warning has generally gone something like this: "Other paths may be valid, but if you truly want God, you have to dig one well deep to the water." The fear is that multiple belonging will only result in shallow skimming. Undoubtedly, this can be the case. But I find myself returning more often

to the words a Hindu swami once shared with me: "Matthew, there's a difference between digging fifteen shallow wells and using fifteen tools to dig one." Wherever God is guiding us in this new future, may we all dig deep to holy water.[84]

Amen.

We also believe an interspiritual path offers an opportunity to build together, in partnership with traditional wisdom paths, an avenue that can serve the burgeoning spiritual awakening of the next generation. If one feels called to the path, one should not feel afraid to embrace it. Alexander Pope, the English poet, once said, "Fools rush in where angels dare to tread." But Cecil Collins reminds us that

> The Fool is purity of consciousness . . . detached from the deadening edifice of clever ambitions, of power, and of the incredible vanity of knowledge, that has already dulled the capacity for the poetry of life in contemporary society. . . . [The Fool] is a divine debonair spirit, whose careless empirical gaiety and overflowing mercy, embraces life; but the Fool is more than this, he is the sorrow of life . . . not a philosophy, but a quality of consciousness of life, an endless regard for human identity; all this lives in the fun of the Fool.[85]

We have seen the impulse to walk an interspiritual path continue to grow, and our intuition is that it will only broaden in the decades to come. We feel, therefore, a call to begin forming some tentative structures for this path, including a supportive network of mentors and fellow wayfarers as well as the methodologies we put forward in the following sections. A spiritual home is a special container for growth. It is the need for such a dwelling, one which abides in grace and partnership with traditional wisdom paths, that inspires our work. We all wish to feel at home. Perhaps, in the fullness of time, a more formally developed interspiritual path can serve many of the same purposes that traditional frameworks and formation processes have. The cultivation of such service is a major impetus for the Foundation for New Monasticism, which aims to provide mentorship and guidance for the larger movement.

This interspiritual path and the larger new monastic movement need varying communities where these frameworks and methodologies can be more fully explored. They need spiritual elders and the accumulated wisdom of our spiritual traditions, and they also need new ways to pass down that wisdom. Too many in the younger generation are no longer drawn to the theological structures or formulaic dogmas that have played such a large role in the past—or worse, feel in them a violation of their deepest selves. For many, being embedded in a particular path or tradition feels more like a straightjacket than a warm, comforting home. What is most needed is a sense of the sacred, an unwavering commitment to one's path, and an intimacy in which life is shared deeply. Then they can be mentored in a way that brings them into the depths of their own life experience and aspirations, and from where they can begin to articulate a new, more universal story line that springs from their own inner contemplative unfolding. The Manifesto and this book are but one example of this process.

The guidance of the Spirit simply reflects an aspect of reality that we all experience in some way in our own lives. It cannot be bound within any one tradition, and while indeed working in mysterious ways it is not apart from reason and discernment. It has led many into the depths and heights of spiritual maturity, guided revelatory insights in modern science, psychology, and sociology, and it now invites us to embody new paths born of its work. This aspect of reality has a special role to play in actuating our unity as a human family—it is as if the Spirit is at play within all these various streams of wisdom, catalyzing new dances of divine attributes, synthesizing varying and unique gifts, incarnating harmony among us as we look to build our civilization with a heart.

DIALOGICAL DIALOGUE

The ultimate human horizon, and not only differing contexts, is at stake here. The method in this third moment is a peculiar dialogical dialogue . . . piercing the logos in order to reach that dialogical, translogical realm of the heart . . . allowing for the emergence of a myth in which we may commune, and which will ultimately allow under-standing (standing under the same horizon of intelligibility).[86]   —Raimon Panikkar

The crossing over into the religious world of the other can be a moment of revelation or enlightenment in which the encounter between different religious or cultural [or individual] worlds reaches a new stage of being. Such dialogue . . . is not only a growth in human consciousness but "the whole universe expands."[87]   —Ilia Delio

The dialogical dialogue is not a mute act of love. It is a total human encounter.[88]   —Raimon Panikkar

I mean the personal-universal. The most incommunicable and therefore the most precious quality of each being is that which makes him one with all the rest. It is consequently

by coinciding with all the rest that we shall find the centre
of ourselves.[89]   —*Pierre Teilhard de Chardin*

The process of dialogue, of understanding, of crossing over into
the sacred realms of another tradition is the medium of transformation which draws the divine cosmic-human encounter toward
the cosmotheandric goal.[90]   —*Beverly Lanzetta*

Dialogical dialogue is fundamental to the new monastic movement
and the vision unfolding throughout this work. Our vision itself, including the Manifesto, was born through this process. It could perhaps be
said to be the rhythmic movement that underlies our own journeys. It
embodies the movements of the Spirit, emerges out of them, and allows
for a new sense of communion and religious ritual to be incarnated. Dialogical dialogue is an emanation of the contemporary movement toward
the Feminine, the Spirit, Wisdom, Sophia. It manifests spiritual democracy—and is a necessity for a Second Axial Age consciousness.

Dialogical dialogue is a way of relating to one another, such that we
allow ourselves to be changed in the light of the wisdom of the other. It
is a dialogue that is always an exploration. Its philosophical roots stem
from an understanding that the other is not really other, but participates
in a shared reality of which we ourselves are a part. "The thou is a source
of self-understanding that I cannot assimilate from my own perspective
alone. . . . Our participation is always partial, and reality is more than
just the sum of its parts."[91]

The other is not the same as our self, but is not separate from our
self either. Together, we both participate in a shared reality, and we affect
and change that reality through our interactions with one another. Dialogical dialogue is made possible because we are both individuals and
exist in communion and interdependence with one another. It means
that a constitutive part of our being, our I, is caught up in, is part and
parcel, of others. Therefore, the dialogue is primarily "neither a strategy
for peace nor even a method for better understanding. It is all this, and
more, because it implies, first of all, a vision of reality. . . . I am not the
other, nor is the other I, but we are together. . . . We *are* in dialogue."[92]

If we are to be true to our own religious quest, our own spiritual
journey, we must then take the revelations of others seriously. We have
to view other persons as unique beings endowed with their own wisdom
and integrity, and also know that in some way we need their wisdom in
order to bring our own into greater fullness.

The rationale for the dialogical dialogue is that the *thou* has a
proper and inalienable ontonomy [being]. The thou is a source
of self-understanding that I cannot assimilate from my own per-

spective alone. It is not as if we would all see "the same thing" but from a different vantage point. This may be true, but the dialogical dialogue is not just a locus for perspectivism. . . .

In order to have an undistorted view of reality, we cannot rely exclusively on "our" consciousness but have somehow to incorporate the consciousness of other people about themselves and the world as well. . . . It is not that I do not examine my partner's credentials (he could be wicked or a fool), not that I fall into irrationalism (or any type of sentimentalism), giving up my stance, but that I find in his actual presence something irreducible to my ego and yet not belonging to a nonego: I discover the "thou" as a part of a Self that is as much mine as his—or to be more precise, that is as little my property as his.[93]

We must be discerning in what is another's truth, not merely taking his or her word for it, but exploring together the nature of the insight. The basis is that we share a portion of Reality, a part of our Selves, a ground in which we both "live and move and have our being."[94] It is about coming to know others in the depths of their being, and thereby coming to understand our own depths more fully through their reflection. It is reciprocal, we are able to reflect back to others their own process and help them to discern which lines of thought, understanding, and action are arising from their divine core. However, first we must come to truly understand them, and "we cannot understand a person's ultimate convictions unless we somehow share them."[95]

Dialogical dialogue can only take place when both parties are willing to enter into the worldspace of its enactment. To understand others means to "stand under their horizon of thought." One must enter into their way of seeing the world, the way in which the world is revealed to them. In this, one is laying one's life on the line. When we truly enter into another's understanding we may not return the same; we may find that new truths are revealed to us that we must now incorporate and integrate into our own horizons. It must be a two-way street. If one is unable to open oneself in this way, then the communion is aborted, and the transformative communication that emerges cannot be brought to bear.

We cannot assume too early in the process that we know what the other person means or what their understanding is purely through the words they use. We must come to know what they signify by those words, what those words mean to them. Too often we categorize the words of another within our own constructs, which might differ from another's in profound and revealing ways. We have to continue to engage others until understanding dawns and we come to see the world through their eyes. We must not cut the process short through misunderstanding or through judgment.

This type of dialogue emerges when our encounter with another begins to touch the "depths of our intimate beliefs, when it reaches the ultimate questions of the meaning of life."[96] We engage with others in a way that is inviting them to reveal their wisdom to us, to enlighten us, opening a new road of discovery. Our understanding of Reality remains open to inspiration, fluid in its discernment, ready for insight and revelation; acknowledging that we are but one instance of universal experience graced with the opportunity to commune with another instance of equally valid experience.

The dialogical dialogue is a dialogue that is absent a solid ground for either party to stand on, at least in terms of beliefs and understanding—faith may be another matter. Faith, as a constitutive dimension of the human being, may be the only solid ground that truly exists for such a life-giving dialogue. Faith in Life itself, in its progression, communion, and divine underpinnings, offers an unshakeable foundation to engage in this dialogue. This type of faith allows us to reveal our own sacredness while receiving that of others, and in this intimate communication to be born anew. The dialogue must contain the genuine possibility of transformation, emerging from it with inner thoughts and even an inner being reshaped, with subsequent consequences for the trajectory of one's life.

If one enters into the dialogue on solid ground, knowing what one's beliefs are and that these are nonchanging, static—then one cannot enter into the dialogical dialogue. Implicit in that view is a subtle ego game. It says that the revelations of others are not revelations for me—they cannot affect me. But the "me" in this case is only the self-centered ego. The true I has a constitutive part which is one with the other, not separate—the Thou of my I. In reality, the authentic revelations of the other are not separate from one's own Self.

Therefore, "I trust the other not out of an ethical principle (because it is good) or an epistemological one (because I recognize that it is intelligent to do so), but because I have discovered (experienced) the '*thou*' as a counterpart of the I, as belonging *to* the I. . . . I trust the partner's understanding and self-understanding because I do not start out by putting my ego as the foundation of everything."[97] The dialogue requires a "listening attitude toward my partner, the common search for truth . . . the acceptance of the risk of being defeated, converted, or simply upset and left without a north."[98]

Ilia Delio, in her book *Christ in Evolution,* offers a beautiful description: "It begins with the assumption that the other is also an original source of human understanding and that, at some level, persons who enter the dialogue have a capacity to communicate their unique experiences and understandings to one another. . . . It calls for a 'cosmic confidence' in the unfolding of reality itself. Such confidence, however, does not arise from intellectual understanding alone but from the maturity of a deep inner spirit rooted in God."[99]

Dialogical dialogue does not require or necessarily produce an overarching philosophical understanding that can be articulated in language (though it might), but it does demand a philosophical openness, a loving awareness that is able to recognize the presence of the Divine in others and allow oneself to be changed in such an encounter. It is having enough confidence in the movements of the Spirit to let another's revelation into the deepest recesses of our being. It is becoming comfortable with allowing our own understanding to evolve, which requires that we do not identify with our conceptual belief structures. Then it can be a revelatory, joyous experience. As the astronomer searches the night sky, relishing the ever-expanding mysterious happenings of our universe, so the dialogical dialogue becomes an exploration of our own interior and collective depths. It is a catalyst for emergent insights and intuitions into the hidden destiny of the human being. It is an exploration tinged with existential questions in which the very meaning of our lives is caught up. In a word, it becomes an adventure.

"The dialogical dialogue assumes a radical dynamism of reality, namely that reality is not given once and for all, but is real precisely in the fact that it is continually creating itself—and not just unfolding from already existing premises or starting points. . . . This creativity constitutes the locus of the dialogical dialogue."[100] Our dialogue with one another assumes the possibility of weaving together a new pattern in creation, of creation proper, and it occurs when each of us is able to reveal in integrity, love, and truth how the divine nature of the Kosmos has revealed itself to us, which is to say to speak from our own Divine core. Then, in communion with the divine cores of others a synergism occurs in which creation is born anew and understanding emerges. It is creation through relationship. The Spirit, the *pneuma,* exists *among us—between us*—and "where Spirit, freedom. And where there is freedom, thought cannot dictate, foresee, or even necessarily follow the 'expansion,' 'explosion,' life of Being. . . . The dialogical dialogue makes room for this sovereign freedom of being to speak new languages—or languages unknown to the other."[101]

In this, one discovers a novel realm of the mind, one that synthesizes and arranges according to reason, heartfulness, and sensitivity a marvelous understanding of various interior perspectives. This will be the basis of our next section on dialogical sophiology. The Thou to my I strikes a note of shared resonance, and the mind synthesizes this new note into an expanded horizon of understanding, a new *mythos,* out of which one's life is lived. The underground impetus of one's life is changed. Our consciousness integrates another's insight into Reality, incarnating our interdependence in a more concrete way, deepening and expanding our minds and hearts. The dialogical dialogue is a methodology for entering into the reality of interdependence in a most conscious and tender way; a way of building a world that takes seriously unity in diversity. Ewert Cousins said of it, "We will be evoking and nurturing the complexified form of religious consciousness that will be characteristic of the global community of the future. We will discover that this kind of interreligious dialogue is itself a spiritual process, *it is the characteristic collective journey of our time.*"[102]

The need for this dialogue in our times is immense. We believe that dialogical dialogue should be taught in our schools and seminaries as one of the primary ways of relating to others, to differing traditions and cultures, and to the world at large. We see dialogical dialogue as a ritual center around which new monastic communities can develop, a location where religious traditions can meet in respect, understanding, and mutual enrichment. It is a place where men and women can come together to better understand one another, building healthy and mature relationships, and within which new political, social, and cultural realities can be born. It is an integral part of the movement toward new institutions, novel forms of governance and political philosophies, and real-world communities that are sustainable, life enriching, and supportive of society at large.

> [The dialogical dialogue] is itself a religious act—an act that neither unifies nor stifles but re-links us (in all directions). It takes place in the core of our being in our quest for salvific truth—in whatever sense we may understand these too-loaded words. We engage in such a dialogue not only looking above, toward a transcendent reality, or behind, toward an original tradition, but also horizontally, toward the world of other people who may believe they have found other paths leading to the realization of human destiny. The search becomes an authentic prayer, a prayer open in all directions. . . . It is not research into a different worldview out of curiosity, or with a sympathetic mind. In this dialogue, we are in search of salvation, and we accept being taught by others, not only by our own clan. We thus transcend the more or less unconscious attitude of private property in the religious realm. Intrareligious dialogue is, of its very nature, an

act of assimilation—which I would call eucharistic. It tries to assimilate the transcendent into our immanence.[103]

DIALOGICAL SOPHIOLOGY

On the heights, beside the way, at the crossroads she takes her stand. . . .[104]

She is a tree of life to those who lay hold of her; those who hold her fast are called happy.[105]

For she knows and understands all things, and she will guide me wisely in my actions and guard me with her glory.[106]

— *Proverbs, Wisdom*

She was, in the first place, a central figure of mystical experience, and within that experience she represented the divine-human feminine.[107]   —*Christopher Pramuk*

I believe that personality is, ontologically speaking, the highest entity in the vast Sea of Being which we apprehend about us. To that degree, the person is the supreme attestation of the Divine.[108]   —*William Everson*

The organization of elementary human energy, whatever its generalized methods, must culminate in the formation, within each element, of a maximum of personality.[109]

—*Pierre Teilhard de Chardin*

So she does in us a greater work than that of Creation: the work of new being in grace . . . [110]   —*Thomas Merton*

For whoever finds me finds Life.[111]   — *Proverbs*

Sophia

Dialogical sophiology is our term for how the new monastic develops a complexified-religious framework for understanding her journey. Since the new monastic no longer simply inherits a theological framework from her forerunners in the spiritual life—nor can she choose to disregard the revelations of our religious traditions—she must have a methodology for coming to terms with her own journey, for merging her intellect with her emotions, her insights with her body, her spiritual realizations with those of others, and with the world around her. Dialogical sophiology is a methodology which allows for this deeply personal, organic development to occur in such a way that one's unique framework can serve to guide one's journey into maturity, while at the same time it substantiates and advances our unity as a human family. To better understand this methodology, let us first look at Sophia, Wisdom herself, and the theological tradition, sophiology, she has inspired.

Sophia is the enigmatic character found in the Old Testament in Proverbs and Wisdom, and of course the perennial "love" of the philosopher *(philo-sophia)*. We are told she was "set up, at the first, before the beginning of the earth . . . When he established the heavens, I was there, when he drew a circle on the face of the deep."[112]

"Sophia is also a kind of real symbol and revealed Name for what Orthodox theology calls 'divinization,' meaning the *fullness of participation in the life of God*. . . . [S]he is 'the Humanity of God' . . . a certain humanness *in* God."[113]

That was from theologian Christopher Pramuk in his book *Sophia: The Hidden Christ of Thomas Merton*, which takes us on a journey through the theology of Thomas Merton, arguing that the breakthrough of Sophia into Merton's consciousness throughout the years 1957–1961 proved a pivotal movement in Merton's life, setting the stage for his final years and the intensely engaged mysticism that comes out of his later writing: "it was *Sophia,* the 'unknown and unseen Christ' within all things, who both centered and in many respects catalyzed Merton's theological imagination in a period of tremendous social, political, and religious fragmentation."[114]

Pramuk argues that Merton's theological method was inherently sophiological:

> Indeed, with respect to Merton's central concern for everyday Christian spirituality, it will be emphasized through this book that the sophiological tradition implies not the embrace of an elaborate theology so much as a way of life: a commitment to prayer, community, simplicity, solitude, artistic and vocational creativity, asceticism—all tested means . . . for cultivating a wider love in relation to the world, or what monastic spirituality calls purity of heart, poverty of spirit.[115]

The sophiological tradition developed in modern Russian Orthodox theology with such passionate and poignant expressions as those of Vladimir Soloviev, Sergi Bulgakov, and Nicholas Berdyaev, as a reaction to the modern world and the struggle to understand how the Orthodox tradition can and should engage with it. Though they wrote in the second half of the nineteenth and early twentieth centuries, we see profound parallels with the new monastic movement in their struggle to relate the process of "theosis," or divinization, and the "humanity of God" to contemporary life, and their eventual conclusion that God's Wisdom,

Sophia, was active in all spheres of life, including secular pursuits and even other religious traditions. The sophiological tradition's founder for all intents and purposes was Soloviev. Paul Valliere, in *Modern Russian Theology*, describes Soloviev's thought:

> If the evolution of religion is a divine-human process, every stage must embody the humanity of God to some extent. Does this mean that all religions are in some sense true? Soloviev says yes, " . . . not one of the moments of the religious process, can be in itself a lie or delusion. 'A false religion' is a contradictio in adjecto. . . ." The working assumption of Soloviev's theory of religious evolution is that every positive religious claim contains a measure of divine truth.[116]

In Merton, this tradition helped him to understand the need for engagement with the struggles of the larger world. "Russian sophiology seems to have carved out something rather new and unexpected in Merton, a space and a language in which there was enough room, both conceptually and imaginatively, to envision God's unbounded freedom, love, and presence to peoples and cultures everywhere."[117]

The greatest parallel of the sophiological tradition with the new monastic movement, however, is its affirmation that spiritual maturity and growth occurs within the world, and not just through leaving the world behind. It broadened the Orthodox concept of *theosis*, or the divinization of the human being in God—"enlightenment" as it is known in other Eastern traditions.

> While Soloviev affirms the Orthodox doctrine of theosis, he also broadens it. The traditional doctrine, formulated almost exclusively by monks, is an ascetical theory which envisions the image of God stripping itself bare of worldly attachments. . . . For Soloviev human beings are divinizable not just as primordial image but as creative agents engaged in the pursuits that fulfill humanity in the flesh, such as politics, science, education, the arts, technology and so on. To put it another way, Christ as the humanity of God has the power to divinize human "wisdom," i.e. culture, and in this capacity is appropriately called Sophia. The name fits the function.[118]

"Sophiology is not a gnostic quest for truths beyond the world but reflection on creative processes taking place within the world. It does not warrant an ethic of detachment or stillness *(hesychia)* but 'an ethic of joyful and creative labor.'"[119] (Though we note here that for those vocationally called to a life of *hesychia*—such as our good friends Sister Michaela Terrio and Brother Francis Ali, the hermits of Sky Farm

Hermitage in Sonoma, California—this also can be "joyful and creative labor," and for us is surely *sophianic* to the very core.)

Perhaps most clearly:

sophiology "is oriented to the actual world [which] is always under construction. . . ." In its open engagement with the natural and human sciences, the sophiological tradition, as Rowan Williams observes, "dissolves crude oppositions between spirit and body, and allows us to imagine a world that is not only self-aware but *sensually* aware of itself. . . . [It] sees the basis of ethics in the call to active co-operation with the sophianic transfiguration of the world . . . [a world] in which the characteristic *human* business is the transforming of an environment."[120]

When we attend to her tender voice and give our quiet consent, she effects in us a work greater than that of Creation: the work of new being in grace, the work of mercy and peace, justice and love . . . The remembrance of Sophia opens onto a mystical political spirituality of engagement with the world.[121]

Clearly, the resonances with new monastic life are pronounced, as are parallels with the evolutionary thought of Pierre Teilhard de Chardin. Interestingly, the whispers of Sophia can be heard in Teilhard's beautiful autobiographical story of his faith, "The Heart of Matter," where he confesses to us, "As I tell the story in these pages of my inner vision, I would be leaving out an essential element, or atmosphere, if I did not add in conclusion that from the critical moment when I . . . began to wake up and express myself in terms that were really my own, I have experienced no form of self-development without some feminine eye turned on me, some feminine influence at work."[122]

The connection between Teilhard's theology and Sophia is made explicit by Kathleen Duffy, SSJ, in her essay "Sophia: Catalyst for Creative Union and Divine Love," in *From Teilhard to Omega: Co-Creating an Unfinished Universe*. In it, Duffy takes the liberty to rewrite a poem by Teilhard titled "The Eternal Feminine" which was based on the Sophia of the Bible. Duffy tells us that "Teilhard's eternal feminine personifies the cosmic unifying and spiritualizing force at work in creation; like Wisdom, she is at play in creation and delights in its every facet; like Dante's Beatrice, she is a guide for the journey into God."[123] Let us listen in to Sophia as she speaks through Duffy in her rewriting of Teilhard's poem:

I am the principle of union, the soul of the world. . . .

The process of creative union is a gradual process, and it is often beset with failure. Therefore, from within the fragments of matter, I encourage all possible combinations since I know that not every combination will be productive. Whenever fragments of matter are able successfully to unite, I make sure that they do not lose their identity. However, as they come together and begin to operate as a unit, I evoke in them new possibilities for creativity, for more fruitful interactions, and for further union. Under my influence, these new creations always become more than what they would have been had they failed to unite. Each step toward union drives the cosmos toward greater spontaneity and freedom, toward greater novelty, greater integrity, and ultimately toward greater consciousness.[124]

Dialogical Sophiology

We began this chapter with the introduction of a new term, *dialogical sophiology*. We explored the dialogical relationship in our previous chapter, and now have the context to understand *sophiology* as not only a positive engagement with the world, but as a *"divinization by participation"* in the world.[125] It also connotes a democratization of the spiritual life, broadening "the traditional concept of theosis from the individual (e.g. monk, artist, prophet) to 'all human beings living in the world.'"[126] Finally, and perhaps most important, we recognize the living presence of *Sophia*, of Wisdom—her gifts of intuition, gentle but attractive power, and synthesizing communion—here and now, in our midst, "delighting in the human race."[127] It is from this foundation—together with a faith in the integrity and uniqueness of the other—that the new monastic builds her spiritual/theological/philosophical framework. By "other," here we mean Wisdom or Truth found outside of own phenomenological awareness, or our personal experience, from wherever it may arise: other people; other religious, wisdom, and cultural traditions; modern scientific, psychological, and sociological insights, etc.

Dialogical sophiology is related, then, to a specific vocation that is very important to the new monastic movement, the vocation of a theologian. Just as all new monks embody various vocations in differing degrees—for we are all activists, contemplatives, artists, and, yes, as we will see, even theologians—dialogical sophiology is our term for the universal "theological" vocation of building a solid framework within which one's spiritual journey can find a home. This framework must help one to avoid pitfalls and distractions, must be informed by the great truths of the wisdom traditions, and must emerge out of one's own experience, yet in a dialogical relationship with one's mentors and sangha.

Therefore, even though the framework is unique to oneself, it cannot be said to be owned or even created by one's self—for it comes into being among us, in harmony with all that we have spoken: personal experience, the wisdom of others, our religious traditions, modern scientific, psychological, and sociological insights, and the very presence and action of Wisdom, Sophia.

Each new monastic is called to be a dialogical sophiologian. This entails a reflective way of being with the other, where we remain aware that Wisdom is present, evoking her synthesizing beauty among us. This other can be persons, philosophies, religious traditions, mentors, art, political and social theory, poetry, nature. As we form and cultivate our intellectual framework we are careful to remain aware that it is not purely rational or intellectual, but it is also wedded to the heart. It develops through the lens of the heart, the depths of our humanity, and the revelations of others, including our wisdom traditions. Neither is it to be easy. We must struggle intellectually in order to actualize this integration of mind and heart. It "involves *both* 'realization' (contemplation; mystical experience) *and* intellectual struggle, the two movements circling and informing each other as perhaps in a fugue or carefully patterned dance."[128] In addition to realization and intellectual struggle, it involves taking seriously the revelations of others as well, so that what emerges is the product of dialogical relationships.

Nor does it at some point become a closed framework. It is an ongoing process, entailing an unending philosophical openness, where we are confident enough in the presence of Wisdom and her evolutionary work in the world to allow our current framework and understanding to evolve and be informed by others and by the guidance of the Spirit. It partakes of what Blessed Cardinal John Henry Newman called the illative sense, "the process of growing into the truth about the mystery of God."[129]

Or as Soloviev taught, "The contents of revelation accumulate gradually and grow richer as the meaning of the humanity of God is revealed. In other words, 'religious consciousness is not something finished, ready-made, but something emerging and in process, and thus the revelation of the divine principle in this consciousness is necessarily gradual.'"[130]

Some may feel (or even think) that building a theological framework for ourselves is too intellectual, and may worry that it is a movement away from our body and emotions, from the heart and our Mother Earth. However, we fail to see that that in itself is an intellectual framework, one that will guide us to make certain decisions and take certain actions, and prevent us from fully integrating our intellect with the rest of our humanity. It would be a great mistake for us to assume that we do not experience the world through our own metaphysical and religious understanding—even atheism is its own form of this. We all live our lives according to our own philosophy, that is to say according our own understanding of the world, the Kosmos, and our place within it.

Unfortunately the majority of us allow our philosophical framework to form unconsciously, subtly in the back of our minds, or perhaps we simply accept a framework that is given to us—by society, by our religious tradition or spiritual teacher, by a close-knit group of friends or coworkers. Our own philosophies are not really our own at all, but rather a mysterious mix of social and cultural conditioning, impersonal forces inherited through various structures of consciousness, and faint or not-so-faint notions of our divinity. The less we take responsibility for what does exist in our minds and being, the more we become like puppets, acting and living not out of a sense of personal integrity, but rather through the inclinations of others, cultural conditioning, and the impersonal motivations of subliminal archetypes. The great tragedy is that many of us trick ourselves into thinking this is who we truly are.

For the new monastic that is clearly not an option. She is required to do the hard work of bringing her personal philosophy and intellectual framework into the light, working on it and merging it with the wisdom of her heart, stretching it, molding it, and making it explicit so that it can function as a road leading her into a life of continual growth and spiritual maturity, allowing her unique talents to flower as benefactions to the whole. In particular, because the new monastic is often creating an individualized framework for her journey, her responsibility for this task becomes much greater. In a certain sense, when she simply relies on a framework given from a religious tradition, she may have the support and guidance of thousands of years of reflective thought and careful cultivation to lean on. This can be a tremendous support. The new monastic must soberly assess these frameworks and the support and guidance they offer, but must give primal credence to that which is arising in her own heart and the living, synthesizing presence of Sophia. In the next section we show why we believe that this personalizing of spiritual frameworks is a necessary step in bringing forth our unity as a human family.

Personalization

One may now ask, how is it that by personalizing my journey, by accenting my uniqueness and building my path around it, I contribute to the unification of the human family? Is this not a movement in the opposite direction? If I become more individualized, how can this help to bring about unity? Once again we turn to the work of Pierre Teilhard de Chardin. We have already spoken of his notion of "reflexion" and "convergence," of the principles of complexity and consciousness, and of the center-to-center meetings which spur the evolutionary process along. Here we come to his reflections as to how in this convergence the unification of the human family is to come about through a *superpersonalization* of each person.

Teilhard had a highly developed notion of personality. Our personality was our most precious gift, consisting of all that was deepest and most incommunicable within us. It was through the phenomenon of reflection, the apex of the evolutionary curve, that this divine gift was able to flower into hitherto unexpected potentials. We can sense and feel its preciousness in the depths of our being. Teilhard saw that his life's work would pass in some ways into "all my fellows: but it is much more fully represented by what I succeed in producing, deep within myself, that is incommunicable and unique. My personality, that is, the particular centre of perceptions and love that my life consists in developing—it is that which is my real wealth."[131] Teilhard noted the beginnings of personality in the animal kingdom, but it is only in the human being, with the full power of reflective consciousness, that it finds its home. In a sense, Teilhard saw the entire evolutionary process as a divergent groping for a physical form where personality could finally incarnate. "Life's task, it seems, was to achieve, by means of increasingly organized elements, the establishment on earth of a higher form of consciousness, a *state of personality*."[132]

Therefore, Teilhard sees our future evolutionary development as moving only in the direction of a heightened, superpersonalized state, where all that is most unique in us is conserved. He even speaks of the law of the "conservation of personality," where "each elementary person contains something unique and untransmittable in his essence" and "each individual nucleus of personality, once formed, is for ever constituted as 'itself'; so that, in the supreme personality that is the crown of the universe, all elementary personalities that have appeared in the course of evolution must be present again in a distinct (though super-personalized) state."[133] Or more directly, "In the final shape assumed by the cosmos, personality, growing with convergence, must be at its greatest."[134]

Yet, we can only develop our unique personality in its fullness through our communion and interaction with others. "In other words it is not in isolation (as we might have supposed) but only in appropriate association with his fellows that the individual can hope to attain to the fullness of his personality, his energies, his power of action and his consciousness, more especially since we do not become completely 'reflective' . . . except by being reflected in each other. Collectivization and individualization (in the sense of personality, not of social autonomy) are thus not opposed principles."[135]

It follows then that our unity as a human family can only occur through the deepest development of our personality, our uniqueness in God, because our unity as a human family cannot function without that which is most precious in us. But that uniqueness can only be found and developed through our relationships with others, "in the field of personal relationships, where friends and lovers can only discover all that is in their minds and hearts by communicating them to one another."[136]

Through "the process of our growth we find ourselves under the double necessity of deepening ourselves and simultaneously passing in some way into our surroundings. . . . [T]hese two actions . . . are linked in the harmony of a single underlying movement."[137]

We come now to Teilhard's important insight that union differentiates. Rather than unification causing a fusion or merger with the various elements to be united, it differentiates. Teilhard contrasts this notion with that of a fusion of elements, where distinctiveness is lost and a merger occurs. "True union does not fuse the elements it brings together, by mutual fertilization and adaptation it gives them a renewal of vitality. . . . Moreover, as we have seen, this gift he makes of himself has the direct result of reinforcing his most incommunicable quality, that is to say the quality of super-personalizing. 'Union differentiates.'"[138]

Teilhard makes a distinction between the more mechanized unity in diversity that we see in nature (such as bees in a hive or ants in a colony), and what we can expect from a unity in diversity in the realm of the human being, which we recall is of a higher, psychic order. While in nature this differentiation in unity results in specialties of mechanistic function, e.g., queen, drone, and worker bees each pledged to performing specific functions for the hive, in the human family it takes a much different course, with the differentiation in unity corresponding "to what might be called a function of personalization. Operating in such a field, the tendency of union to bring about differentiation, far from giving birth to mere mechanism, must have the effect of increasing the variety of choice and the wealth of spontaneity."[139]

Unity and uniqueness are not opposing movements, but in fact grow in accordance with one another, "which amounts to saying that true union (that is, spiritual union, or union in synthesis) differentiates the elements it brings together. This is no paradox, but the law of all experience. Two beings never love one another with a more vivid consciousness of their individual selves than when swallowed up in the other."[140]

This personalization and subsequent unification is only engendered, in the end, through the center-to-center unions of individual human beings accomplished through love. "Only union *through* love and *in* love (using "love" in its widest and most real sense of 'mutual internal affinity'), because it brings individuals together, not superficially and tangentially but center to center, can physically possess the property of not merely differentiating but also personalizing the elements which comprise it."[141]

We have delved into this aspect of Teilhard's thought in order to better understand how the cultivation of our own unique gifts, understandings, and spiritual maturity not only develops that which is most precious and incommunicable in us, but also effectuates our unity as a human family. As we touch that deepest center inside of us we find that we enter into a divine milieu. Here it is as if a divine ambiance suddenly reveals itself to all of our senses, and we find ourselves operating in the world in a way which not only acknowledges our unity but manifests it. This act partakes of the totality and uniqueness of our being, our bodily and emotional energies, our intellect, our spirit; it takes us outside of our selves while at the same time radiating from our deepest core, putting us in touch with our most sacred gifts that we have to offer in a palpable atmosphere of communion.

In relation to dialogical sophiology, we can now understand how an individualization of our journeys contributes to the manifestation of our unity. Seeing this demands that we also offer support and guidance for others to cultivate their own unique frameworks and spiritual paths. Teilhard's understanding was certainly unique, even though he participated fully within the Catholic theological tradition and respected its boundaries, and therefore his gift to the world was that much greater—it manifested our unity that much more, specifically to the degree he was able to find and express this uniqueness within him. When we find our vocation we begin to live from this place inside of us, deepening our personality, our unique way of being in God, and therefore incarnating our unity. Dialogical sophiology is therefore an evolutionary methodology that allows for a hyperpersonalization of each person, but in such a way that it brings us closer to the eschatological unity that our souls seek.

The Archetype of the Theologian

The practice of dialogical sophiology is a universalized, democratized practice of theology (reflection and speech on the Divine) and philosophy (love of Wisdom). As we used the monk as archetype in order to delve into that same dimension within ourselves—that inner dimension of complete commitment to the transformative journey—we now turn to the archetype of the theologian in order to better understand this dimension within ourselves. The theologian embodies the importance of shaping, integrating, and divinizing our intellect so that it becomes a living organ of our journey. As always, when dealing with archetypes we cannot approach them with only the mind, but we also have to allow them to enter by the back door, as it were, via the subliminal, watery pathways of our emotions and spirit.

Every new monastic is called to marry the silent with the reflective, but the theologian is called to fulfill this special task in a very specific way. Each movement needs this task fulfilled or else it is in a danger of not recognizing the dream that is unfolding in its heart. A theologian is one who can be present to what is unfolding and recognize the gentle whisperings of the Spirit in people's hearts—and then name them with intellectual precision and poetry. The theologian connects what is recognized and named to the religious unfoldings of the past and present, thereby providing a vision that connects the past with the present and thus seeing clearly God's incarnational presence in our history and lives. The theologian then offers this vision in service to the movement as a whole, enriching every organ of it, encouraging every stone of the mosaic to ponder this vision in his or her heart, and through this maturing the understanding and direction of each of the members. This inspires a general deepening and reauthenticating of the movement as a whole. The theologian, then, is in a dialogical relationship always engaged with what's unfolding in the movement's heart, in an I-Thou dance between each heart, the movement as a whole, and the currents of religious history, bringing everyone to greater and subtler possibilities of what can be so that God's face can be reflected in each heart and the movement as a whole. The work of completing each individual soul and the world goes on.

Father Thomas Keating calls to light one of the problems with how we moderns envision theology:

> the science of theology and the practice of spirituality appear to be two distinct categories of religion. Traditionally, they are two aspects of one reality, two expressions of the Word of God that are complementary and presuppose each other. The unity between them was better understood in the early centuries of the Church. One example of this understanding was the use of the term *divine* as a synonym for a theologian, as in the case of John the Divine. A theologian was one who had been divinized by the Word of God and who consequently spoke of the mysteries of God with the unction of divine wisdom.[142]

For Raimon Panikkar, who did not separate theology from philosophy, "Philosophical activity is not like scientific inquiry; everything is interconnected. You cannot investigate a portion of reality without being involved with all of it. In a word, the vision of the whole is not the sum of its parts. It is another type of vision."[143] It requires "solitude, nonattachment, distance, and even a certain avoidance of others [when needed]. . . . The thinking activity forges reality somewhat in the way that the smith forges the iron."[144]

> Authentic philosophers have to be in solidarity with the entire universe. . . . [Embodying] an active and intelligent listening to reality itself—to the Rhythm of Being. . . . The philosopher's task is to place one's mind and heart in tune with reality, allowing the very throbbing of Being to pass through one's spirit, and by so doing change its rhythm.[145]

In short, it is an act of prayer, the word become flesh.

Yet theology should do more even than this. Thomas Merton said that theology could only be done by first becoming "impregnated in our mystical traditions," but then went further: "theology meant even more than to 'become fully impregnated in our mystical tradition,' it is also to . . . help us to do what we must really do: live our theology . . . fully, deeply, in its totality."[146]

Or as Panikkar says: "Then authentic philosophy will crystallize into a life-style."[147]

Perhaps most important, it must be understood that this methodology of dialogical sophiology is inherently an artistic act. It is an artistic act that includes the mind, the intellect, merging it with the archetypal world of the artist, feeling passionately the cry of the poor and oppressed, and wedding it to the *praxis* of one's life and the practical details demanded by it. Since dialogical sophiology is an inherently artistic act, let us bring our archetypal exploration to a close by turning to Cecil Collins, as he describes the artist and the creation of a work of art.

> The artist . . . like the priest and monk . . . is the representative of the affirmative integrity of life. . . . By dreaming the dreams of man—because the artist does not speak for himself—he speaks for all men, by dreaming the dreams of man he then begins to change man's dreams from within. This is the most important point of all. . . . And for an artist the greatest happiness is to have failed at doing the perfect, and the greatest misery is never to have attempted it.[148]

In the creation of a work of art, Collins makes a distinction between creation and self-expression:

> self-expression is not creation . . . Creation is transformation, something quite different, and no transformation takes place unless the energy is qualified and denied by limitations. For

self-expressionists there are no limitations. But the real creative artist immediately has a vision and a perfection . . . You imagine something is infinite but then it has suddenly got to be in concrete shape. The shape, the size, the whole thing resists you, and this qualification is pain, and the pain purifies the energy and transforms it . . . [It is] the problem of incarnating it in a denser way. . . . That is where the purification comes in. The energy becomes transformed through this mutual qualification and then it's in a state of grace.[149]

As for the creative act itself, "art is not a place but a condition where the life of the soul is reenacted. When I say the life of the soul I mean the real life of the soul, what is happening in the life of the soul."

Real creation of a work of art has nothing to do with having ideas that you wish to put in action, or having a programme, no matter how grand—it is a revealing, an unveiling of the nature of reality through evocation and through climate, atmosphere, through musicality. And therefore it's always active, always alive . . . the idea or the vision is already within me in a seed form and the working of the material excites the seed and it unfolds within me. And I participate in this unfoldment, knowing when to come in, I hope, and trying to come in when it is necessary to give it a little bit of form in this way or that way, and not trying to interfere with it too much—to let it reveal itself. The whole problem is one of becoming sensitive to its intention, its unfolding. It knows perfectly well what it wants to do, and I mustn't interfere with it. On the other hand one has to control the energy, to give it form, to be participating all the time in it. It is a wonderful balance between revelation, as it were, and form.[150]

Our framework emerges, then, in the creative, artistic act of dialogical sophiology. We do not need to understand our framework and *then* work on articulating and forming it. Rather, we are constantly working on it, expressing it, courageously exposing it and letting it come into being, allowing it to be what it wants to be, to guide us, and to emerge as understanding in the act itself. "It is not necessary to understand in order to create but it is necessary to create in order to understand."[151]

And creation is always incarnational.

Return to Sophia

As a quintessential expression of theology as artistic act, we offer here excerpts from Thomas Merton's passionate and haunting prose-poem "Hagia Sophia" (Holy Wisdom), dedicated to our ever-present guide, playwright, and eternal breath of inspiration, Sophia. Listen and hear her gentle whisperings in our soul:

> There is in all visible things an invisible fecundity . . . a hidden wholeness. This mysterious Unity and Integrity is Wisdom . . .

> This is at once my own being, my own nature, and the Gift of my Creator's Thought and Art within me, speaking as Hagia Sophia, speaking as my sister, Wisdom. . . .

> It is like the first morning of the world (when Adam, at the sweet voice of Wisdom awoke from nonentity and knew her). . . .

> She is the candor of God's light, the expression of His simplicity. . . .

> All that is sweet in her tenderness will speak to him on all sides in everything, without ceasing, and he will never be the same again. . . .

> As Father He stands in solitary might surrounded by darkness. As Mother His shining is diffused, embracing all His creatures with merciful tenderness and light. The Diffuse Shining of God is Hagia Sophia. We call her His "glory." . . .

> I do not speak of her as a Beginning, but as a manifestation. . . .

> She wills to be also the unseen pivot of all nature, the center and significance of all the light that is in all and for all. . . .

> Hagia Sophia in all things is the Divine Life reflected in them, considered as a spontaneous participation, as their invitation to the Wedding Feast. . . .

> The feminine principle in the world is the inexhaustible source of creative realizations of the Father's glory. She is His manifestation in radiant splendor!. . . .

> So she does in us a greater work than that of Creation: the work of new being in grace.[152]

"The work of new being in grace." That is the heart of the new monastic journey. A new monastic comes into being as a response, as a saying yes to the emerging spirit within her. As she says yes, certain characteristics begin to emerge. One of her characteristics is that a different relationship to one's experience is born. She becomes a *sophiologian* and is in a dialogical relationship with others, with traditions, and with Reality. Her presence evokes this emergence in others, and the emergence of others evokes more of this emergence in her. It's a relationship of reciprocity and constant dialogical deepening, where everyone participating is locating his or her truth. And so she lives and articulates her dialogical sophiology from that place. Her life and articulation are not separate from eath other; both are part of this emerging.

MEDITATIONS ON VOCATION

There is one thing in this world that must never be forgotten. You may forget everything but that one thing without there being cause for concern. But if you performed and remembered everything else, yet forgot that one thing, then you would have done nothing whatsoever. . . . It is just as if a king sent you to the country to carry out a specific task. If you go and accomplish a hundred other tasks, but do not perform that particular task, then it is as though you performed nothing at all . . . as though you used a priceless Indian sword to slice rotten meat. . . . You say, 'Look at all the work I do accomplish, even if I do not perform that task.' You weren't created for those other tasks! . . .

A poet once said:

You are more precious than heaven and earth.

What more can I say?

You do not know your own worth. . . .   —*Rumi*

"You are . . . the inheritor of a unique set of gifts. Never before in the world were they created. There is a certain transection of energy which has reached an apex utterly in you.[153]
                                                            —*William Everson*

A new monastic is both a contemplative and an activist; she is also a sophiologian and a dialogical organ of the emerging new monastic movement. She is a presence in search of transformation, diving deeply into the traditional tools for spiritual deepening, inviting the Spirit in so the divine therapist can do the work of healing on her, so that a consent can be produced with every part of her being, a consent to enlightened love and action in her—and through her in the world. But, just like every new monastic is all of those things—in that wholeness and integration of active with contemplative, contemplative with intellectual, silent with reflective, evolutionary with revolutionary—each of the emerging new monastics feels a call to a specific task. Each of us is a stone in a mosaic that reveals the face of God. While all are called, each is called in specificity.

For some, as consent to the Divine's love and action in us deepens, God's dream wants to live through us by following in the footsteps of such spiritual luminaries as Mother Teresa and Dorothy Day, where care for the poorest of the poor can be merged with deep awareness of the need to reconcile our socioeconomic systems with ever-present values of compassion and justice.

For some, as the river of God's love expands their minds and hearts, a resonance begins to flower with the great theologians and articulators of the divine life, the Raimon Panikkars and Teilhard de Chardins, the Chandrakirtis and Nagarjunas and Shankaras, and they find themselves called to follow in their footsteps. Through what is unfolding in their hearts and within the whole, they connect us to the historical trends of religious unfolding, name new emergences with intellectual precision, and offer a vision that enriches and deepens the understanding and direction of those experiencing this call to newness that we call new monasticism.

Still others may be called to one of the great vocations of teaching, parenting, being a social worker, an artist, or a simple silent hermit.

In our favorite book on vocation, William Everson's *Birth of a Poet*, vocation is presented through a series of meditations arranged on various aspects of the process and fulfillment of our calling. As Everson describes the work, "Taking a common subject, one of concern to all my students, the problem of vocation, I began to meditate on it as I would on the Word of God. . . . In meditation the art is to transcend what one knows by immersing oneself in the inexhaustible depths of the subject under contemplation."[154]

Partly in tribute, more as methodology, we present our section here on vocation, of cardinal significance for the new monastic, through a series of meditations—some ours, many those of others.[155] The meditations are divided into five sections, representing various facets of the vocational journey. Each individual meditation is a whole in and of itself, a distinct contribution to the whole, and should be read as such. Each must have an opportunity to find its own resonance within, for only then can the melody be heard and the symphony embraced. Therefore, they are meant to be read slowly, deliberately, mythically, knowing that the feeling they produce in the heart is more important than the intellectual clarity they bring. We recommend taking each section one at a time, staying with only that section for a day or even a week or more, meditating on it, letting it sink into one's soul. There are many subtleties to the reality of vocation, subtleties not easily assimilated. At times paradoxical, passionate, and poetic, demanding and uncompromising, these meditations, when read in the depths of our being, will continue to linger with us for many days and months, even years, appearing in our dreams or in the synchronistic happenings of life, as we struggle to find and incarnate our vocation in this world.

Meditation One: What Is Vocation?

Vocation is like love—until it is awakened in you, you don't know what it is. When you are a child, you don't know what sexuality is, yet once it awakens within you there is no going back.[156]

* * *

Every vocation is controlled by a symbol, and that symbol comes not from the individual but from the race. The human race cannot go forward unless vocations arise to constellate the collective energies into true realization. It is the race which creates the vocation. All an individual can do is answer the call . . . which is why it is so important to listen for what your true calling is.[157]

* * *

A knowledge of myth is crucial to a knowledge of vocation. In some way vocation is an enterprise, an enterprise of service or discovery, and the moment it becomes that, it becomes mythic. It is this dimension which changes vocation from career to witness. . . . *You must have faith*—faith in yourself as a human being and faith in your creative destiny in its myth-like dimension.[158]

* * *

Recall Teilhard: while building our souls we collaborate in "another work, in another *opus*, which infinitely transcends, while at the same time it narrowly determines, the perspectives of our individual achievement: the completing of the world."[159] That greater *opus* is infinitely transcending yet narrowly determining our individual achievement, the arena bestowed upon us by the collective in which to build our souls. Our spiritual journey can never be complete without a carnal energy for humanity to blossom in its fullness. It is the great vow of the bodhisattva—to serve—but here not only by removing suffering but also by bringing forth new creation.

* * *

Vocation does not come from willfulness. It comes from listening. I must listen to my life and try to understand what it is truly about—quite apart from what I would like it to be about. . . . Vocation does not mean a goal that I pursue. It means a calling that I hear . . . not as a goal to be achieved but as a gift to be received.[160]

* * *

Our vocation is the answer of the Spirit to our prayers to serve, taking into account all the needs of the collective, all of our gifts, and then offering: "This is how you can most copiously contribute." Only in consent to this offering do we find the place through which our most precious, most unique, most inexpressible energies will flow. Our role is to offer ourselves, to listen, and then to consent.

* * *

Vocari. To be called. We always speak of the most noble of the professions of mankind as *callings.* . . . You are called, you respond, you surrender; and when surrender is complete, you profess. All of these meditations are an exploration of that equation—the meaning of call and surrender, the meaning of profession.[161]

* * *

Vocare. Vocare. The calling. A call from the deep of the night in the inner soul. The dark submergence of the soul. The inner being is opening its eye, trying to see. The inner nodes are birthing, flowing. Messages of supreme consequence, implicit urgency. The great cross-over point in your life. The Threshold."[162]

* * *

Meditation Two: Finding Vocation

We are moving into the calling of a new monastic, traveling within to that place where it is known, as the *tzadiks* of old did, that a piece of this world has been waiting for our soul to repair it . . . and that we are here to offer our life, our gifts, in service of completing our special task. We are here to do the work of *tikkun olam;* we are here to heal and complete the world.

* * *

Your dreams throw out possibilities to you every night, the possibility of what you are to be, of the nature of your vocation. Every night you get clues as to your calling, the measure of yourself in your responding witness of profession.[163]

* * *

Nothing in a dream is trivial, or it wouldn't be there. The more deeply you regard the contents of your dream, even the apparently trivial contents, the more deeply will they begin to take on their archetypal character. . . . The idea most difficult to accept, and most necessary, is that the dream is the agent of wholeness.[164]

* * *

Your quest is spiritual, and what will be tested is your immortal soul, but tested only in the sense of verification, and to the ends of verification. . . . Therefore, you must expose yourself to the dangerous kingdom, knowing that the resources for your survival are intrinsic in yourself, the essential spirit. No one has ever been guaranteed survival of anything. . . . Your freedom is your Light.[165]

* * *

As May Sarton reminds us, the pilgrimage toward true self will take "time, many years and places." The world needs people with the patience and the passion to make that pilgrimage not only for their own sake but also as a social and political act. The world still waits for the truth that will set us free—my truth, your truth, our truth—the truth that was seeded in the earth when each of us arrived here formed in the image of God. Cultivating that truth, I believe, is the authentic vocation of every human being.[166]

* * *

A calling is a special thing. Some people just come to this world knowing what it is. There are many examples of people who have always felt that a specific thing is part of their soul's DNA. Others have to spend years searching. Our journey into vocation is unique and can't be fully named or described. And yet there are tools that are useful, tools that enable us to go deep into the depth of our hearts and touch there the collective. Dreams are one way to do this, work with a seasoned spiritual director is another. But remember, mentors are there not to give you answers. The community is not there to give you answers. They can help you in your own discernment—and when you find yourself in your vocation, they can affirm it.

* * *

Separation, Initiation, and Return. . . . Everyone is going to have to go through it. . . . Vocation is one of the essential ways which, in this competitive world, the problem can be met, embraced, and resolved. . . . You should be able to arrive at the end of the process not only with the inner journey achieved, but also with your tools and techniques in some degree of development. Only then will you be able to effect the thing you set out to do, even though it was a mystery when you began it.[167]

* * *

We live in a world that paralyzes us. The devastation of the earth we stand on, the hunger of children, the proximity of war, violence, and poverty are making it more and more difficult for us to believe in the dream of self-actualization. We do not know how to respond. The problems are so big and yet our actions so small. How does one solve the ongoing devastation of our Mother Earth? How does one deal with the fact that one in five children in this country live in poverty? How does one respond to the deepening crisis of homeless youth? Or gay youth too often ostracized for being who they are? How does one do anything when we are surrounded by so many crises?

* * *

Loud voices of politicians tell us that voting will solve all of our dilemmas. Intriguing images produced by marketing gurus scream loudly that all can be solved by shopping green. Otherworldly spiritual celebrities encourage us to not pay attention to the illusive nature of this world; after all, it is only maya. Focus instead on cultivating your own personal inner peace. How does one move forward with all this pain and the noise of contradictory voices? How does one one not get stuck in confusion and helplessness? How does one make use of one's spirituality and one's life?

* * *

The goal is not to answer these questions. The goal is to be present to them with all that we are. We are following the poet Rilke's advice in counseling a young artist, "be patient toward all that is unsolved in your heart and try to love the questions themselves. Perhaps you will then gradually, without noticing it, live along into the answer."

* * *

In most cases the spiritual journey begins with either falling in love or heartbreak. With finding vocation, it is similar. These questions take us into the reality of heartbreak and aliveness, and there we hold them simultaneously with all that we are, with every part of our being. Then we just wait faithfully, trusting that if we stay with these questions and what they evoke long enough, something will emerge—an insight of the heart, a direction for our lives. It's not enough to follow our passion. It is both what makes us alive and what breaks us. To stay with that dichotomy, to stay with the tension—if we stay long enough something will crack—then grace begins to guide us. We must give ourselves permission to embrace what life is offering and where it is leading. Once this happens, the work of embodying our vocation in the world begins.

That can almost be said to be a methodology.

* * *

Do not forget to take heart in the unknown. As Everson tells us, "You must not let that outside world, with its emphasis on the linear, deny you your deeper self, which is of the cyclical mode. Your course in life must always be to hold both realms in your being. Your vocation is the process by which you bring them together."[168]

* * *

Finding vocation also requires a certain freedom from our cultural conditioning. Otherwise you will be putting your own ideas on what your vocation should look like. It can help to have an awareness of what our cultural conditioning is and where its biases lie, for instance, a bias toward "doing." Not only doing, but also doing big. And the need to see in a physical, materialistic form the fruits of one's actions. We feel we have to become a fictional somebody, bigger than life, who can address all the overwhelming issues. The real answer, however, is in going back to one's life in prayer and discernment, feeling one's self, embracing one's self, and engaging all that one is. The only way to address big problems is to be familiar with small problems first. Otherwise, we end up with policies and models that are detached from reality and therefore inadequate.

These biases can take you away from a sense of confidence in your own discernment process, and it takes a tremendous fidelity to what is arising within you to go through the process.

* * *

It is also important to remember that this need to be bigger than life is a way of preventing ourselves from feeling the real pain that we see around us. In order to get to the core of things, we have to approach them in a prayerful way. Touch their pain, perhaps even be broken by it, and then in that brokenness something mysterious will happen. It is only when we touch that pain that our truth will be evoked.

* * *

Our goal is to be an instrument of God's loving impulse in the world. Only then will the best of our abilities come to be. We have to work hard on developing our talents, yet we also have to work hard on letting them go. When God's grace enters our lives and takes over, all that is uniquely ours will flower. It will flower in a way that we may not have known was possible.

* * *

Our deepest calling is to grow into our own authentic selfhood, whether or not it conforms to some image of who we *ought* to be. As we do so, we will not only find the joy that every human being seeks—we will also find our path of authentic service in the world.[169]

* * *

It's the most personal thing that there is—saying yes to what this journey is, saying yes to what it means to follow the spirituality of vocation. It is so significant because there is no one else who can give birth to what you and I and everyone else are here to give birth to. For one to miss that is a tragedy for all.

* * *

Timing is important, too. Sometimes you may know what your vocation is, but it has to ripen. Both you and the collective must be ready for it to incarnate. It can only happen in a dance between you and the collective.

* * *

How do we know if we're on the right path?
Is the work that we're doing dedicated to justice and compassion?
Is the path transforming us into a healing presence in the world?
Take the advice of Abhishiktananda: "In the end, love is the final test."

* * *

Rootedness within transmission, there it is. There are many ways to be called, yet only one calling.

* * *

Rootedness—from the core of your being roots grow down, down into the very core of this Earth, with its molten, liquid fire. You become one in spirit with the indigenous peoples, with their nonseparation, their organic belonging. Like the great sequoia tree, rooted deep in the ground, you belong here, impervious to the ravishing winds that may come your way.

Transmission—your heart reaches up to the Divine with confident supplication, your head opens and widens so the sky may pour in. It is a funnel into your heart. You receive that which descends, bear it, endure it, until you become impregnated with it. Your solar plexus opens, gracefully, blossoming as you radiate outward, giving birth to that which was given. It is gentle, purified, eternally fecund.

When one finds the place of rootedness within transmission, then one has found vocation. The above merges fruitfully with the below. One finds one's place not only on Earth, but in Heaven as well.

* * *

Never forget that only the acceptance at the close will yield the mystery of wholeness to you, the thing you desire most of all. You have to lose your life in order to save it. You have to expend yourself in order to find yourself. You gain your life only by giving it up.[170]

* * *

Meditation Three: Incarnating Vocation

If you want,
the Virgin will come walking down the road,
pregnant with the holy,and say,
"I need shelter for the night,
 please take me inside your heart,
my time is so close."
Then, under the roof of your soul,
you will witness the sublime intimacy, the divine, the Christ
taking birth forever,
as she grasps your hand for help, for each of us
is the midwife of God, each of us.[171]

* * *

In the recognition of a sacred space you are founding your world, endowing existence with significance. And in your recognition of vocation you are finding your purpose in life. There it is; the significance of reality is recognition, the purpose of existence is fulfillment.[172]

* * *

Do you go where you belong, and then start from there? Or do you go where the opportunities *seem* to be, and cut yourself off from your roots? Often you will find that your greatest strengths come not from being where the opportunities are, but from where you belong.[173] One may find one's vocation, but if it "is not supported by the authority of sacred space" then we "must insist that the process is not complete." And the founding and the finding "seldom occur simultaneously."[174]

* * *

No one
knows his name—

a man who lives on the streets
and walks around in
rags.
      Once I saw that man in a dream.
He and God were constructing
an extraordinary temple.[175]

* * *

There was a hermit who lived in the Sahara in Algeria, a Christian hermit, Charles de Foucauld. He lived as a hermit among Muslims and throughout his lifetime never found any disciples. One day he was killed by a band of marauders. By all accounts he was a failure according to any conventional measurement of the world. Years after he died, people were inspired by his writings and vision and gathered and prayed to him, forming the Little Brothers of Jesus. So you never know how it will come into being. It was the same with Abhishiktananda—it's now that we can appreciate him. This is important to ponder. Parker Palmer said that there are thousands of ways of being *almost* yourself. If you sway to the enticements of society, or a need for relevancy, then you move only further from your truth.

* * *

One of the biggest lessons that a new monastic must learn is what Henri Nouwen called the "temptation to be relevant." In a world where everything gets compartmentalized and specialized, where human suffering needs to be labeled and classified into pathologies, a new monastic is here to first witness what is happening. To show up fully with all of her being—without any preconceived notion of what is needed. To be in a curious not-knowing, waiting for the impulse of God to break into her life, into the situation she is bearing testament to.

* * *

Thomas Merton captures this temptation to be relevant well in his letter to a young activist:

> Do not depend on the hope of results. . . . You may have to face the fact that your work will be apparently worthless and even achieve no result at all. . . . As you get used to this idea, you start more and more to concentrate not on the results but on the value, the rightness, the truth of the work itself. And there too a great deal has to be gone through, as gradually you struggle less and less for an idea and more and more for specific people. . . . In the end, it is the reality of personal relationships that saves everything. . . . You are probably striving to build yourself an iden-

tity in your work, . . . using it, so to speak, to protect yourself against nothingness, annihilation. That is not the right use of your work. All the good that you will do will come . . . from the fact that you have allowed yourself, in the obedience of faith, to be used by God's love. Think of this more and gradually you will be free from the need to prove yourself, and you can be more open to the power that will work through you without your knowing it.[176]

* * *

When I think of being in vocation, it is being in that space where the Spirit can live through you, where the Spirit can do with you whatever it needs to do. As the Spirit enters you and lives through you, a unique quality emerges in you along with unique gifts. Then you live as an expression of those gifts. All of us is used in this process. We develop expertise but then put it aside. Somehow it is reassembled and utilized in unexpected ways, ways we need not even be conscious of. We become instruments of a transmission that is taking place. That transmission brings us peace in action, funnels our energy, removes obstacles, tames us, integrates us. It feels like prayer.

* * *

It happens in moments of grace—the Spirit just breaks in—and those are common experiences. But to incarnate one's vocation we are talking about a sustained way of living. It takes a lot of energy, a lot of courage, and a lot of contemplative practice to allow this. It doesn't just happen. It requires a lifestyle, because a lifestyle is required for you to sustain that state of being. You take active steps toward being a receptor and transmitter for grace.

* * *

I have stopped at many oases in my life. Vocation is the force that carries you beyond them, that won't let you rest, that seizes you and possesses you and carries you along. . . . No matter how much you try to rest in an oasis, sooner or later it evacuates you. You might be willing to settle for everything it offers because you are tired of the journey, but at that time something else comes to your rescue, the innate disposition of what you are. It is your vocation, and that is what sets you apart and says *go*. You feel that spiritual craving which is a different thing from either sensual or intellectual thirst; that spiritual thirst to be with your own kind, to associate with them and participate with them, sends you once again on your way across the desert.[177]

* * *

Saying yes to one's vocation may mean struggling financially; it may mean making decisions that family and friends might not fully understand, or even reject. "Prophets are not without honor, except in their home town, and among their own kin, and in their own house."[178] It may mean choosing roads that are counterintuitive to the mind, so conditioned by the culture we live in. Doing this can be a direct challenge to the way most people live.

* * *

They will sense it, even if only unconsciously. They will work against you, bless their souls. People will be threatened because deep down everyone who is not living an authentic life, deep down knows it. When someone is making decisions for an authentic life, it exposes others' shallowness, threatens their lifestyle, implicates them in an unknown conspiracy. The response is to attack the source, denigrate the source, dismiss it, invalidate it.

* * *

However, "if you do have the vocation, you can survive anything that comes at you . . . because it has conferred that role on you. I am what you have conferred upon me, no more. If I touch you, it is because I have been touched."[179]

* * *

Each vocation also has a shadow, and that needs to be addressed. The shadow of a contemplative is not to want to take action; the shadow of an activist is not to want to be in a state of inaction. And so again, it's an integration. And remember, "One great thing about your vocation is that even if you sabotage it, it still is the one thing that can take you forward to redeem your losses. Only the naked authenticity of vocation can do that."[180]

* * *

We learn as much about our nature by running into our limits as by experiencing our potentials. . . . Our created natures make us like organisms in an ecosystem: there are some roles and relationships in which we thrive and others in which we wither and die. . . . God asks us only to honor our created nature, which means our limits as well as potentials.[181]

* * *

"Burnout is a state of emptiness, to be sure, but it does not result from giving all that I have: it merely reveals the nothingness from which I was trying to give in the first place."[182] True vocation produces a different kind of giving, grounded in a different way of being, a way that results not in burnout but in fecundity and abundance:

"As slowly as the ripening fruit
Fertile, detached, and always spent,
Falls but does not exhaust the root. . . ."[183]

* * *

Freedom in acceptance—that's a powerful thought, that freedom lies in acceptance. . . . We refuse to accept unless we understand, and that is our error. If we chose to accept, understanding would be given to us.[184]

* * *

We can take solace that there is a whole tribe of people who have gone before us. Some of those people become our mentors; some become our guides through their journals and writings; some—we do believe in the communion of the saints—become our guides through prayer and the grace that descends.

* * *

Ultimately though, we are all hermits in the depths of our soul. It is the problem of uniqueness. And in our vocation we will always find ourselves to some degree in the great Alone. We must make friends with the abyss, for it will carry us through the darkest of times, bring us solace when most needed, and be the one place where we are truly understood.

* * *

In that Aloneness, in our vocation, we walk with the archetypal Hermit: "the solitary man with the lamp, mantle and staff. For he possesses the gift of letting light shine in the darkness—this is his 'lamp'; he has the faculty of separating himself from the collective moods, prejudices and desires of race, nation, class and family . . . in order to listen to and understand the hierarchical harmony of the spheres—this is his 'mantle'; at the same time he possesses a realism which is so developed that he stands in the domain of reality not on two feet, but rather on three, i.e. he advances only after having *touched* the ground through immediate experience . . . this is his 'staff.' He creates light, he creates silence, and he creates certainty. . . ."[185]

* * *

The Hermit is neither deep in meditation or study nor is he engaged in work or action. *He is walking.* This means to say that he manifests a third state beyond that of contemplation and action. He represents . . . the term of synthesis, namely that of *heart.* For it is the *heart* where contemplation and action are united, where knowledge becomes will and where will becomes knowledge. The heart does not need to forget all contemplation in order to act, and does not need to suppress all action in order to contemplate. It is the heart which is simultaneously active and contemplative, untiringly and unceasingly. It *walks.* It walks day and night, and we listen day and night to the steps of its incessant walking.[186]

* * *

The heart . . . will become a traveler, a visitor and anonymous companion of those who are in prison, those who are in exile, and those who bear heavy loads of responsibility. It will be an itinerant Hermit, traversing ways leading from one end of the earth to the other, and also ways through spheres of the spiritual world—from purgatory to the very feet of the Father. Because no distance is insurmountable for love and no door can prevent it from entering—according to the promise which says: "and the gates of hell shall not prevail against it" (Matthew xvi, 18). It is the heart which is the marvelous organ called to serve love in its works.[187]

* * *

Because we find that love is work enough for us, we don't take the time to categorize what we are doing as either "contemplation" or "action." We find that prayer is action and that action is prayer. It seems to us that truly loving action is filled with light. It seems to us that a soul standing before such action is like a night that is full of expectation for the coming dawn. And when the light breaks, when God's will is clearly understood, she lives it out gently, with poise, peacefully watching her God inspiring her and at work within her.[188]

* * *

Thus, every new monastic is an activist, for she is here to be an instrument through which God's dream of love, solidarity, and healing can be brought into the world. Every authentic calling is deeply personal and intimate. Even though at first it seems like it requires a loss of self, it ultimately allows one to be one's most authentic self. What is lost is regained in its transfigured fullness. What is needed is returned, so again it can be given.

* * *

Meditation Four: Vocation as Transformational and Revolutionary Act

We live and create when we understand and obey our key nature, our key nature is our path to Reality, to God.[189]

* * *

All creation is awakened and called. It boasts a calling, a vocation, a reason for being, an invitation to participate and make things happen. This is true of stones and rocks, of trees and animals, of birds and sun and moon. And it's surely true of humans. We are called to "co-create," to live out our awakening, our calling, our greening power, our creativity and verdancy.[190]

* * *

I do not divide your life into a religious life and a secular life. I see your vocation as the heart of your religious life, and that the fulfilling of your vocation is the fulfilling of your religious life.[191]

* * *

A "spirituality that is only private and self-absorbed, one devoid of an authentic political and social consciousness, does little to halt the suicidal juggernaut of history. On the other hand, an activism that is not purified by profound spiritual and psychological self-awareness and rooted in divine truth, wisdom, and compassion will only perpetuate the problem it is trying to solve, however righteous its intentions. When, however, the deepest and most grounded spiritual vision is married to a practical and pragmatic drive to transform all existing political, economic, and social institutions, a holy force—the power of wisdom and love in action—is born.[192]

* * *

Each one of us has a seed of Christ within him. In each of us the amazing and dangerous Seed of Christ is present. It is only a Seed. It is very small, like the grain of mustard seed. The Christ that is formed in us is small indeed, but he is great with eternity. But if we dare to take this awakened Seed of Christ into the middle of the world's suffering, it will grow. Take a young man or a young woman in which Christ is only dimly formed, but one in whom the Seed of Christ is alive. Put him into a distressed area, into a refugee camp, into a poverty region. Let him go into the world's suffering, bearing the Seed with him, and in suffering it will grow, and Christ will be more and more fully formed in him. As the grain of mustard seed grew so large that the birds found shelter in it, so the man who bears an awakened Seed into the world's suffering will grow until he becomes a refuge for many.[193]

* * *

The deeper one is drawn into God, the more one must . . . go out to the world in order to carry the divine life into it.[194]

* * *

Dream Me, God
It's not you who should solve my problems, God,
but I yours, God of the asylum-seekers.
It's not you who should feed the hungry,
but I who should protect your children
from the terror of the banks and armies.
It's not you who should make room for the refugees,
but I who should receive you,
hardly hidden God of the desolate.
You dreamed me, God, practicing walking upright and learning
to kneel down more beautiful than I am now, happier
than I dare to be
freer than our country allows.
Don't stop dreaming me, God.
I don't want to stop remembering that I am your tree,
planted by the streams of living water.[195]

* * *

"To worship was formerly to prefer God to things. . . . To worship is now becoming to devote oneself body and soul to the creative act." By witnessing, respecting, and responding to God's creative impulse in us, the highest of theological virtues, *caritas,* charity or love, attains "its full meaning in life given for common progress."[196]

* * *

"The great artist has a divine impatience with the way things are."[197] So does the prophet!

* * *

The collective does not have the power to save itself; only through the individual, through the creative personality, then back down into the collective. The race can only go forward through . . . individuals who rise out of the common level and go through a certain psychic process of crystallization. . . . As kind of a fruitful off-giving they then pour back into the collective the substance of their penetration.[198]

* * *

In that "fruitful off-giving" one "exercises a spiritualizing influence in the world . . . which is in accord with *the creative wisdom of God* in things and history."[199] Thus, a new monastic's activism is not just about joining causes. You don't become an activist by stepping outside of yourself and taking on a cause. Your true self, at its deepest, connects you to the cause.

* * *

Meditation Five: Vocation as Community— Notes in the Symphony of Life

A mosaic consists of thousands of little stones. Some are blue, some are green, some are yellow, some are gold. When we bring our faces close to the mosaic, we can admire the beauty of each stone. But as we step back from it, we can see that all these little stones reveal to us a beautiful picture, telling a story none of these stones can tell by itself. That is what our life in community is about. Each of us is like a little stone, but together we reveal the face of God to the world. Nobody can say: "I make God visible." But others who see us together can say: "They make God visible." Community is where humility and glory touch.[200]

* * *

God's will is one of infinite love and compassion and is trying to initiate us into our particular contribution to the evolutionary process. We can't do that without a community. . . . We need the support, the encouragement, the trust, the love of a community to become fully human.[201]

* * *

The key to this form of community involves holding a paradox—the paradox of having relationships in which we protect each other's aloneness. We must come together in ways that respect the solitude of the soul, that avoid the unconscious violence we do when we try to save each other, that evoke our capacity to hold another life without dishonoring its mystery, never trying to coerce the other into meeting our own needs.[202]

* * *

In our aloneness, we need the support of others in this world. Not only as part of our spiritual awakening, but on a practical level as well. Our vocations are sacred, and can't be "valued" by our world of economics and enterprises. A lot of vocations don't produce a livelihood at this point. That doesn't mean they shouldn't be done. It simply means that we need communities whose primary role is to create environments in which gifts, talents, and vocations are evoked, welcomed, authenticated, and supported to reshape our world. We need communities that can make it easier for people to become who they were born to be.

* * *

We need this desperately, because it is only through each of us living out our vocations together that we make God visible. And it is only through making God visible that we complete the world, even, some may say, we complete God. For as Panikkar tells us, "The Absolute is only absolutely incarnated in the Relative."[203] What greater incentive could there be to come together in supportive communal life?

* * *

I am a bird. I am a nightingale. If they say to me, "Make some other kind of sound," I cannot. My tongue is what it is. I cannot speak otherwise. However, those who learn the song of birds are not birds themselves— on the contrary, they are the enemies of birds and their captors. They sing and whistle so others will take them for birds. . . . It is not truly their own.[204]

NEW MONASTIC COMMUNITIES

A common bonding takes place in all who are attracted to the transformative process. Such is the ultimate lineage of all spiritual lineages emerging in the various religious traditions. We are partners/companions in the search, moved by a common perspective and inspiration. Inklings of the contemplative dimension of life are reflected in the world's religions. . . . Monastics move toward the Unknowable by witnessing to it in a common lifestyle of complete dedication.[205]   —*Thomas Keating*

Community is first of all a quality of the heart. It grows from the spiritual knowledge that we are alive not for ourselves but for one another.[206]   —*Henri Nouwen*

Without the context of community, prayer and resistance easily degenerate into forms of individual heroism. . . . Only when we belong to a supportive, as well as self-critical, community is there a chance that our peacemaking effort may be more God-serving than self-serving.[207]   —*Henri Nouwen*

Albert Nolan, the South African Dominican priest and activist, considered Jesus to be a revolutionary. However, this was not a typical revolutionary in the political sense of the word. For Nolan, Jesus did not simply want to replace people in power with those who are not in power. His revolution was much deeper. It was one that called for a spiritual conversion and a radical shift in human relationships. In the same way, the new monastic movement calls for the revolution that takes place on a personal level, and subsequently in all of our relationships. It calls for a radically new way of being with each other in which love and not power are at the center. It organically demands the creation of small communities of friends, worlds within the world, in which people are brought into the heart of who they are, evoking their uniqueness, goodness and authenticity. It calls for a world based on reciprocal and networked global relationships, founded on mutual aid and caring. New monastic communities are containers—experiments—in which we learn how to live that, containers in which we learn how to practice truth and forgiveness with one another, how we come to a place of shared heart, and how we cultivate relationships in which we can evoke and affirm each other's gifts containers in which we can discern the guidance of the Holy Spirit for our lives together. New monastic communities, then, are our way of seeing and living into a world of authenticity, solidarity, and heart.

When new monastics gather in communities, their communities reflect the calling of every member. The community is there to support the unfolding of every vocation present in the prayerful gathering of talents, and each person is there to enable this flowering of community. The two are interdependent; one is a reflection of the other. New monastic communities are not like typical communities of the past, where at times individual callings were neglected in favor of focusing on the greater whole. Rather, these communities embody a deep trust in each person's unique calling, pledged to support what emerges in another's heart. While at first this way may seem individualistic, new monastic communities are endowed within a new paradigm—one which sees clearly that individual callings do not move people away from their communities; instead, they are what make authentic communities possible. Our uniqueness, in maturity, never prevents us from achieving greater unity; it is rather, as Teilhard saw, indispensable for this achievement.

These communities are mosaics where each stone is deeply cared for, where there is a profound knowing that the community is there to support everyone who wants to truly say yes to the Divine dream unfolding in their hearts. They are not based on everyone subscribing to the same theology. They are not based on everyone performing the same spiritual practice. They are based on a commitment to contemplative life and dialogical processes, the dialogical processes we spoke of previously, and to the support and discernment of each individual's unique vocation in the world. The centers of these communities are dialogical gatherings which allow friends to be present to each other in a way that locates them in their truth.

Once our identity is established in the heart of who we are, we no longer feel a need to play worldly games based on a constant reinvention of our personal brands, manipulating the world to affirm that we matter. New monastics know that in order for a new world to come into being they have to become new people first; and that "to be is to be in relationship."[208] Knowing this, new monastics give a profound importance to every gathering and every community, no matter how small. They understand these communities to be laboratories for personal transformation and social change, containers of reciprocal care in which the best in people can be evoked and nurtured. They understand these communities to be experiments through which the Spirit begins to breathe in our midst by engaging one another in a prayerful, heartfelt way.

New monastics also understand that these communities become containers for the emergence of our dark sides, our shadows and faults, for us and for the others we gather with. As Father Bede Griffiths tells us, "As soon as we form community the ego in each person begins to come out. . . . The closer we come to people the more we are in conflict." Therefore, new monastics enter into community with an awareness of this emergence of one another's shadows, and in order to become transformative containers for this emergence, new monastics must learn patience, fortitude, and clear discernment of the members of its community.

Sometimes this may call for difficult decisions, tension-filled exchanges, and extended dialogues. New monastic communities must be wary of idealistic visions, particularly at the beginning. Members must get to know one another and feel out the depth of resonance present, which only reveals itself in the course of time. All of this must be done *before* entering into community. When this is done, and a strong core resonance can be formed at the center of the community, then it can play the transformative role of bearing one another's burdens—but this core must be formed first. Without it, communities are in grave danger of degenerating after a number of years, and disillusioning the participants in the process. In the beginning, it only takes one person in the inner circle with whom the resonance is not strong enough, and this can be enough to prevent a sufficient communal bonding to occur. With a committed, resonate, and strongly developed core, new monastic communities can bring others in, with a firmly established center of gravity around which new members can orbit and to which in time they can contribute their part. In this way, these communities can serve as cells of a new world, giving birth to novel ways of political, spiritual, and economic life.

New monastic communities, then, are about building the Kingdom of Heaven, one friendship and one community at a time. They are about building collages of everyone's calling, collages that reflect beauty and radiate compassion and justice into the world. When new monastics gather in these communities, either live-in communities or prayer groups, they understand that they are following in the footsteps of great spiritual pioneers like Dorothy Day, Lanza del Vasto, Father Bede Griffiths, and Gandhi-ji, who made community the center of their revolution for a better world. They understand that what they do in their communities affects the whole world; that we are all in the process of building a civilization with a heart that struggles to be born in our midst.

Yet different communities do and will have different charisms necessitated by the differing endeavors needed to complete the world. Some communities are prophetic testaments to the plight of the poor and oppressed, alleviating suffering and bearing witness to the brutality of our current unholy economic inequalities, communities such as Sewa Ashram in India where, under the direction of Ton Baba, this community of the poor focused on serving people broken by poverty, taking them off the streets of Delhi and healing them back into life, incarnating one of the holiest places one could experience. Other communities are containers for contemplative writing, reflection, and art, following the inspiration of some of our mentors, such as Father Bede Griffiths and his Shantivanam Ashram in India, and Sister Michaela Terrio and Brother Francis Ali of Sky Farm Hermitage in Sonoma, California. They too may cultivate places of holy silence where pilgrims from all walks of life, including new monastics who are called to ministry in urban areas, may come for renewal.

Still other new monastics, when they choose to gather in communities, may find inspiration in evangelical new monastic communities, such as Shane Claiborne's the Simple Way community in Philadelphia and Jonathon Wilson-Hartgrove's Rutba House in Durham, North Carolina. These communities are often formed by moving to places of great poverty "abandoned by the empire," and through prayer and social action see their mission in bringing qualities of new and resurrected life to these forgotten places. There may also be communities, such as our friends at BlueStone Farm in Brewster, New York, brought together by an Episcopal new monastic ideal; feeling the urge to become part of a movement that bridges interspirituality with organic farming and permaculture, envisioning what an ecofriendly and socially responsible economy could look like. These communities are experiments in what the world to come may be, exploring the foundations of new economic and spiritual synergies, concerned with offering a model for where we may be headed. Finally, there may also be communities like Canticle Farm in Oakland, California, more actively engaged in helping to change the current structural systems of economic and spiritual violence and oppression. Formed in the spirit of Dorothy Day by Anne Symens-Bucher, Canticle Farm combines the radical witness of the Catholic Worker movement with the contemplative wisdom of Buddhist philosopher and elder Joanna Macy, participating in movements such as Occupy, and embodying a commitment to nonviolence and peacemaking in all the broken and violent parts of our world.

All of these varying types of community are necessary, all are evolutionary, all are contributing in their own way to the completing of the world, and all are united therefore in that endeavor. As with individual vocations, communities of different charisms are needed. It is also possible for communities to be formed by members who each have different callings in one or another of these varying vocations, some members with an activist calling, others with more contemplative, ecological, artistic, or administrative vocations. These types of communities hold within them a creative mix of tensions, and perhaps demand a greater reservoir of flexibility and fortitude, but in this they become synergistic, diverse, and fascinating containers to creatively build upon the wide-ranging talents of the members. They must struggle to find and hold a common ground, not by reducing the differences among themselves to this ground, but rather by using their love for one another and dialogical processes to skillfully give birth to new emergences among them. This book could be said to be an embodiment of this type of "process in community," with Adam's more activist vocation, Rory's more contemplative and philosophical leanings, and the legion of mentors and elders whose wisdom is quoted and assimilated throughout.

All of these communities are based on a deep knowing that our destinies are linked. What holds them in harmony is a complete transparency and mutual dedication to the truth that is emerging in everyone. They go even beyond community, because what we are really talking about is communion. This can only be done when each person shows up, fully present, fully honest, and in humility. In these new monastic communities the idea of shared belief and practice is replaced with process-based activity, in particular with the dialogical dialogue and support for each other's vocations. This moves us beyond what traditionally has been conceived of as community. When all of those components take place it manifests as a coming together of lives where brokenness is transfigured into wholeness. An opening for grace is made, a certain positioning of human endeavors that gives the Divine permission to break into this world in a new way. The presence of God is invited in, and a container is created into which grace can pour. Some of it manifests as silence; some of it as conversational prayer; some of it as a removal of masks; some of it as fortitude, patience, and even failure. These are places where pain, aspiration, and intimacy can be welcomed and embraced. These communities help all of us to begin working together in a way that brings us into a deeper discovery of our truths, allows those truths to then interact, and in this gives birth to the new.

MOVEMENT 3
A Dialogical Interlude

He observed the graciousness of one, the earnestness in prayer of another; he studied the even temper of one and the kindheartedness of another. He fixed his attention on the vigils kept by one and on the studies pursued by another. He admired one for his patient endurance, another for his fasting and sleeping on the ground. He watched closely one man's meekness and the forbearance by another.[1]

—*St. Athanasius in The Life of St. Anthony*

We introduce here an extended dialogue between Rory and Adam, recorded in Steamboat Springs, Colorado, in 2014 and subsequently edited. As we mentioned in "Beginnings," we feel that the dialogue adds considerable context to all we have articulated, and allows readers to gain insight into many of the ideas presented through a different medium and rhythm. In addition, it offers an inside feel to the differing personalities behind our vision, and the close friendship and interaction they have grown out of. However, perhaps the most important element is that they offer a taste of the dialogical interaction and emergence we have spoken of so often, embodying the power of prayerful dialogic creativity and its ability to evoke what is most authentic in us, under the integrating depth and heartfelt guidance of the Spirit.

In our dialogues below we will receive an intimate view of some of the insights that have emerged from the Snowmass dialogues and their meaning for new monasticism. The Snowmass Dialogues are formally known today as the Snowmass Interspiritual Dialogue Fellowship (SISD), and were previously known as The Snowmass Conference (and sometimes as the Snowmass Interreligious Conference). They originally began in 1984 as Father Thomas Keating convened a group of committed contemplatives and spiritual practitioners from varying religious traditions to come together for deep dialogue during an intimate five-day retreat. The idea was to share personal experiences of the transformative journey, rather than to represent one's tradition. As such, it was decided that the dialogues would be kept completely private so that participants did not have to worry about representing their traditions. The dialogues were so successful that they have subsequently met for a five-day retreat every year since, and are respected in many circles as one of the most authentic inter-religious dialogue experiments to have ever taken place.

ON THE SNOWMASS DIALOGUES,
GRACE, AND INCARNATION

RORY: So let's discuss some of these elements we have articulated thus far.

ADAM: I think it's important to give some context, to go back to the idea of interspirituality and some of the experiences that gave birth to it. I think it would be good to focus on one specific experience that we know of, that in many ways is part of the lineage for this particular project, which is the Snowmass Dialogue: how a group of spiritual leaders were able to gather together for thirty years now, once a year, with the goal not to meet as representatives of their traditions, but rather for them to meet as human beings who clearly have been formed by their traditions. The understanding being that they will share deeply with one another in a spirit of friendship. As Father Thomas mentioned, the goal was that there were lots of spiritual teachers coming to this country, and they simply didn't have support—they were often alone, and it's tough to do this. So for him the gathering was a way for them to almost take a break from their identity as teachers, and to meet on a heart-to-heart level and share deeply about their struggles, about their journeys, about their questions.

And what's interesting about this is that I think through whatever they did, whatever methodology they used to connect with each other and to share, clearly that methodology led them to this experience of a shared heart. And I wanted to ask you some questions about that process, so that's one: It led to something, right? Where they felt that together they discovered something—I know you used the term *love*—where you almost fail at articulating what's happening, and through that failure something happens, and in that this grace descends where you just feel connected, present, *in love*.

It's also very clear that the reason why they were able to arrive at that is because there was this deep dialogical sharing, where people were able to essentially take off their masks and be with each other in a very direct and intimate way. And so through that process, through that love they experienced, this experience was born. And then it's also very clear that whatever was happening there really influenced Brother Wayne. And in many ways, I don't know if it would be fair to say, but perhaps interspirituality would not have been articulated if it weren't for that particular group and experience.

RORY: I think it certainly informed Brother Wayne and, for him, was one of the more powerful experiments in interspirituality and in the phenomenon he was naming, even though he never was able to personally participate in it. Father Keating was of course his spiritual father, so he was intimately related to it through that connection. And Brother Wayne made extensive use of the Points of Agreement in his development of interspirituality, a series of eight (and later extended to twelve) principles on the spiritual life and Ultimate Reality that members of the Snowmass group were able to come to agreement on. I think the genius of the Snowmass Dialogues, when they originally started back in 1984, was that Father Thomas had this idea—he was going to many conferences where other spiritual teachers would be, and they would do a dialogue or give talks to an audience—and as he went around to these conferences, he found that it was in the side moments, maybe over dinner or as they went for a walk following their presentations, with no audiences present, that he always felt the best exchanges occurred.

And so he thought: What if I convened a group to meet, simply with the purpose of just getting together as friends in a private, intimate way and sharing our experience of the transformative journey? And what he was looking for was not representatives of the theology, dogmas, or beliefs of the traditions, but for people who were living a deep, experiential, transformative, spiritual, mystical path *within* the traditions, so that those who participated would be bringing with them the insights and the tools of transformation from the traditions that they had cultivated in their own lives. In other words, they would share the experience of their transformative journeys, and the techniques they used for that experience and the insights that came about as a result of that process, and then see what came out of that.

ADAM: So when you attended some of those meetings, what was your experience like? And how did that experience differ from some of the other experiences that you've had when people meet and share?

RORY: I have been to the dialogues the last five years. And the process itself has gone through some stages. For the first twenty years the participants, which was usually somewhere in the vicinity of ten to twelve people, got together for basically a week, five days, once a year, usually up at Father Keating's monastery, St. Benedict's in Snowmass, Colorado. Though they went to a few different places in the early years, St. Benedict's became the settled place and held for them a special energy that the group members felt contributed mightily to the dialogue and the process. During these twenty years they decided to not speak publicly about what was going on there for the most part. Nothing was recorded, nothing was put out for public consumption, except perhaps the Points of Agreement that they came to after the first few years, and which were highlighted in Brother Wayne's work. After the first twenty years a book was published,

The Common Heart, where members discussed some of their experience of the conference through interviews in a dialogue format. That was the first thing made public. At that time, they also decided to change the format of the conference. Instead of just members meeting for dialogue, they decided that each member would bring one or two mentees to the conference, and they developed a format to lead the mentees through a dialogue process as well, essentially using the methodology and insights they had gained over the years and then attempting to pass that down each year to a new group of mentees. I first attended the conference as a mentee of Father Thomas back in 2010. The following year the members invited me to be become the administrator for the group, and so I have participated in the dialogues since that time. In addition, in 2013, a reunion was held as part of the Dawn of Interspirituality conference, with both mentees and members who had participated throughout the nearly thirty years of retreats.

One interesting thing to note is that it was always very important to the members for people to come out of traditions. If you weren't embedded in a particular spiritual tradition, you weren't invited to the conference.[2] I was one of the only people who attended and didn't claim to be embedded in a particular tradition. There were some amazing people throughout the years who wanted to be part of it—it was and is one of the most respected interreligious dialogue groups we have seen—but they were consistently turned away if it was felt they were not embedded in a particular tradition. They also, interestingly, tried to stay away from people who were too famous (even though a number of people who ended up becoming quite famous were with them in their early years, such as Bernie Glassman and Pema Chodron), actually turning away a few people who they felt were too famous because they felt it could affect the intimacy of the dialogue.

So that is a little bit of the background. As for the experience itself, for me, one of the things that most stands out is the level of depth and sharing and communion that is palpable in these retreats. It was much deeper than I had seen in other places. Part of that is the smallness of the retreats, anywhere from ten to twenty-five people together for five days in a stunning spiritual setting, not with a leader teaching them—Father Thomas was always very clear that he was not a leader of the group, or even a founder, but merely a convener—but with the intention of simply sharing and learning from one another. And remember, these are people, when we talk about the members, who for the most part had worked very seriously on their spiritual lives, and some of them had been getting together like this for almost thirty years. So when I went, I experienced a level of dialogue among the wisdom traditions that I just hadn't seen before.

ADAM: And so when you say a dialogue, what do you mean by that?

RORY: Well, they could get into some really tricky points and difficult questions. For instance, the first time I was there, there was a discussion going on, and I remember Venerable Tenzin Priyadarshi, who was a Tibetan Buddhist representative and is the founder and director of the Dalai Lama Center for Ethics and Transformative Values at the Massachusetts Institute of Technology—at one point Tenzin asked concretely, in the context of the Christian path with the idea of having a soul which is moving toward a union with God, how does one protect oneself against an aggrandizement of the ego? In other words, "because *I* am being transformed, the grace of God is coming through *me*. Isn't it dangerous that this leads to an inflation of the ego, and how is that then handled?"

What's interesting about these questions is that present in the dialogue is someone like Father Thomas, who clearly has been transformed by the Christian spiritual path. In other words, Tenzin was not necessarily pointing out a flaw in the Christian path, but was wondering how, within that framework, this problem of ego-aggrandizement could be handled. And what I realized in that moment was not so much a response to his question—I was already fairly familiar with how that is handled in the Christian tradition, mainly through the "dark nights" and the understanding that "only God is good," as Jesus taught; and also understood Tenzin's framework and where his question was coming from, mainly how in Tibetan Buddhism this problem of an aggrandizement of the ego is handled with the doctrine of "no-self" and eventually a direct cognition of the reality of that doctrine, that there really is no "self," at least not in any permanent way that we normally tend to cognize it—so it wasn't an answer to the question that piqued my interest but rather an insight in that moment that allowed me to see deeply and clearly into the primal integrity of each tradition.

In each tradition there's a certain integrity to the structure and the teachings that make up the magisterium, the collection of teachings, dogma, lore, rituals, and techniques of a tradition, and this integrity allows one to walk a mature path, a path that leads one through a transformative process that in the end endows one with qualities such as compassion, wisdom, mercy, love, etc. And so there is this type of integrity in all the different traditions. The various practices and frameworks they have developed are very particular, and can address very specific occurrences, problems, and potentials that arise during one's transformative journey. That is why, as a whole package, if one commits to them with all of one's being, one gets a developed and integrated system that leads to substantive spiritual growth.

It is also interesting to note here what Panikkar called homeomorphic equivalents between traditions. *Homeomorphic* is a math term in the relatively new field of topology that describes two objects as homeomorphic if they can be bent or molded into one another. For instance, a circle and a square are homeomorphic because if the circle was flexible it could be bent into the shape of a square and vice versa. However, neither are homeomorphic to a circle with a hole in it (a two-dimensional doughnut), since no matter how much you bend and shape it, it will always have a hole in the middle of it, therefore it could never be molded into a circle or a square. So Panikkar had this notion of homeomorphic equivalents between the traditions, where in one tradition, for instance, the problem of ego aggrandizement could be handled by a doctrine, and specific practices related to the doctrine, of, say, no-self, whereas in another tradition the problem is handled differently, for instance by the notion of a soul that is utterly dependent on God. Then, in looking at the various transformative outcomes of particular practices in traditions, we can begin to see how they are performing similar functions within vastly differing frameworks. Also very interesting, I think, is that these are actually more than just doctrines (no-self and a soul dependent on God), primarily because they are insights into Reality that paths are built around. So different frameworks for the journey can be built around different insights into Reality, but they tend to form many of the same functional equivalents in terms of the transformative path.

All this was very fascinating, but then also, coming from where I was, which was not being embedded in any particular tradition, I could experiment with and actually use notions from varying traditions. So, for instance, the notion of no-self: at the time I had already attempted to cultivate a fairly deep understanding of it through struggle and study and practices of techniques that Buddhism (mostly Tibetan, though some Zen as well) has developed around it, and had also had some slight personal experience in its direct cognition, the *yeshi* experience (or an experience of *sunyata*, emptiness) as it is known in Tibetan; but also clearly my journey is very informed by a guidance of the Spirit and a relationship with Life, the cultivation of a soul, and the growing of my soul into God and in conjunction with others, so that in me in a direct way there lives a synergistic combination of the wisdom of different traditions.

ADAM: That's interesting. In a way, for you, one corrects the other.

RORY: I think that is very true. I also think it can lead to new insights, new understandings, that are informed by the different traditions, especially because not everything in one tradition has a homeomorphic equivalent in another tradition. In other words, each tradition is not necessarily doing the same thing just in different languages and frameworks. Each also has its own uniqueness, and their own special gifts, and has also in certain ways cultivated, even incarnated, differing divine attributes. For instance, the Buddhist understanding of compassion is unique, and the quality they articulate as "compassion" is unsurpassed, as is the Christian understanding of love. And these two are not the same thing! When Buddhists talk about love it is a very different concept from when the Christian uses the word, with very different qualities, and you don't necessarily find a corollary for it in Buddhism, just as you don't necessarily find a corollary for what Buddhism has named *bodhichitta*, often translated as compassion but that in its essence means "mind of enlightenment," in other traditions, at least not in the way that Buddhism has developed it—what I would call a divine attribute. So the traditions can be carriers of these unique attributes in a profound way that we don't quite understand yet. My intuition is that, as Brother Wayne said, the traditions complete each other. At least we can agree that in the sense of having a more holistic view of our humanity, we need the insights of all of them, which means we need to recognize both the similarities that exist and the differences. In these types of deep, dialogical dialogues among mature spiritual practitioners I think that process can begin to occur. You see the universality of the process of transformation, and the stages one passes through during this process; you see homeomorphic equivalents, how different practices and different theoretical understandings address the same problem in unique ways, but then you also see fruitful differences as well, and can reflect on those.

And coming from the standpoint of an interspiritual path, you are able to allow those influences and insights into yourself in such a way that a new emergent framework and understanding is created, and as this process is guided by the Spirit, by Sophia, by Divine Wisdom (and this of course also means in consultation with mentors and the sangha, perhaps Spirit's most effective way of guidance), its creation and synthesis naturally, organically, resonates with both your own spiritual maturation and the collective destiny of humanity, as well as the role you can play within that.

ADAM: And so what is the goal for that? Is the goal for that for us to have an understanding and to basically be able to relate to each other in a new way? Is the goal for that to enable us to see that there is a certain structure of transformation that one needs to go through, that's more or less universal, even though each tradition relates to some of those issues differently? Or is the goal of this all experiential—that somehow we struggle with these questions, we wrestle with them, and in the process something happens and something cracks in us? And as a result, we reach a deep communion that is beyond our understanding. Or perhaps the goal is for those three things to all happen simultaneously or at different times.

RORY: Beautifully said. . . . I think that there are different goals—though I don't know if *goals* is the right word, but rather different *fruits* that emerge out of it. We've spoken a bit about the first few fruits you mentioned, about how a new way of relating to each other is present in the dialogue, essentially it is the dialogical dialogue discussed previously, and the recognition of a universal process of transformation, and also how the traditions might relate differently to some of those aspects of the transformative process. The last fruit you mentioned, of deep communion beyond understanding, is perhaps at the heart of the whole experiment.

One of the processes the mentees are now led through, because this was so foundational to the formation of the original members of the group, is one of dialoguing among themselves on the Points of Agreement, and perhaps even coming up with their own articulations. And what is often found, to the surprise of some, is that it is a difficult, almost herculean task! As they try to put things into words, significant tensions usually arise, and jettisoning your most intimate beliefs and experiences in order to find common ground or relieve the tension in the room is not allowed. You have to stay true to yourself and to your own understanding.

Eventually then, if you don't just call it quits, you come to a sort of breaking point, where the language and the words you want to use to communicate just aren't working. And if you passionately want to connect with the other person's experience, it occurs at some point that you simply fail in that endeavor. And then something cracks open—and through that crack, through that failure, grace comes in.

A deep, palpable communion begins to arise in the silence, bound by the love that everyone feels for each other . . . simply beyond words, though it took a struggle with words to get there. And what happens within that experience is each person's respect for another's path is heightened and deepened at the same time, because the communion, the reality of the unity of our human family, becomes an existential experience to everyone there. It becomes a love that surpasses understanding.

And that, really, is the heart of the Snowmass experience, entering into that space as an experiential reality. And people are changed in the process. Some of the mentees had never really known someone from another tradition, and the ideas they heard from each other seemed very foreign, even threatening. Others had had lengthy experience with multiple traditions. Some had been on a path for a long time, others not so much. But in this experience none of that mattered; the simple love of hearts broken open transformed everyone present.

So, on a foundational level, that type of experience is of utmost importance.

In my opinion, though, there is a further dimension to this work that can only open up after such an experience. It is that of going beyond respect and awe for spiritual paths which are not our own, to learning from them, allowing them to change our path, struggling to understand the structures and language and experience they are built around. Language is important, and if we are to eventually incarnate our unity in this realm, language is an intimate part of that.

So for me, I'm interested in how that direct spiritual experience of unity comes into being in terms of historicity, in terms of its incarnation in our human family, especially if we don't view our human lives as simply a training ground to have transcendent experiences. My guess is that this process will have some surprises for us along the way. As our entire human experience is brought to bear on questions that must be answered by the whole of our human family, and not any one particular religious tradition, what emerges? New frameworks? New understandings? Emergent spiritual paths? Revelations as to our place as humanity within a greater Kosmic community? Who or what, really, is the human being?

So some of the things we find ourselves exploring are these: What are these common core structures of the spiritual path and spiritual formation that everyone goes through? What are the advantages of varying perspectives as to how different problems and potentials are addressed? What insights are present? What divine attributes cultivated? But then also, is there some synergy? I mean, when we talk about combining different frameworks and different practices, is this really giving birth to something new?

ON THE SNOWMASS DIALOGUES
AS METHODOLOGY

ADAM: That's what I'm interested in. Essentially we are establishing that the Snowmass process, historically, enabled traditions to get a sense that perhaps there is a universal structure for transformation, and compare notes on it and see how it connected.

RORY: And also to acknowledge that transformation itself is at the heart of all the different traditions.

ADAM: And essentially that process led people to experience communion with one another. And perhaps in that communion they were even seeing how each of their paths has a unique gift to offer that has a place in this communion, right? All of that happened, and it was very important for us because now it allows us to have this conversation. That was a historical development, and this development will continue to happen.

But now we're talking about something considerably different, because what we're saying is that there is a new path emerging, a new path that is outside of the traditions, and that this way of communicating with one another no longer has to be about traditions sharing with each other, but actually people sharing with each other, whether they are in traditions or not. And somehow this way of relating to each other, somehow that can be a primary way of guidance, where one is guided into the core of one's being—and that a Snowmass-like process could be a methodology for that. So what this dialogical way of being did for the traditions in terms of reaching this communion with one another, on this new path it can do the same for us in terms of reaching that communion with God, or with the deepest parts of ourselves, and therefore, by definition, communion with everyone else who's involved in the process.

RORY: Yes, I agree. One thing it has done, I think, is helped develop the skill set Ewert Cousins called "crossing over" and Panikkar called the dialogical dialogue, where we enter into the other person's experience in a way where we listen deeply and where literally, when the authenticity of their experience becomes present to us, it changes our own experience. It changes our framework of what the Divine is, of what this journey is, of its possibilities. And this then has consequences for how we live our lives, which is really what it comes down to. And so this skill set was developed within this interspiritual dialogue, but now it becomes a sacred way of relating to each other, not just between traditions but simply between people, between individual souls.

Beyond that, it becomes a way of guiding and mentoring people into their own unique experience and their own unique journey, whether that's embedded in a tradition or not. And so it becomes a way to relate to mentors, and it becomes a way to form a community, because you essentially learn to imbibe of the gifts of others and reflect back their authenticity, and also share yours in a way it can be received and affirmed.

Something became clear to me during the most recent Snowmass dialogues, something I felt deep in my soul, and I shared it with the group at the time. As we sat together in a circle I said, "Each of you gets to leave here and go back to your traditions, but for me, this is my tradition. What you have incarnated here, what has bloomed in the between among you, in your sacred interactions over the many years, through your disappointments and heartbreaks and steadfastness and deep, palpable communion, this is my tradition." And it was striking, I think, for the members, because they are giving birth to something that they don't even necessarily understand, yet it emerges out of the Spirit they have made present among them. And for myself as well, to realize that in many ways my "tradition" has been birthed out of the sacred interactions of the depths of the traditions in communion with one another.

ADAM: But now a difficulty that arises is this: Before, it was seasoned practitioners who, through their traditions, were able to experience God or whatever name we have for it. Now we're talking about people starting from scratch, without being rooted anywhere. And essentially what we're saying is that relating to each other in this way almost evokes God.

In a sense, this is for me where Buber plays a big role, where, at least in my experience, it's possible to relate to other people in such a way where you become the liberator of their soul, so to speak—where you give them permission to be their most sacred element. As they start becoming who they were born to be, somehow the awareness that emerges in them begins to liberate you. And in this dialogical process of mutual freeing, God actually becomes the "between" between friends, and in the process begins to guide where this goes. And that's really beautiful. But is that the same as what they were doing at Snowmass?

RORY: Well, I think in some ways there's a hindrance in . . . I mean, at Snowmass, you're starting the process with some people who have a very developed spiritual life in terms of the members themselves and who have gained a certain maturity on the path, and who have an ability to drop into a deep state of listening and openness, and they already have a certain confidence in their own paths. And so they are able to pick up on new insights at times, and these have a revelatory feel. For instance, Swami Atmarupananda told me a wonderful story once about how when he first attended the Snowmass Dialogues he felt he knew what it meant to worship Jesus, and so he felt he understood, to a large degree, the Christian revelation. Swami Atmarupananda is from the Vedanta tradition, specifically the Ramakrishna order, and they recognize varying pathways to the enlightened state and venerate multiple spiritual teachers, in particular Ramakrishna, Sarada Devi, Jesus, and the Buddha. And so he felt he knew what the experience of Jesus was. Then, at Snowmass, through this deep dialogue, he realized, for instance when Father Thomas, as well as others, spoke that his experience of

Jesus, and how he viewed the Christian experience through the lens of his universal Vedanta, was not necessarily what the actual experience was for those coming through the Christian tradition.

And inhaling whiffs, if you will, of this different divine fragrance was enlightening for him. So the members and mentees, I think, are able to learn a lot from this deep level of sharing. But I guess my point is that you have a certain container for that experience there, and some fairly mature spiritual guides who have cultivated and held that space for almost thirty years now, and so the process works. And you usually don't have this when just beginning with people who are coming to the path for the first time.

Though as people's spiritual lives deepen, the discussion will deepen. I think when you're not just coming from traditions, as well, there's perhaps also a greater openness to a framework that the Spirit may be constucting. When you are coming from a particular tradition there's a certain fidelity to your own theological framework, a certain container for your experience. As people come to it new, and a younger generation comes to it without these particular developed containers, perhaps there is a greater openness. As people learn to listen more deeply, as people grow in their own spiritual disciplines, then these frameworks can perhaps emerge organically from each other's insights.

ADAM: But that's what I'm saying. And it could be facilitated. Quakers have this where your presence calls the other into being. And this, of course, is also connected to spiritual direction. Can you do that with a group, when you gather a group, and teach people how to be present to each other in such a way that they call each other into the deepest levels of being? And whatever emerges, again, calls everyone else. It's this kind of a dance where whatever is evoked in the person that you're relating to, that then evokes more of you. And somehow it's this constant deepening, with God really just incarnating in that process and taking over and guiding and guiding and guiding.

RORY: It reminds me of story that Gayan Macher once told me of the Sufis, the origins of the magic carpet ride. The whole idea comes from Sufis who used to gather together, and they'd usually sit around a carpet, probably some beautiful homemade Persian rug, and they would basically engage in the process that we have talked about, where you're in a group and you're relating to each other but you're also paying attention to what's between you and what's trying to be born in the "between." And so you're very gentle with it, as with a newborn baby, and slowly God's grace and presence flows in and begins to move and dance with everyone there. But everyone remains attentive to it, and moves with it, and essentially it builds and synthesizes something beautiful, which then emerges out of the dance. Beauty itself, one may say. And so they called this the magic carpet ride because they would start relating to each other in this way, and that would take them soaring into these mystical heights and insights and revelations as a group. There is also a very similar idea in the Hasidic traditions, where they stay up all night in study and prayer and dance with God as a group. And so what we're really talking about is this kind of group formation but with people of varying traditions and even no tradition at all. . . .

ADAM: Right, where we give birth to God, metaphorically speaking, in the midst of what's happening, and God takes birth and then takes us into a specific direction. And it's the same Spirit that we talked about in terms of interspirituality and the guidance of the Holy Spirit. So we're really saying dialogical dialogue becomes a methodology which allows us to welcome this Spirit, to open to this Spirit, be touched by this Spirit, be taken by it, and directed into where we need to serve, as a group and individually. And that becomes, in this new path, one of the main ways of learning.

RORY: Yes, and one of the main centers of community life.

ON DIALOGICAL INTIMACY IN SPIRITUAL DIRECTION, SUPERPERSONALIZATION, AND ENLIGHTENMENT

ADAM: This takes us into the question of mentorship and spiritual direction, because essentially, if we look at spiritual direction, traditionally speaking, at least within the Christian tradition, that's what it was. It was not that the spiritual director is necessarily a teacher who gives wisdom. A spiritual director is someone who essentially is able to guide his mentees into that deep unfolding that is always happening within, and make them conscious of what that movement is, how to feel it, and then slowly encourage them to sense it more and more and more, and then encourage them to live according to it.

RORY: And in this, if we are talking about spiritual direction, I think are some basic tendencies, that continue to occur, regardless of what tradition or path one may be walking. And one of these is the fact that the spiritual path has stages, which don't necessarily have to be gone through consciously, but a mentor can many times recognize what stage or state you are operating from and reflect back to you an understanding of this, and then help you to relate in a healthy way to that unfolding and movement inside you. This seems to me to be of inestimable help, since many times out of ignorance or fear or doubt we react to these movements in a way that can stunt the process, whereas by reacting a bit differently, the unfolding is allowed to flower.

As we go along this path and through these different stages, we're also learning different skill sets. We're cultivating various spiritual and psychic techniques, if you will. But once we've cultivated a particular skill set—say an interior movement of our heart, or a certain way of working with energies, or an enhanced fortitude of our bodies—then it seems to be our task to let it go. At that point the skill set will operate in its own way, under the direction of the Spirit, either consciously or unconsciously. If we fail to let it go, it becomes attached to the ego, which can then do a whole lot of damage with some of these gifts. But a good mentor can help us to learn what it is we're dealing with at certain times and stages, how to relate to it, how to cultivate it, and then also let us know when it's time to let go and move on to another stage.

ADAM: Yes, of course. But essentially it's always us in relationship to the Spirit. It's just that there are layers between us and that. And the stages allow us to essentially—I don't know what's the word—to peel those layers back. . . .

RORY: They do. We're also cultivating in a sense our own divinity. We're building our own soul. And we are actually developing abilities that will allow us to be of service to others in more concrete ways.

ADAM: Right, right. But you know, I guess what I'm getting at, what's the relationship between being connected to that impulse of God in us and the stages? And I think that the impulse is always there—it's just that in different stages we experience it differently, we learn different skill sets. And the goal of it is eventually to merge with it.

RORY: I think there are times of merging, and there is a mergence with it, but that mergence is actually eternal, not in the sense of "for a really long time" but in a dimension in which time does not exist. But I think that basic process of continuing through stages . . .

ADAM: Oh, I don't think it ends. And when I say "merging," I don't mean a oneness with it where you become nothing. I mean, yes, in a sense you become nothing, but in the other sense, that's also the full completion of who you are, where your gifts flower completely, because finally you're connected to grace in a way that is not disrupted.

RORY: I do think there is a point on the journey where—perhaps we could call this the "great merger"—where essentially your life has become a spiritual path. And all of a sudden there's nothing in your life that is not also part of the path. You don't even work on it, it just is. But then you also continue to grow and learn and assimilate and mature, and all of this leads to service. Sometimes there are great trials, sometimes times of peace, sometimes great works, and a whole lot of ordinary moments . . . but it is all part of some greater happening that is at once mysterious, interdependent, and evolutionary.

ADAM: Yes, essentially where your life is no longer your life—where there's just divine life. And then, again, it doesn't mean that you don't have your qualities. It means that actually you have your qualities, but in fullness probably for the first time. And the distinction between what's yours and what's God's is almost nonexistent. You simply live as an expression of the Spirit in the world. And yet it seems that that's where you disappear, but paradoxically where your uniqueness is also truly found.

RORY: It's Teilhard's superpersonalization. . . .

ADAM: That's beautiful.

RORY: So you don't actually lose personality, but you become "superpersonalized." You become completely unique, in a sense, and your expression becomes individuated from other divine expressions. It becomes powerful and manifest, and through that a true kind of unity in diversity emerges.

ADAM: Yes, and yet the question then even of service . . . It's just what your life is.

RORY: Yes, so then, you're no longer even thinking, "How can I best serve?" It is integrated in a way where you are just living under the guidance, and you're trusting in it, and you're growing through it, but it is what it is . . . and will be what it will be. . . .

ADAM: Right. And I think what we are saying is that this is actually the final fulfillment of vocation. And that is the final fulfillment of being in the Spirit. That is the final fulfillment of dialogical dialogue. That is the final fulfillment of the mentor and mentee relationship, where both flower into that, in communion. And yet, you know, to get there, even though we're talking about it in terms of a dialogical process and following the guidance of the Holy Spirit, you still go through stages of the "dark night" and everything else needed for the fullness of the transformative journey. And so it's interesting, because we're taking the framework of those stages and essentially combining them with what it means to follow your vocation.

RORY: And laying free all the tools that the human family has cultivated to help in that journey and in that process, without having to commit or embed yourself in a particular framework we are giving you. And interesting as well is that we are not necessarily *a priori* trying to figure out what works where, but we give our guidance over to the Spirit. So we tap into that ever-present wisdom and guidance, Sophia, and the teleological pull or *Eros* of creation itself, and trust in it.

ADAM: So now, I think, what would be useful to talk about are our own individual experiences with mentors.

RORY: First, it might be good to mention one more thing, that state that we just discussed, where things actually become integrated, I think a lot of people have ideas that it's a superspiritual state, or very ecstatic, or it can look like being completely at peace and at one with everything. And I think maybe that is true for some people, but that it can also just be very ordinary. Like you understand that's where your life is, you understand that you're not really doing anything apart from that, and that in some ways you become almost like a superordinary human. You experience all the same sufferings; you may still experience doubt; you may still experience hardship; you could struggle with relationships, with children, with a whole number of things, perhaps actually much more severely than you did before, even though there's a certain peace that always sort of remains in the background. I just think it is important to mention that it can look very different for different people, and that you don't want to expect it to be some kind of explosion of spiritual beatitude. And that is true for this whole process that we are talking about. What is more important is a small, silent knowing in the heart, and all else orbits around that.

ADAM: Right, and also, I think there are some people who just imagine that there's this oneness and bliss, and that everything else disappears and it's all just hearts and flowers. And what we're saying is that no, actually that's not the case—that experience might happen at some point, but it's not a final goal of this.

RORY: And if you're truly going to be part of this Path, until the world as a whole is completed and the human race comes to its fullness in spiritual maturity, there's a discomfort with life whether you're enlightened or not. In fact, if you're enlightened, you actually feel that discomfort more keenly! And so we're all caught up in it. And until, as a human family, as a whole, we're able to come into that fullness, there's suffering. And that's actually part of the drive to keep us moving forward. St. John of the Cross talks about the fact that suffering is actually what we transform, in a sense, into that divine fragrance—so no suffering, no fragrance—at least not of the pungency that is most connected to the evolution of the human family. So if you find yourself in a state of bliss and oneness and totally at peace, be careful . . . you may be missing something!

ADAM: Yeah, it's time to really do some deep work and find out what went wrong.

RORY: (*laughing*) So hopefully we can be aware of this as we journey, so that we can perhaps make some choices and build our determination along the way to stay connected to human suffering. Because you can't leave everyone else behind. Some of the crowning experiences of bliss and transcendence can be awful temptations to do just that, which would be a terrible price to pay for the knowledge and wisdom they bestow. And so in this interspiritual path, you're so intimately caught up with the moving forward of the whole human family that in the end, actually, this integration just looks like working toward that, and that is all there is.

ADAM: Yes, so basically what we're saying, the traditional view of enlightenment in this path is almost irrelevant on some level because it's not about that. Even though thay may happen at some point.

RORY: And that may be how someone can best serve. But it's not the goal unless that's the case, unless it helps us all move forward in the best way possible.

ON MENTORSHIP

ADAM: We have been talking somewhat about the dialogical process and how it's possible to relate to each other in such a way that we're basically being guided into our true purpose, to God, and everything that goes along with it. We've been talking about historically what kind of role that played and how interspirituality really was a result of those kinds of interactions. And we also made some statements about that being a dialogical way of relating to each other, and being a primary way of teaching and guiding and forming communities and mutual support for each other on this journey among friends, spiritual friends.

Now I think it would be important to share some personal experiences. Where is this stuff coming from that we're talking about? We both have had some experiences with mentors that convinced us that this is the way.

RORY: As we start to talk about mentorship I think it's important to mention—and this has certainly been the case in my journey—that because structures on this new path have not been created yet as they have in the traditional ways, mentorship becomes extremely important. So mentorship and having a spiritual guide becomes a way of handling the lack of structure that currently exists for this path. . . .

ADAM: The depth of that relationship and mutual sharing.

RORY: And the ability to guide. . . . I mean, my mentors have played a role where I can't imagine how I could have gained any of the little progress I have made on the path without them. There have been so many times when I was flailing around, and as I think back, especially in the early days of my journey and the first few years, first five years, first decade—and probably the next decade as well—to the understandings I had at the time, the ways I thought of my spiritual practice and journey: I could be off base in so many ways! And it was my mentors that were able to gently let me know that, but also let me know it's okay, and very skillfully guide me into a deeper maturity and more fruitful ways of understanding my experience, and letting me know where I needed to practice and where I was missing the mark, sometimes even to let go of certain practices and just relax. And without these mentors, who all came out of traditions, I just can't imagine making a whole lot of progress, because you can get lost for years and even lifetimes down a barren path, even after committing to a so-called spiritual life.

ADAM: Someone told me that Father Thomas said recently—I think you might have been there; I wasn't—that in thirty years of the Snowmass Dialogues, they discovered that the most effective way of teaching spirituality is through sharing one's stories. Yes? And so, in a sense, my experience with some of my mentors has been that. . . . Yes, I learned some structures from traditions, but the most effective way of learning for me was for my mentors to openly share their lives, their struggles, and their journeys with me. So whatever was shared almost became a container for me to feel my own spiritual unfolding.

And the way that they shared it with me, it wasn't so much that they gave me an outline of what's going to happen, or what needs to happen. But they would rather invite me to share deeply about my struggles and things that are unfolding. And then they would relate elements of their own lives and spiritual journeys as a commentary on what I was going through, and also as a way of naming what was going on in my life. And sometimes that would also include examples from a tradition that they were following, where that would all of a sudden name something that I was struggling with, a place where I was stuck. And then their individual journey and how they navigated through that would then invite an understanding into my heart that would allow me to move forward. But it wouldn't always be the understanding that they had. It would be almost like something would happen and the Spirit would just kind of guide me through it as this deep mutual sharing was happening.

And that's extraordinary—because in a way it's like you practice, you go, you stop; you need help, you relate; they share, they name; some gifts are received; you go further; again. . . . You know what I mean? And it's almost like, the mentorship wasn't about the tradition; the mentorship wasn't about even what are the stages of spiritual life. The mentorship was about my life and what's true right now. And they would just relate to that, and that would be enough for me to move forward. And then after a while I would realize that an understanding or a framework or a structure is emerging out of those moments of communion, and that the understanding was actually very much in line with what the traditional journey is. You know what I mean? It's as if it is basically the same process that has always occurred in mentorship, slightly different now because the times are different, and we have more psychological and sociological insights. So I would say there are perhaps more subtleties to it now, and maybe our lives now are slightly more complex. But nonetheless, it corresponds to what traditional paths have discovered—

RORY: As I'm thinking about it now—and some of the differences in what we are talking about—in the past, perhaps, as one sought out spiritual mentors, one was essentially looking to deepen one's spiritual life. One was looking to become enlightened, one was looking to find union with God, find inner peace. And when people found a mentor, a lot of times they just hung their hat on the mentor—when you found an amazing spiritual mentor it was like, okay, this is it, this is my path. And you stayed with this mentor and this teaching, and that was your path. And maybe at some point way down the road you might have started teaching what that teacher taught you, and that's how lineages were passed on.

And what I'm thinking of, in my experience and in what you just related, that really the integrity, the baseline, of this interspiritual path we are talking about is following the guidance of the Spirit. So we're not just looking for some container to pour our spiritual life into—a particular mentor or a particular guru or a particular teaching. But we're actually in fidelity to this guidance and discernment, and wherever that may take us, which may be into a particular teaching for a period of time, or even for a lifetime; or it may be to different teachers at different times, or it may even be into the guru experience. I mean, I was guided into the guru experience with Joshi Baba. In hindsight, I only really found descriptions of my experience with him in the Tibetan guru literature. It's interesting though, because I also was very clear that it was my decision to enter into the relationship, to give myself over completely, as it were, and in order to do even this I had to check with my own interior guidance. So that the decision to essentially enter completely into that guru experience actually came out of my fidelity to that inner guidance. In other words, the baseline of this path is not lost, even in the midst of a guru experience, so all textures of the path truly are available under the integrity of this guidance. So it is very interesting, what is being born here. I also think the path we are speaking of weaves all of this together in intimate relation with our service to the world.

ON A NEW GENERATION OF SEEKERS

ADAM: Do you think that this new generation, or at least many of them, are essentially already coming to the spiritual search with a baseline of feeling a particular longing or a direction?

RORY: That's a good question. I do. . . . I think somewhat, anyway. I think that for many there's a rejection of being embedded in a traditional path, and there's a rejection of having a spiritual life that is not directly related in some way to serving the world we are living in right now. So I think for the younger generation it's definitely not about "getting into heaven," or even finding an enlightened spiritual peace or bliss, but it's more about helping our world move forward. And there's often a certain spontaneous kind of antipathy at being in a particular tradition to the exclusion of others. Now many people dismiss that as a selfish impulse, but I think one might also interpret it as an organic, if perhaps unconscious, following of an innate spiritual impulse. As you say, a following of what is most alive in their hearts. I think it is hard to say for the general population, but certainly in a wide variety of younger people I have seen who are walking a serious spiritual path, there is a definite inclination to not embed in a particular tradition. Or at least to begin seriously reaching out to other traditions at a very early stage of the path.

ADAM: And it's not out of rejection. There's also, I think, a spontaneous sense of knowing that this is the direction to go. It's not often articulated, not even often understood, but it's deeply felt. And somehow, what's deeply felt is not guiding people into traditions but outside of traditions. And so it's almost like an evolutionary guidance that young people are downloading, so to speak. And what we're articulating is very much in line with that.

RORY: And so we have to be willing to recognize that fragance of genuine spiritual inspiration and trust it.

ADAM: Even if it's not named as spiritual inspiration, you can feel it. You can feel it in certain social movements, when initially people gather, there's an energy, and it's pure spiritual transmission. They might not name it that, but if you give them something that is not of that same nature, they immediately reject it because it contradicts the thing that is most true in them.

RORY: So in a sense, without building a path around that impulse, we are hopeless to serve the spiritual maturity of this younger generation.

ADAM: Exactly. So now, in a way, we're talking about mentorships that can respect that initial feeling that many young people nowadays have, of something that is guiding them.

RORY: Yes, and within that guidance is a longing for depth and service. Everyone feels it in a certain way. And people respond to it with different degrees of understanding and maturity. And I guess what we're seeing is that, as people authentically respond to it more fully and more deeply, they're not necessarily walking traditional pathways. And so then new ways of mentorship are needed.

ADAM: So now a new mentorship is needed, and so we've had some experiences of what that new mentorship would be like. Such as the one I just articulated in terms of mentors not giving me a framework but just relating experiences, and out of that a framework started emerging for me that then I realized was very much in line with all of this we are talking about. What about you?

RORY: Well, another thing that comes to mind is that there are actually new responsibilities for the mentees as well. As a person who's feeling this longing and then beginning to explore it and engage it, one is bound to come upon spiritual mentors—and let's just warn people here of the mind-boggling amount of inauthenticity out there, perhaps we will get to talk about it later, but their name is legion, and bless their souls, many people with good intentions are working hard to abort a spiritual emergence while convinced they are its progenitors—but you know, there are true, authentic, real, mature spiritual mentors who are simply extraordinary beings. In my experience, I've come upon a number of such people, where I just met the person but yet there is a certain spiritual gift present. In some cases extraordinary things can happen—perhaps they seem to know everything that's happened in my life, they know where I am at spiritually, they know what I am dealing with in this moment, and

I haven't even spoken a word to them yet. And it's like . . . I'm an open book and they can read my whole soul and my life. And they make a few comments. Like you said, they maybe tell a story, look at me in a certain way, touch me in a certain way, energetically affect me in a certain way.

And in a certain sense, I think a lot of people can be overwhelmed by some of the gifts that manifest around very mature mentors. And so, part of the responsibility of the mentee is to begin to recognize this. To follow up on these occurrences, make adjustments in one's life to accommodate them. Give them priority. Recognize these occurences, learn how to bow to them, how to accept them. Learn interior postures that allow transmission to come through. A constant process of letting go . . . But that is not the only responsibility. On the flip side, it can be a temptation to say, "Okay, just tell me what to do. You obviously understand me. Let me do whatever it is you think I should, and I'm just going to stay by you and stick around and follow whatever you teach me."

But what we're saying is, even when these things happen, you check back in with your guidance, and you learn a sort of spiritual dance, even a spiritual aikido with the mentor, where you're going back and forth and they're reflecting your experience, but you're also developing your own discernment and your own understanding, and expressing your own insights and opinions, some of which will turn out to be false, but some of which will turn out to be genuine, and sometimes these will even go against the understanding of the mentor with these amazing capabilities.

So the mentee has to maintain the integrity of her process and her choices and her insights. Even at the point of going through the guru experience and completely giving yourself over to a teacher, this is still done in a way where you take the responsibility for that decision, you let it emerge out of your own inner guidance. So that there's a core to this path and a responsibility that you undertake that becomes the place for you to assimilate and develop your own uniqueness and your own expression of God in the world. And you can't give that over to a mentor.

ADAM: I completely agree. And when I think of some of my mentorship experiences, one of the things that I think was very valuable to me happened in a psychotherapeutic context, which I think was one of the biggest gifts I received. It was a Zen-like methodology, and the person that I worked with—truly it was a miracle. In a sense he kept on refusing to give me what I went there for, and kept pointing me back to my inner experience, my inner guidance and inner life, and then helped me to be present to it. So layers and layers of stuff that separated me from that could be removed, and I could actually just know how to pay attention to that inner movement. And so it became almost habitual where I could just stop and tune into it and sense it.

And I don't even know if that was the purpose of it. Maybe it's just that that's the role it played. . . . It's like God used that person for that experience for me. And his training as a Zen teacher, I think it was very presence-based, helped. But I think that it was a tremendous gift, because what I realized is that how I related to my own heart changed. It reminds me of Llewellyn Vaughan-Lee's writing . . . where you can almost feel the flame from his heart that is present in the words. And it's beautiful. . . .

So I feel like, in a sense, one of the things that we can learn from mentors is how to pay attention to the movement of our soul, of our spirit. And it takes a while to learn.

RORY: Yes, discernment. . . .

ADAM: Discernment, yes. How to be present with it, how to recognize it. So that's one thing.

RORY: We should also know that on some level the ego knows when it is threatened, it knows when we have discovered something that could begin to oust its foothold on us, and it will begin to throw up all kinds of emotions and defensive thoughts to move us away from that guidance.

So this takes work. It's not something that just happens. . . . And you have to respect the integrity of what you're drawn to enough to give it a chance to open a space in your own being, and to work its alchemy on you. And that takes humility, and it takes letting go of your predispositions and your preconceptions, and it also takes an authenticity where you don't just swallow down the frameworks you are given, but you struggle with them in your being until Wisdom dawns. You wrestle with the angels, as Jacob did.

In all of this, too, there's a, what to call it . . . a mysterious, mystical, magical aspect. A deep sense of the interconnectedness of all of life, and at times a ceremonial, ritualistic aspect of the Kosmos can emerge, and within that there is present an intuition of a mysterious plan being worked out.

And our elders and mentors are carriers of these divine, spiritual transmissions and lineages that contain within them powerful attributes. It can be a graciousness, a joyfulness, a fortitude, or earthy solidity; a relationship with an animal, or plant, or the wind; a tremendous peace; even an insight into particular hidden dimensions of reality.

ADAM: Or the spiritual energy of the warrior.

RORY: Absolutely . . . or wisdom, or spiritual timing, all these divine attributes. And they can pass these on to us when we're ready—actually it just happens, as Joshi Baba would say—or we could think of it as occurring under the direction and inspiration of the Spirit.

ADAM: They infuse us with those gifts. But what's interesting is that again, if we're formed properly, we're aware of the integrity of our own journey, our own spiritual path. And some of what surrounds the transmission, we accept—and some we leave behind. And it's our responsibility to know what to take and then to work on integrating those insights, which at times are almost conflicting insights.

And those elders—and this is something that Netanel Miles-Yépez said—it's not necessarily their work to figure this out. They might not even fully understand it. It's our responsibility. They prepared the foundation, but this is our job. And some elders have certain insights about what is happening, and they may say things that will direct us, but it's our responsibility to form it. And they might not even fully understand it on some level.

My beginning was fairly traditional. I embraced certain paths and followed them according to the book. And it reminds me of the Jungian idea of two halves of life, how in the first half of life you embrace the rules, you follow the rules, maybe you even enter a tradition and stick to it; only when a certain level of maturity happens can you break those rules and you're freed from those rules. It doesn't mean that you don't respect them. You still respect them for what they've given you and what they can give others. But by then, you have been formed, so you can recognize what the guidance is. And so that's also part of the stages.

So the key is to give yourself over to the process completely, with all of its integrity.

MOVEMENT 4
The Path

Faith that the divine light is present within us—a conviction, not necessarily an experience—is the primary foundation . . . [1]

—*Thomas Keating*

As we discuss the nature of the spiritual path itself, we do so not with the hope of providing an overall framework for the journey, but rather with the goal of providing a general orientation for the new monastic. We will discuss some basic elements of any comprehensive framework, which includes an understanding of various states of contemplative experience, the difference between those states and developmental structures or stages of consciousness, as well as insights from modern psychology with a particular emphasis on the shadow, the "dark nights," and fruits of spiritual maturity. There are a number of books which have already developed these insights in great detail, much more clearly than we could hope to here, and so we will reference these books and encourage any new monastic to take up a study of them. In particular, we will be making extensive use of the work of Father Thomas Keating, along with the work of Ken Wilber and the writings of St. John of the Cross, whose insights and articulation of the dark nights are unsurpassed and of great importance in particular for those on an interspiritual path. The dark nights are, for us, safeguards for many of the dangers one encounters along the way, helping to purify unconscious motivations and prepare us for subsequent stages of spiritual maturity.

Throughout we hope to elucidate why we have chosen to present the path in the context we do, and why we believe the insights we have chosen to highlight are of special importance for the new monastic. In terms of books to help build a solid overall framework for a spiritual path wedded to modern psychological insights, we recommend Father Keating's *Invitation to Love, The Human Condition,* and *Intimacy with God,* as well as Ken Wilber's *Integral Psychology* and *Integral Spirituality.* We also hope to be able to more fully flesh out the somewhat bare-bones presentation that we offer here in a future work.

In all of this, we will present each piece in the context of how it corresponds to some of the unique challenges new monastics face, particularly for those on an interspiritual path, both in terms of positive potentialities and perilous pitfalls.

ORIENTATION: THE WAY OF THE NEW MONASTIC

As we have emphasized throughout, a new monastic journey is keen on developing one's relationship with Life. As this relationship develops, one finds a maturing sense of guidance, interdependence, and integration with all realms of being. One also finds one's uniqueness beginning to blossom, a process of superpersonalization. For those on an interspiritual path, the sense of the guidance of Life, what we refer to as the guidance of the Spirit, takes on a primary importance. It is the hidden drumbeat at the foundation of one's path, the inner heartbeat of one's journey, and where the integrity of this way lies.

As such, to begin we would like to follow along the stream of Father Thomas Keating's description of the spiritual journey, which is described in the context of his development of the practice of Centering Prayer. Father Keating, along with William Meninger and Basil Pennington, developed Centering Prayer as a Christian meditation practice designed in conjunction with traditional understandings of contemplative prayer and modern psychological insights. Father Keating then developed his own conceptual framework around it as a way to "bring the Christian contemplative tradition into dialogue with contemporary science, especially developmental psychology, anthropology, and physics."[2] We use Father Keating's work because we feel it captures in an essential way the general orientation of a new monastic. While designed within the Catholic contemplative tradition, and formed by its theological formulations, at its heart is a sublime development of the guidance of the Spirit. Therefore, its inner heartbeat harmonizes with the way of the new monastic.

As we begin the journey, Father Keating reminds us, "We have no idea of where we are going. There are all kinds of difficulties we cannot foresee. . . . The spiritual journey is basically a surrender in blind trust to our conviction that what we hope to find on the journey we either already have or will certainly find. But there is no guarantee that we will arrive safely on the basis of the evidence or our circumstances. We must let go and let the wind (the Holy Spirit) take us where we hope to go."[3]

The journey requires a complete commitment to the transformative process, a courage to expose and surrender all parts of one's life to it. In time, everything in one's being comes under the searing light of the Divine, as we grow through its graces and purifications.

> Contemplation involves a surrender of one's whole self, not just a period of time set aside each day for some form of prayer or meditation. It is a commitment of immense proportions and requires an eminent trust. . . . It does not matter how many difficulties there are, we have to go. There is no turning back once we have started. . . . It involves a commitment of the whole person—body, soul and spirit. . . . Without having accepted the trip into the unknown, one is really not a candidate for contemplation because that is what is presupposed. . . . [It] involves a complete reversal of our prepackaged values, a complete undoing of all our carefully laid plans, and a lot of letting go of our preconceived ideas.[4]

All of our practices along the path are "in the service of sustaining us in a transforming process which is anything but secure, easy, or certain."[5] That is their purpose, to propel and continue our maturity as divine human beings. It is not to realize a particular state, not to have a nondual experience, not to become enlightened. All of that may or may not happen, but fundamentally our practice is in service of our own spiritual maturity and the maturity of our human family. We have the humility to say that it is fundamentally a journey into the unknown. Therefore we remain ever open, both in our work and practice, to the guidance, discernment, and movement of the Spirit.

As Father Keating begins to describe the inner depths of Centering Prayer practice, he captures the orientation of a new monastic to the spiritual path:

> Centering Prayer is both a relationship and a method to foster that relationship at the same time. . . . Every prayer is inspired by the Spirit. We say that the Spirit gradually takes over our prayer and that Centering Prayer is in service of that project. . . . Purity of intention is the primary focus of the practice. It is a matter of love. . . . The Spirit has now taken over our activity and prays in us. Our will is mingled with God's will in some mysterious way. . . . [It] becomes contemplation when the work of the Spirit absorbs our prayer and takes over. This can eventually be our habitual state of prayer, which is resting in God. . . . Our uniqueness remains and becomes the vehicle for the divine expression, which was why we were created.[6]

THE IMPORTANCE OF MODERN PSYCHOLOGY

Carl G. Jung, the great psychologist of the twentieth century, traces the actual discovery of psychology to a world where our religious imagery and symbols, our metaphysical understandings of the cosmos and humankind's place within it, have for many people fallen to the wayside. In all previous civilizations and cultures, a certain religious understanding was always taken for granted by the masses. There was always an essentially unquestioned, shared worldview. For instance, a member of an indigenous culture did not question that she was part of a tribe, or the mythological understandings her tribe professed. Being unquestioned, these worldviews were participated in almost unconsciously, as no one was choosing consciously to believe in them. The idea of a free-thinking human being, who interprets his or her own experience in a unique way and creates a novel framework out of this experience, only came about with the rise of the First Axial Age, and did not happen on a widespread scale until the modern age.

The interior psyche of human beings, therefore, was always in the past projected into the religious understandings of the age. In his essay, "The Spiritual Problem of Modern Man," written in 1933, Jung says that a modern person is not simply one who lives in the modern age (Jung actually says "there are few who live up to the name"[7]), but rather is the man or woman who is moving clearly beyond the unquestioning assumptions of his or her culture. Such people want to experience things for themselves, to test assertions and dogmatic postulates, and hold them "valid only in so far as their knowledge content seems to accord with [their] own experience of the deeps of psychic life. . . . Our age wishes to have actual experiences in psychic life. It wants to experience for itself, and not to make assumptions based on the experience of other ages."[8] The modern man must "stand alone . . . for every step toward a fuller consciousness of the present removes him further from his original *'participation mystique'* with the mass of men—from submersion in a common unconsciousness. . . . Thus he has become 'unhistorical' in the deepest sense and has estranged himself from the mass of men who live entirely within the bounds of tradition."[9]

In past ages, there was never a question of psychological issues. People were possessed by the gods, or by demons, or by God himself or the Great Spirit—whatever made sense within the cultural understanding of the time. The human being experienced life through the prism of metaphysical and religious understandings. It is only in the modern age, where we no longer have a shared story to turn to, that the psychic processes of the human being become something in their own right, something that can be studied objectively and from which universal conclusions can be drawn. "All ages before us have believed in gods in some form or other. Only an unparalleled impoverishment of symbolism could enable us to rediscover the gods as psychic factors."[10] It was a certain distance that the modern person gained from past religious symbolism that allowed for the objectification of our psychic processes, i.e., the birth of psychology as a realm of study. Therefore, for Jung, psychology itself arose out of the need of modernity to find religious meaning through new symbols. "As the modern person has outgrown whatever local form of religion he was born into—as soon as this religion can no longer embrace his life in all its fullness—then the psyche becomes something in its own right which cannot be dealt with by the measures of the Church alone. It is for this reason that we of today have a psychology founded on experience, and not upon articles of faith or the postulates of any philosophical system."[11]

As such, psychology, at its best, becomes part and parcel of the very language of modern theology, that is, of how we understand ourselves, our relationship with the Divine, and our relationship with the world and other people. It is an indispensible tool for those on the spiritual path, whether a traditional path or otherwise. The insights of modern psychology must be integrated into traditional spiritual paths, and any new emergences must make skillful use of the insights of modern psychology. These insights include the shadow, developmental models of consciousness, cultural, anthropological, and sociological constructions and insights, a personal and collective unconscious, and universal psychological complexes which form in each of us throughout childhood and which we all hold more or less unconsciously. All of these insights allow us to better understand how we are connected with all of humankind and its historical unfolding, within the experience of our own psyches. They also show us how we are responsible for this inheritance and for its spiritual transformation and continued maturity. They link us, in the most intimate way, to all human beings who have lived, and speak to a universality of the human condition. It is telling that in Jung's essay "Psychotherapists or the Clergy," he relates, "Among all my patients in the second half of life . . . there has not been one whose problem in the last resort was not that of finding a religious outlook on life. It is safe to say that every one of them fell ill because he had lost that which the living religions of every age have given to their followers, and none of them has been really healed who did not regain his religious outlook. This of course has nothing whatever to do with a particular creed or membership of a church."[12]

AN INTEGRAL FRAMEWORK:
LINES, STATES, AND STAGES

No one has done more to analyze, codify, and develop insight into the relationships between traditional spiritual paths, modern psychology, scientific truths, and cultural and sociological methodologies than American philosopher Ken Wilber. In so doing, he has developed by far the most comprehensive model for bringing to light what he calls the partial truths of each of these into a more all-embracing, integral framework. Of particular interest to us is his development of a vast psychological model of spiritual development, complete with subtle insights into many of the problems, and potentials, of our current cultural and spiritual milieu. We have already recommended four of his books: *Sex, Ecology, and Spirituality* [*SES*]; the popular version of that same book, *A Brief History of Everything; Integral Psychology;* and *Integral Spirituality.*

These are some of the best complements one can have in developing an overall framework for one's journey.

For us, we will stick to outlining a few elements from his overall spiritual/psychological system developed in *Integral Spirituality.* This outline is hardly meant to be an involved development of an overall view of the path. Nevertheless, we do wish to give a very general overview, with another recommendation to consult and study the books mentioned in the introduction to this movement. We will use these elements to highlight some specific features of an interspiritual path and the new monastic movement, and how some of the methodologies we have previously developed specifically address certain modern spiritual problems that arise when viewed from an integral framework. One of the reasons it is so important to incorporate modern psychological analysis into any spiritual framework is that, as Wilber has been at pains to emphasize throughout his work, there are insights into Reality that modern Western psychology has discovered and that no spiritual tradition has. Of main concern for us here are the discoveries of developmental stages of consciousness, various interior lines of development, states of consciousness, and the shadow.

"Stages" and the Pre/Trans Fallacy

One of the best ways to understand developmental stages of consciousness is to understand how they were first discovered. Researches began to gather large groups of people and asked particular questions, questions that had, say, moral or aesthetic or cognitive implications. They discovered that the answers they received could usually be categorized (in other words, people's answers tended to fall into particular groupings or classes that could easily be matched up). Then—and this is the real discovery—as they followed people over time, they realized that sometimes people's answers changed, but always in one particular direction. If you labeled your classes of answers A, B, C, etc., then you could see that people who changed their answers always moved from A to B to C and so forth. In other words, these classes were really stages of growth, in the sense that people would always move, or progress, or develop, from one stage to the next. This was found to be true in various settings and cultural conditions, and with many different types of questions, ranging from cognitive development to moral development to stages of faith to self-identity to values to worldviews.

This research became known as structuralism, which to summarize, involved this: "Pose a series of questions to large groups of people. See if their responses fall into any classes. If so, follow those classes over time and see if they emerge in a sequential order of stages. If so, attempt to determine the structure or makeup of those stages."[13]

Wilber then classifies the general results of these many experiments in increasingly subtle ways, but the most general classification is "pre-conventional," "conventional," and "post-conventional" responses; or perhaps more telling, "egocentric," "ethnocentric," and "worldcentric." The egocentric or pre-conventional responses tended to be something along the lines of "Whatever is best for me is right," or "Whatever I think is the right answer." Ethnocentric or conventional responses were, "Whatever my tribe says is right," where one's tribe could be one's country, religion, family, socioeconomic status, academic colleagues, friends, etc. And worldcentric or post-conventional responses tended toward thinking in terms of whole of the human family, and taking various circumstances into account to try to maximize the most benefit to the most people—essentially a utilitarian standpoint.

Notice that each development to a higher stage is not a matter of leaving the previous stage behind, but a process of transcending and including. For instance, in a worldcentric or post-conventional view, my opinion is still important, as are the opinions and truths of various tribes; it is just they are no longer the only things that matter. So we do not totally leave behind previous stages, but transcend and include their truths in a higher stage within a wider expanse of compassion, consciousness, and complexity. Wilber, in line with Teilhard, sees these expansions or stages as moving ever in the direction of increasing complexity and consciousness.

Perhaps we should note here that many people out there, readers of this book and otherwise, will have an internal negative reaction to any concept of development or hierarchy—perhaps even a fear of such things, or of labeling anything better than something else—but here we must understand that these are researchers who have performed these experiments many times over, including cross-culturally, with similar results. So however one would like to view the results within their own sophiological framework, no new monastic can simply deny that these results occur, nor deny a general progression of maturation in their own lives, and therefore must account for a general notion of successive growth, or stages, that include greater expanses of wisdom, compassion, communion, and love.

This allows us to point out a classic problem in many modern conceptions of spirituality, the "pre/trans fallacy." This is the confusion of lumping both pre-conventional and post-conventional states into the same heap, since neither are purely rational or conventional, and essentially equating them as the same, when they are actually on opposite ends of the spectrum. For instance, the worldview of children is equated with a mature spiritual consciousness simply because both are nonrational, or, on the other hand, highly developed transpersonal spiritual realizations are equated with magical or fundamentalist religious beliefs, simply again because both are nonrational. This latter problem is an especially acute one in the secular humanist movement.

As Wilber says, "This is a constant problem with, and for, spirituality. Particularly when you deal with the meditative, contemplative, or mystical states of spiritual experience—most of which indeed are non-rational—it might seem that all of the non-rational states are spiritual, and all the rational states are not spiritual."[14]

For those in spiritual circles, this can lead to an anti-intellectualism that "fosters and encourages a narcissistic approach to meditation and spiritual studies . . . extremely common in popular culture. . . . Egocentric feelings are confused with worldcentric feelings, just because both are feelings . . . and anything is considered spiritual if I just feel it and emote it really hard. If I can just feel my narcissism with great gusto, I'm getting closer to God (or Goddess or Buddha-Nature). . . . This fearless and exuberant embrace of shallowness has marked too many of the alternative approaches to spirituality."[15]

As the new monastic movement and an interspiritual path are emergent ways, we must be vigilantly aware of such problems, which have almost universally affected the vast majority of New Age spiritual paths. Wilber is articulating, with loads of scientific research and psychological studies to back it up, the problem we have been consistently referring to, that of adopting a spiritual practice and framework that in the end comforts one's ego rather than dismantles it. The pre/trans fallacy is a classic way to fall into this trap.

One last remark on stages: this concerns the further postmodern and post-postmodern insights regarding the underlying structures that lie behind these stages, structures that consciousness itself seems to breathe through in these various stages, creating numerous worldviews at each stage. These structures are not preexistent, but rather have been constructed by human beings, cocreated in community, as they have been grown into throughout history. In other words, there is a heavy and significant intersubjective and historical element to these structures of consciousness, and as we develop even higher structures of consciousness in the further reaches of our human potential these will also be cocreated in an intersubjective and historical fashion. For the new monastic, this means taking seriously the intersubjective component of one's journey, which the new monastic does through the practices of dialogical dialogue, dialogical sophiology, and one's actions toward others. The adoption of an evolutionary spiritual framework that embeds itself in our historical development and works for the continuation and culmination of that development is also part of this practice of inclusion. (New monasticism within Wilber's integral framework is discussed further in note 16.)[16]

States of Consciousness

Not only do there exist structures and stages of consciousness, but also states of consciousness. The relationship between these, Wilber feels, is *"the single most important key to understanding the nature of spiritual experiences."*[17] While structures can never be discovered through first-person experiences, say through meditation or reflection, states "are directly available to awareness, under various circumstances."[18] In addition to the natural states of consciousness that we all experience, those of waking, dreaming, and deep sleep, other states have been explored in depth by our mystical traditions. They consist of first-person experiences of what might best be described as various meditative and spiritual realizations, such as a spiritual experience of a deity or spiritual guides such as Jesus or the Buddha, various experiences of spiritual oneness, nondual realization, and more. What we want to recognize for our purposes is that there is a difference between states and stages. Spiritual, meditative experiences fall into the category of states, but not stages, and this includes continuous, stable realization of a state of consciousness.

Therefore (and this was nearly impossible to understand prior to Wilber's insight), one could have a nondual realization, but still be at a relatively low *stage* of development. And all of us will interpret our spiritual experience according to our stage—and not only according to our stage, but also according to the conceptual framework we have developed. For instance, two people could have very similar, profound spiritual-state experiences of an encounter with Jesus. A person who is at a worldcentric stage of consciousness might interpret that experience as an invitation to higher levels of spiritual development and translate it into a need for a greater love for all humanity. However, a person at an ethnocentric stage of consciousness might interpret it along the lines of "I have finally been saved! This confirms that my religion is the only true religion, and that anyone who hasn't been saved by Jesus is destined to burn in hell. How sad for them; they just don't know the truth."

In other words, two very similar state experiences can lead to two very different results based on the stage that one is in. Therefore we find here both the importance of a solid framework that can keep us moving forward on the path and the danger of equating any spiritual experience with spiritual growth. The two are related, but not equivalent. One of the great benefits of state experiences is that they can occur at any and all stages, and therefore can be harbingers of future development. For instance, one could have an experience of transcendent oneness, while still at a lower stage of development, and this can greatly serve one's journey, concretizing the reality of transcendent states of consciousness and molding in one a great determination to commit completely to the transformative journey.

The great Eastern traditions have become particularly good at training individuals to experience various states of consciousness, which do tend to unfold as stable experiences in a sequential pattern, similar to stages. But they have been less successful at moving people through stages, perhaps because in many of these spiritual frameworks, once someone has attained stable "nondual" realization, they are essentially done—no need to keep growing. A consequence of this can be seen in India, hailed as the spiritual center of the world, with literally thousands of highly realized people, experts at attaining and even transmitting these subtle spiritual states of consciousness to others; yet at the same time it has a caste system that tells people if you are born an untouchable it is perfectly acceptable for you to be condemned to cleaning toilets for the rest of your life, for it is simply your karma.

This is possible because training yourself to experience even the highest states of spiritual experience does not necessarily move you through various stages of development. One could literally have nondual realization while finding the abuse of women perfectly acceptable. Take, for instance, the case of Joshu Sasaki Roshi (who recently passed away at well over one hundred years of age), highly regarded as a Zen master of tremendous realization and a teacher for many Westerners, yet it was recently discovered that throughout his teaching years he had consistently asked female disciples to show him their breasts and let him touch them during their private koan sessions with the master![19]

Few would doubt that Joshu Sasaki Roshi had attained a tremendous realization of spiritual consciousness. Therefore, his case should stand out as a warning to us all. For the new monastic this means that one must be vigilant of falling into the trap of simply training to reach various meditative states, and certainly one should not regard particular spiritual experiences as denoting an attainment of what we have called throughout our book *spiritual maturity,* the elements of which will be discussed extensively in an upcoming section. You will notice that nowhere in our book do we highlight the ability to reach various states of consciousness. That does not mean that we do not hold them as effective tools or in high regard, but it does mean that in and of themselves they mean not much. It is only within the framework of a comprehensive path, and a foundation of service to others as well as a dialogical orientation toward other people, religious traditions and teachings, and sociological and scientific insights, that these trained states of consciousness and spiritual experience in general have a most fruitful outcome, both for the individual and for the greater human family.

Lines of Development

Recall that in our discussion of various stages and structures of consciousness we referred to the discovery of stages by researcher who asked various questions which dealt with things like cognitive, moral, aesthetic, emotional, spiritual, and kinesthetic development.[20] What we did not mention was that each of these lines of development can be at different stages. This is the idea of multiple intelligences, which can grow at more or less different rates (though research seems to suggest that cognitive development to a certain stage is necessary before other lines of development can also grow into that stage).[21] For instance, someone could be at a very high cognitive stage, but a very low stage of moral development, such as the systematic organizers behind the Nazi plan to eradicate Jews. Clearly they had a high cognitive development combined with a horrifically low level of moral development.

This does not mean that a high development in every line is necessary, but an integrated development is. One can be a wonderful human being and still be aesthetically challenged. One cannot be such a wonderful human being when one's moral developmental line does not continue to progress forward. New monastics can be aware of these various lines of development, and cultivate some self-knowledge about where they are strong or weak. They then can and should take an active stance toward increasing general overall development, particularly in the areas of body, mind, and spirit. For those on an interspiritual path however, in the end our overall development is left to the guidance of the Spirit, for we are allowing that guidance to do the work of transformation within us. When putting oneselves under the guidance of the Spirit, we understand that we will be led into situations and events that will require us to constantly grow in one or more lines, as the Spirit sees fit. This, in particular, is what we mean when we say *integrated* development.

One last important understanding about lines of development: one can be highly developed in a certain developmental line, say, a spiritual line, which may manifest as powerful psychic gifts, reading minds or telepathy, even the ability to radiate spiritual transmissions and divine experiences to others, but this does not necessarily mean that one is highly developed in other lines (particularly along moral and relationship lines). This is a particularly important understanding in our current spiritual milieu, often giving a premium as it does to those with psychic gifts and abilities. This should also help us to be wary that likely no one "master" will be able to offer us a complete program of integrated development.

For the new monastic on an interspiritual path (as well as others), the great mechanisms to protect one from unintegrated growth will be the "dark nights," mysterious processes whereby the Spirit reaches into our inner being and performs powerful work upon us. Before we get to those, however, let us first take a quick look at one of the most important and well understood psychological dynamics discovered with the birth of modern psychology, the shadow.

The Shadow

One insight of modern psychology that is essential for anyone walking a new monastic path is an understanding of the shadow. The shadow consists of the parts of ourselves that we have repressed into our unconscious, pieces of our personal development that we found too painful to process, or aspects of our personality, positive or negative, that are deemed unworthy of who we are. Perhaps they were not spiritual enough, perhaps they were too spiritual, too feminine or too masculine, too sexual; or perhaps they are too powerful and wise for us to accept. We are so afraid of these aspects that we repress them, we demonize them, we reject them and force them back into the darkness of the unconscious. However, there they do not disappear. Instead they are often projected out into the world, onto the people and things that resonate with their qualities, causing us to simply hate them—or in the case of our projected better parts, to give various divine statuses to others who are perhaps not so deserving (particularly partners in the beginning stages of an intimate relationship, or our spiritual teachers, another common projection). [22] Or instead of projecting them we may begin to experience them interiorly, as energies of depression, anxiety, and fear. (What is posttraumatic stress disorder other than an inability to process horrific life experience?) The shadow often emerges in the subtle realm of our dreams; dreamwork, or the proper interpretation of one's dreams, is one of the best ways to work with these personal unconscious energies. [23]

Ken Wilber is very clear that an understanding of the shadow is "something contributed exclusively by modern Western psychology. . . . The great wisdom traditions, for all their wisdom, have absolutely nothing like this. . . . Consequently, even advanced meditators and spiritual teachers are often haunted by psychopathology, as their shadows chase them to Enlightenment and back, leaving roadkill all along the way." [24]

The optimal way of working with the shadow is to befriend it, to recognize the aspects that one has been repressing, to acknowledge that these are parts of one's own self, and to allow those parts to then be reintegrated into one's conscious sense of self. Even the parts of the shadow that we deem negative have gifts to offer us; Buddhism speaks of the transmutation of the negative energies into aspects of wisdom, as does Father Thomas Keating's spiritual framework. The dynamics of the shadow are fairly well understood today, and there are many ways of working with these banished parts of ourselves to reintegrate them in a healthy way. Ken Wilber details the development of the shadow in detail in his chapter by that name in *Integral Spirituality*. This is not meant by any means to be full discussion of how to work with the shadow (for which there are vast resources), but rather to point out the fundamental importance of doing so.

Dealing and working with the shadow is a must for any new monastic, no matter what tradition or spiritual practice he or she is working with. It is work which must be integrated into the spiritual path, and for the most part the new monastic should not expect to find an understanding of these dynamics within our wisdom traditions. It is inherently dealt with in Father Keating's framework that we present below, but beyond that Wilber makes clear that many, if not most, meditation techniques can actually make shadow dynamics worse. Without dealing with the shadow we create a very unstable foundation as we move along the path, and lurking just under our conscious awareness it waits for the right moment to come to the surface and topple all the hard work we thought we were accomplishing. Not working with the shadow is like cutting off one of our arms before entering into a playoff basketball game, chopping off essential aspects of ourselves that are needed for this path, parts of ourselves that are meant to be divinized as we progress, not thrown in the waste heap. Father Keating tells us, "This is why I say one can't do the spiritual life nowadays without some working knowledge of one's own psychology. Unless one develops a healthy self-identity, the psychological resources for the journey are lacking."[25]

We are now ready to take a further journey on our overview of the path as we peer into the conceptual framework for the spiritual journey designed by Father Thomas Keating.

THE PSYCHOLOGICAL MODEL OF FATHER THOMAS KEATING: THE DIVINE THERAPIST

Father Keating also has recognized the fundamental importance of modern psychological insight for our times. In *Invitation to Love*, a book Father Keating wrote "to provide a solid conceptual background for the practice of contemplative prayer and the spiritual journey for our time," he states,

> It is my conviction that the language of psychology is an essential vehicle in our time to explain the healing of the unconscious. . . . For one thing, it is a language that is better understood than the traditional language of spiritual theology. . . . It also provides a more comprehensive understanding of the psychological dynamics which grace has to contend with in the healing and transformation process. . . . Thus psychology has become the new "handmaid of theology."[26]

In his work of renewal of the Christian contemplative path, Father Keating has developed a universal psychological framework with the explicit goal of forming a basis for the spiritual journey. As such, it is one of the great gifts of our times, allowing us to peek closer at the dynamics at work inside each of us and how those are related to our spiritual search. It offers us a new way to understand our journeys in terms of modern language and with essential insights that traditional paths did not have access to. In this way, it also opens up new avenues of spiritual work that were not available as traditional paths developed, such as shadow work and a growing awareness of the psychological damage done to each of us during childhood. We will present a shortened overview of Father Keating's work here, and highly recommend his many books for further development, particularly *Invitation to Love*, for an in-depth overview of both his psychological framework and how it relates to various stages of the spiritual journey.

Stages of Consciousness and Evolutionary Development

Father Keating has made extensive use of Ken Wilber's work as well in developing his conceptual model, particularly in terms of the stages of consciousness we each pass through from childhood to adulthood. Father Keating then analyzes what can go wrong as we mature through that process, mainly the development of a "false self system," that then is in need of dismantling by what he refers to as "the Divine Therapy." We begin with Father Keating's adoption of Ken Wilber's stages of consciousness: "The developmental model is actually a subset of an even more comprehensive model, the evolutionary. The infant experiences the same developmental pattern and value systems that the human family as a whole experienced. In other words, each human being is a microcosm of where the human race has been—and where it might be headed."[27]

Father Keating goes on to describe the various levels of consciousness that we all pass through on our way to adulthood. When we are born we are immersed in an archaic, or what Father Keating calls a "reptilian," consciousness. This consciousness is one of complete immersion in nature, with no sense of a separate self. As we saw in our discussion of a pre-Axial age, this was the consciousness of the earliest inklings of primitive humanity. There was a unity with all of life around one, but no sense of individual identity. Life is dominated by instinctual needs for survival. This is the state of consciousness of the first year of life for all human beings, and it seems that we can reexperience this state of unity in later contemplative or mystical states. In addition, we experience a continual yearning at some level to return to this state. "As adults we yearn for the kind of un-selfconscious unity that was actually present in the first year or two of life, but was lost during the development of the separate-self sense. It is to be recovered in an immensely superior form in the transforming union."[28]

Notice the difference Father Keating makes between an experience of unity before a separate-self sense develops and an experience of unity after this development, with the latter being "immensely superior." This is a recognition of the pre/trans fallacy we mentioned earlier. It is important to recognize that not all experiences of unity are the same, and that the unity experience we strive for is not a return to an undifferentiated consciousness, but a move forward into a more complex unity, a complexified unification. We should also note that somewhere in our being we still yearn for a return to an undifferentiated consciousness, for the simplicity of life in the womb. But it is ever forward we must march—not a return into a fantasized past, but a movement into the further reaches of the Kosmos, into a creative unknown.

Between the ages of two and four we begin to experience typhonic and magical modes of consciousness. Our bodies become recognized as distinct objects from other bodies around us, and our world takes on a magical, dreamlike nature. We dream about, and have waking visions of, animals and other strange creatures; our toys magically turn into spaceships, and fantasy stories become real for us. It is a beautiful time in our development, and also corresponds to a pre-Axial consciousness.

Then we begin to move into modes of consciousness that have particular importance for us in today's world:

> Between the fourth year and eighth year, the child enters the period of socialization and accesses the mythic membership level of consciousness where possessions, competition, success, belonging to a group, and interiorizing the values of a structured society are the order for the day. The child at this age absorbs unquestioningly the values of parents, teachers, peers, and the predominant society in which he is being raised. . . . Overidenti-

fication with the group is the dominant characteristic of mythic membership consciousness.[29]

This is essentially a tribal level of consciousness, still pre-Axial, which many or even most of us today have not completely grown beyond. Whether it is an unhealthy loyalty to our religious tradition, our country, our friends, the new spiritual teaching we have discovered, our economic status or field of work (the recent movie *The Wolf of Wall Street* typifies the strong tribal nature many of us embody in our occupations, particularly in jobs that are lucrative or ones that appear to be doing the most damage to our Earth and our human community), we are literally acting out of humanity's childish tendencies.

The next stage of development is the "mental egoic," or rational consciousness. Despite what we may think at first, this development is unfortunately one we are still struggling with:

> Theoretically . . . the mental egoic is the era we live in now, and the level of consciousness that we attain in the normal course of our human development after about eight years of age. It would be comforting if this was so. . . . Unfortunately, this is not the case.

> Mental egoic consciousness is the movement beyond the self-centered instinctual drives and gratifications of the prerational instincts into full personhood. It is to take responsibility for ourselves as well as to respond to the needs of our families, our nations, and the human race, including the generations yet to come. But this level of consciousness is still not accessed by the vast majority of humankind.[30]

Father Keating then describes the overall process of growth from one stage to the next:

> Every movement of human growth precipitates a crisis appropriate to the level of physical, emotional, or spiritual development at which we find ourselves. Each major crisis of growth requires letting go of the physical or spiritual food that has been nourishing us up to then and moving into more mature relationships. In such a crisis we tend to seek the feeling of security. It is characteristic of reptilian and typhonic consciousness to react to frustration by choosing the line of least resistance, or whatever seems to be the easiest security blanket in which to wrap themselves. The capacity to go forward into personal responsibility is constantly challenged by the temptation to revert to lower levels of consciousness and behavior. Human growth is not the denial

or rejection of any level, but the integration of the lower into more evolved levels of consciousness.[31]

The Development of the False-Self System

One of the monumental discoveries of modern psychology is the discovery of the unconscious, that mysterious nexus of shadows, energies, and dreams that motivates our activity and decisions to a much greater degree than one imagines. All modern psychotherapy is based on this discovery. Within our unconscious, as we move through the various stages of cognitive development mentioned above, arises what Father Keating calls the false-self system, a system of programs designed around our instinctual needs for survival, control, and affection, and based on our intrinsic drive for happiness. Unfortunately, it arises out of problems in our development, and hence represents childish fixations on selfish notions of obtaining happiness, backed up by our emotional states. Of these unconscious motivations, Father Keating declares, "If we don't face the consequences of unconscious motivation—through a practice or discipline that opens us to the unconscious—then that motivation will secretly influence our decisions all through our lives."[32]

"One of the biggest impediments to spiritual growth is that we do not perceive our own hidden motivations."[33] These hidden motivations, as mentioned, begin for Father Keating in childhood with the development of this false self, "our injured, compensatory sense of who we are."[34] This false self is based around three main instinctual needs we are all born with: security and survival, power and control, and esteem and affection. To the degree that each of these is not provided for adequately in childhood we develop compensatory needs to offset the emotional pain we experience from their deprivation. This compensation evolves as we develop a full-blown, mostly unconscious, system of psychological complexity aimed at providing and protecting those instinctual needs. In essence, we develop a false sense of self, a compensatory personality that treats other people and the world around us as a means to fulfill those needs, and we are ever in fear that we will be deprived of them once again. This false self is built around a sense of deprivation and lack rather than a sense of fullness, adventure, and one's true identity as a divine being.

Using the insights of developmental cognitive psychology, Father Keating shows in intimate detail how these instinctual needs, when not fully met, bloom into full-grown "emotional programs for happiness," and how they sabotage our lives and spiritual growth. When these emotional programs are not met within the circumstances of life, they pour forth all of our afflictive emotions: fear, anger, frustration, anxiety, etc., along with a ticker tape of interior commentaries that reinforce these emotions and with them our perceived need for these emotional programs to be met. Unfortunately, these are programs designed not for human happiness, but for disaster. As Father Keating tells us, "The homemade self, or the false self, as it is usually called, is programmed for human misery."[35]

The Divine Therapy

As a result of this false-self system, we come into mental egoic consciousness with these lingering dysfunctions in our unconscious, and they continue to influence all we do. Rather than using the power of full rational consciousness to build a better world and prepare the ground for even further development of consciousness, the false-self system is used to prop up our emotional programs for happiness.

> Instead of developing the capacity to relate to other persons and to all reality with honesty and compassion, we use the immensely creative energy of rational consciousness to develop more sophisticated ways of controlling people, extracting greater pleasures out of life, and heaping up more security symbols. Thus we reinforce self-centered motivation appropriate to childhood but totally inappropriate for adults.[36]

The solution for this problem is what Father Keating calls the divine therapy. "The divine therapy, like Alcoholics Anonymous, is based on the realization that you know where you are and that your life is unmanageable."[37] It is unmanageable because our motivation remains unconscious, which means that we cannot get to it through simply making resolutions to change. We need more than this; we must undergo the confrontation with our own unconscious motivations. That question, "Where are you?" Father Keating puts forth as the first great question of the spiritual journey.

> "*Where* are you?" is, indeed, a question of great magnitude. Are you still at the age of one or two, where your emotional program for security is the chief energy that determines your decisions and relationships, especially the relationship between God and you? Are you so enamored with your religion that you have a naïve loyalty that cannot see the real faults that are present in a particular faith community? Do you sweep under the rug embarrassing situations and bow to the security or esteem needs of the community?[38]

The divine therapy is a call from the Spirit to begin exploring and letting go of our selfish unconscious motivations, and to move into the full adulthood of reflective consciousness, where we can take responsibility for our actions, for the way we treat others, and for the first time, take full responsibility for our spiritual journeys as well. By submitting ourselves to the divine therapy we begin to move into the adulthood of our spiritual path. "God invites us to take responsibility for being human and to open ourselves to the unconscious damage that is influencing our decisions and relationships."[39]

Father Keating's main practice to enhance our opportunity to receive the divine therapy is Centering Prayer, a highly receptive meditation technique, combined with practices for integrating its effects into ordinary daily activity. Being a receptive method of meditation, it brings one into a deep relaxation of our bodies and psychological defense mechanisms. By resting in silence, we begin to allow the divine therapist to do its work of healing. Father Keating has said, quoting St. John of the Cross, that God "spoke the eternal Word in Silence, and it is in Silence that we hear it." As this happens, the undigested psychological damage of a lifetime, warehoused within our bodies, begins to rise to the surface of our consciousness. We begin to reexperience feelings of hurt, anger, and frustration, allowing them to circulate through our bodies and consciousness. By not re-repressing them during their recapitulation, we begin to let go of these damaging experiences. Through continual practice we develop the fortitude and maturity to allow the deepest experiences of pain to resurface, and by doing so evacuate the energetic constrictions that form the foundation of the false-self system.

> Centering Prayer is not an end in itself, but its deep rest loosens up the emotional weeds of a lifetime. When our defenses go down, up comes the dark side of the personality, the dynamics of the unconscious, and the immense emotional investment we have placed in false programs for happiness, along with the realization of how immersed we are in our particular cultural conditioning. . . . To be really healed requires that we allow our dark side to come to full consciousness and then to let it go and give it to God.[40]

Notice the general tone here of the spiritual journey itself. It does not consist of training into higher and higher states of consciousness, but rather begins with a descent into the damaged parts of ourselves in our already-existing layers, or stages, of conscious development. "Our agreement with the divine therapist is to allow the Holy Spirit to bring us to the truth about ourselves."[41] In other words, before heading into higher states and stages, we begin to journey downward, moving not into ecstatic states of realization, but doing the hard work of confronting our unconscious motivations, of purifying and unifying the foundational levels of our consciousness, maturing them, so that they will have the fortitude and wisdom to make the journey into yet higher stages. "This warns us that the spiritual journey is not a success story or a career move. It is rather a series of humiliations of the false self. It is experienced as diminutions of the false self with the value system and worldview that we built up so painstakingly as defenses to cope with the emotional pain of early life."[42]

This allows us to bypass, as it were, some of the more tempting dangers on the path, referred to in the previous section, of cultivating higher and higher states of consciousness without moving into more mature stages of consciousness. In addition, because we place ourselves and this process more and more under the guidance of the Spirit, it becomes less and less of a personal project in the sense of our deciding when we are ready to move on into higher states or stages. The Spirit will bring us there naturally, organically, as we are prepared and catalyzed in its light.

When we put our journey in our own hands, based on what we are capable of doing (as many Eastern paths do), in juxtaposition to being under the guidance of the Spirit, it becomes a high priority to stay within a complete spiritual system and framework that can move us, step by step, through specific processes and stages in the spiritual life, usually under the close direction of a master teacher, so that our growth is truly integrated and developmental. Unfortunately, the completeness of many of these spiritual systems has been lost as they have come to the West, opening their adherents to the very real dangers of falling into the traps of spiritual narcissism and uneven development. This does not mean that they are ineffective, but it does mean that we must be vigilantly aware of the potential pitfalls that can occur.

We may even become "enlightened" according to the criteria of some of these systems but still be at a fairly low level of development in terms of stage. It is not that these paths do not serve a great and tremendous function—they are some of the highest accomplishments of humankind— but we should have a clear awareness that they were not developed within the context of modern life and all of its complexities. Nor were they developed in light of the insights of modern science, psychology, sociology, and cultural studies. They were developed for the most part ideally to serve monks, nuns, or solitary ascetics who were able to practice these techniques unceasingly and within closed environments. In addition, they were developed when human beings believed the cosmos was fixed and unmoving, with no awareness of any evolutionary process in our midst. Therefore, they must be supplemented and reinterpreted in light of our modern discoveries, what many people are calling the need for a "fourth turning" of the religions.[43] They were also developed in the context of an entire magisterium, a collection of teachings, dogma, lore, rituals, techniques, and worldviews which surrounded them, and were meant to be effective within that space.[44] Therefore, they present problems today as we no longer live within those same worldviews, and in the West often do not have access to the magisterium that surrounded these teachings.

It can be hard for one to practice within the full context of some of these systems while living in the world, especially in the West, and if one is not careful one opens oneself to the dangers of uneven development. This has been a major problem for the nondual, neo-advaitic, "already enlightened" movements in the West, where even many of the teachers have developed quirky and downright childish ways of interacting socially, all while (supposedly) remaining in a state of constant oneness and nondual perception.

Of course one can participate in these systems and adopt their practices, and be a new monastic. Our respect for all authentic teachings and spiritual accomplishments is profound. Whether these are enlightened teachings of the Buddha, the revelations of the Hindu sages, the simplicity and beauty of the Tao Te Ching, and countless others, we bow deeply to them. But one has to take into consideration these particular dangers, and consider how one will face up to them maturely. One can also blend one's journey through this landscape with the guidance of the Spirit. The way of the guidance of the Spirit, when discerned in authenticity, has built-in mechanisms to address these very issues. The first of these is a general descent into our unconscious motivations, so that after perhaps an initial foray into mystical experience, or even simply peaceful meditation, one can expect great disturbances and difficulties just around the corner. A researcher once wrote to Father Keating, informing him of a small study in which people who began practicing Centering Prayer experienced less anxiety as a result. Father Keating wrote back: "Centering Prayer will reduce anxiety perhaps for the first three months. But once the unconscious starts to unload, it will give you more anxiety than you ever had in your life."[45]

All authentic traditions acknowledge the confrontation with one's ego, and the subsequent spiritual battle to free ourselves from it. However, many strands of these traditions have been slow to integrate within themselves the insights of modern science, psychology, and sociology, and the new monastic must therefore approach them with this in mind. Let's take a closer look now at these built-in mechanisms we speak of on this path—better known as the "dark nights."

THE DARK NIGHTS

One dark night,
fired with love's urgent longings
—ah, the sheer grace!—
I went out unseen,
my house being now all stilled.

In darkness and secure,
by the secret ladder, disguised
—ah, the sheer grace!—
in darkness and concealment,
my house being now all stilled.

On that glad night,
in secret, for no one saw me,
nor did I look at anything,
with no other light or guide
than the one that burned in my heart.

This guided me
more surely than the light of noon
to where he was awaiting me
—him I knew so well—
there in a place where no one appeared.

O guiding night!
O night more lovely than the dawn!
O night that has united
the Lover with his beloved,
transforming the beloved in her Lover.

Upon my flowering breast,
which I kept wholly for him alone,
there he lay sleeping,
and I caressed him
there in the breeze from the fanning cedars.

When the breeze blew from the turret,
as I parted his hair,
it wounded my neck,
with its gentle hand,
suspending all my senses.

I abandoned and forgot myself,
laying my face on my Beloved,
all things ceased; I went out from myself,
leaving my cares
forgotten among the lilies.[46]

—*St. John of the Cross*

The Dark Night of Sense

Our central thesis here is that the "dark nights" of sense and spirit, when proceeded through under the guidance of the Spirit, produce in the human being an integrated development, or what we call spiritual maturity. It is spiritual growth that is aligned with one's vocation in the world, produces in one an integrated psychograph of the various lines of development, and most important, allows one to proceed fully prepared for further stages of growth, and not just states. We describe the "dark nights" here in the light of this thesis. As we will see, the "dark nights," particularly as described by St. John of the Cross, a sixteen-century Catholic monk in Spain and one of Christianity's most celebrated mystics, seem to be experienced in stark contrast to the attainment of states of consciousness. Wilber describes the "dark nights" as tending to appear

> at the boundary between those general states [denoted as gross, subtle, causal, and nondual in Wilber's work, representing successive attainments of states of consciousness] as *attachment* to, or *identity with*, those states is let-go of or surrendered. The states themselves (and their general realms of being and knowing) remain and continue to arise, but identity with them is stripped, and that "stripping" constitutes the respective dark nights of senses, soul, and self—causing a dark night of the senses, a dark night of the soul, and a dark night of the self.[47]

We are positing here that the dark nights can be utilized to accomplish more than this movement between states of consciousness, preparing our being in a more complete psychological fashion, and moving us between stages in a unique way, and not just states.

Father Keating introduces the "dark nights" in the context of beginning to move beyond full mental egoic consciousness. The "dark night of the senses" is essentially the Spirit's way of shining a light on the hidden motivations formed during our childhood.

Little do we realize when we embark on the spiritual journey that our first fervor is itself immature and under the influence of these programs; it will have some growing up to do. . . . The night of sense heals the malformations that took place in the growing from childhood to early adolescence when we felt that our basic needs were not being met and we responded with insatiable compensatory demands.[48]

The spiritual journey is characterized by the ever-increasing knowledge of our mixed motivations, the dark sides of our personalities, and the emotional traumas of early childhood.[49]

Often this night of sense will begin to occur after an initial breakthrough into higher states of consciousness. After committing completely to a spiritual journey we may enjoy a so-called honeymoon period, where we enjoy the graces of mystical experience and gain a trust in the reality of spiritual growth and our divine nature, a trust that will be much needed on this path as we reverse direction and begin to peer into some of the more unseemly parts of our nature. These initial breakthroughs in the spiritual life, the springtime of spiritual life, are meant to prepare us for this looming confrontation with the unconscious. They are not to be mistaken for a mature attainment of higher stages of development. To progress healthily to those higher stages is the goal of these "dark nights" when progressed through in the manner we will explore here as described by Father Keating.

It is for this reason we believe these "dark nights" guard us from some of the tragic results of uneven development as we allow the Spirit to do its work of healing within us in its preparation of our faculties to receive the higher gifts of the Spirit. Note the difference here again from other paths. Here, we tap into the Wisdom present in the universe at all times, Sophia, the guidance of the Holy Spirit, and we let it guide the process—forming us and shaping us and healing us so that we can become more whole, more complete, and greater transmitters of its beauty and grace in our service in the world. Wisdom itself will not leave us malformed, but if we are branching out on our own, following our own proscriptions of how to proceed, doing so without the guidance of a mature spiritual director, then we are in danger of malformation, despite— or even because of—our zeal.

The night of sense will bring about a tremendous dryness in our spiritual practice. That which we found enjoyable, enlightening, and full of discovery now feels inexplicably boring, arid, and dry. As Father Keating says, "Spiritual reading is like reading a telephone book."[50] Neither do we find satisfaction in any worldly thing.

The Holy Spirit infuses into our minds the insight that God alone can satisfy our boundless longing for happiness. . . . It springs from the realization that no created thing can bring us unlimited satisfaction. In the light of this intuition, we know that all the gratifications we were seeking when we were motivated by our emotional programs cannot possibly bring us happiness.[51]

It is as if the first noble truth of Buddhism, the truth of suffering, *dukkha*, is seared into our consciousness during this night. It creates a tremendous foundation for the remainder of the journey, a necessity, as the Buddha saw clearly.

We may have fears that we are moving backward on our journey during this night. Our enthusiasm for various devotional practices and activities disappears. . . . There is a constant temptation to think we have done something wrong, but we can't figure out what it was.[52]

The will finds no benefit or pleasure in particular acts of love, praise, petition, or any other response. . . . This pulls the rug out from under our plans and strategies for the spiritual journey. We learn that the journey is a path that cannot be mapped out in advance.[53]

The dryness of this night manifests in the outer world as well, for on this path always the inner and outer are wedded to one another. "The Divine Therapist continues the treatment in daily life. God brings people and events into our lives and takes them out again to show us other things we need to see about ourselves. Thus contemplative prayer and daily life work together if we are willing, and mutually reinforce the therapeutic process."

During this night our faith and trust and fortitude and wisdom are ever increasing, even though we may not be conscious of these fruits during the process. What is happening is we are being forced to revisit our psychological foundation, to revisit our developmental process, and to allow the Spirit the freedom to do the work of healing and reintegration all the wounds incurred throughout.

Everything good and of true value in life is reappropriated under the influence of the Spirit. It is as if we were led through our developmental process again, taking possession of the values appropriate to each level or period of life and letting go of the limitations that the human condition and our inability to handle them had imposed on us.[54]

The main fruit of this dark night is humility, as we face up to the dark sides of our personality, as well as bringing "the nature of commitment into clear focus."[55] Our determination to pursue the spiritual path, while at the same time allowing ourselves to undergo the diminution of our false self, is what eventually brings us through this night, solidifying a further foundation for the continuation of our journey. In fact, through this a new realization begins to dawn, one that brings about a certain small, but flowing peace in the undercurrents of our lives, as we find our feet firmly planted on the path. We find that

> the acceptance of our wounds is not only the beginning, but the journey itself. It does not matter if we do not finish it. If we are on the journey, we are in the Kingdom [of Heaven]. . . . It is in bearing our weakness with compassion, patience, and without expecting all our ills to go away that we function best in a Kingdom where the insignificant, the outcasts, and everyday life are the basic coordinates. The Kingdom is in our midst. . . . Perfection, or holiness, it seems to me, should be measured by our commitment to the spiritual journey . . . rather than by attaining some particular goal.[56]

In the words of the Venerable Tenzin Priyadarshi, we can now, perhaps for the first time, truly "take joy in our practice" without overly optimistic expectations of the results.

Fruits of the Night of Sense

There is more than just the false-self system lurking in our unconscious—there are also positive energies and gifts. "It contains within it potentials in ourselves that we are not yet aware of."[57]

"Beside the dark energies of the unconscious, there are all kinds of other awesome energies—for example, natural talents, the fruits of the Spirit, the seven gifts of the Spirit, and the divine indwelling itself—that we haven't experienced yet and are waiting to be discovered." As our energies become freed up from the focus on compensatory motivations, they are able to grow into further reaches of consciousness. The night of sense has helped to prepare the interior faculties to receive some these gifts, opening up upon the intuitive, subtle, psychic level of consciousness.

It is important to emphasize here that we believe the dark night of sense, as described above, functions as more than a boundary between states of consciousness (what Wilber refers to as state-stages). We believe it completes a more integrated action within the soul which prepares one to enter a further *stage* of consciousness, which we describe more in terms of what it has relativized (the false self) than in terms of new phenomenon that may, or may not, begin to arise in one's awareness. This is because our main concern is in stages of development (what Wilber calls structure-stages), and less about states of development. States tend to be defined by the arising of spiritual or mystical or psychic phenomena and realizations, while stages tend to be defined by more of a maturing process that clearly transcends and includes all that came before it. The night of sense is essentially a maturing process of the whole being, advancing the various lines of development within one as well as the overall center of gravity to a sufficient degree as to be able to enter into and participate in the unfolding and creative emergence of future stages of development. As the concern of the new monastic is always with the completing of the world, it is to the building and developing, the maturation and careful exploration, of these further stages to which she is committed—and she knows that they will always be born among us, necessitating an integration of any further growth into all of our relationships in the world.

"Thus, the divine plan is to transform human nature into the divine, not by giving it some special role or exceptional powers, but by enabling it to live ordinary life with extraordinary love."[58]

The Dark Night of the Soul or Spirit

The dark night of the soul is a deeper, more purificatory, and more mysterious experience. Though it parallels the dark night of sense in many ways, it is a movement beyond the realm of our personal unconscious. Carl Jung recognized fairly early in his work that lurking in each person's unconscious was much more than simply our personal unconscious, and he dubbed what was not personal the "collective unconscious." In Jung's words, while the personal unconscious "is made essentially of contents which at one time have been conscious but which have disappeared from consciousness through having been forgotten or repressed, the contents of the collective unconscious have never been in consciousness, and therefore have never been individually acquired."[59] Our personal unconscious Jung calls a more or less "superficial layer of the unconscious," which "rests upon a deeper layer . . . which is not a personal acquisition but is inborn . . . a common psychic substrate of a suprapersonal nature which is present in every one of us."[60]

Father Keating refers to an "ontological unconscious, or level of being, [which] contains all the human potentialities for spiritual development that have yet to be activated. . . . The realization and actualization of this inherent human potential to be 'divinized' . . . might be called the human adventure. The priority we give to this adventure determines more or less the extent of the ontological powers of the unconscious that will be actualized in our particular lives."[61]

Father Keating tells us that even after the night of sense, the residue of the false self still lingers in our "spiritual faculties and manifests itself by the secret satisfaction that we find in ourselves as the recipients of God's favors or of a special vocation."

> The night of spirit is designed to free us from the residue of the false self in the unconscious and thus prepare us for transforming union. . . . It is essential for the final movement into divine union. Without that purification . . . there is a danger of falling into the spiritual archetypes that arise out of the unconscious.[62]

Notice again here how the dark night of spirit is described by that which it guards against, rather than as the perfection of a certain state of being, or the attainment of a particular realization. It protects us from the danger of falling into certain dead ends, or even more tragic circumstances, as it prepares us for further journeys into our deeper depths and those of the Kosmos itself. The many recent (and many not-so-recent) revelations and scandals stemming from such teachers as Andrew Cohen, Genpo Roshi, and Marc Gafni speak volumes about the need to be vigilantly aware of these temptations, and the great need for tools to help navigate these dangerous waters. The dark nights, while sometimes painful beyond imagination, are just such divinely gifted tools. Father Keating describes how the night of spirit protects us from these dangers—once passed through it serves as a thoroughly earned sacred talisman of sorts, protecting us from so many of the problems in our current spiritual milieu, particularly as we talk about emergent ways of walking a spiritual path.

Those who enter into the higher states of consciousness may "experience psychic or spiritual gifts and become gifted teachers or charismatic leaders."

> But the very gifts that attract people to them and to their teaching subtly and insidiously incline them toward a glamorous self-image. Precisely because of their spiritual attainments, the temptation arises to identify with the role of prophet, wonder-worker, enlightened teacher, martyr, victim, charismatic leader— in short, God's gift to humanity. The night of spirit reduces such temptations to zero because, through its purifying action, we experience ourselves as capable of every evil.[63]

Father Keating goes on to list a number of the main fruits of this night of spirit, this humbling existential experience of being "capable of every evil":

> The first [fruit] is freedom from the temptation to assume a glamorous role. . . . It allows God to treat us like everyone else.

> A second fruit . . . is freedom from the domination of any emotion . . . by integrating them into the rational and intuitive parts of our nature . . . extinguishing the last traces of our subjugation to the emotional programs for happiness in the spiritual part of our nature.

> A third fruit . . . is the purification of our idea of God. . . . God reveals himself in the night of spirit in a vastly superior way— as infinite, incomprehensible, and ineffable. . . . This immense energy may be experienced by some as impersonal, although it certainly treats us in a personal way. . . . Our idea of the spiritual journey and the means we should use to pursue it, and our ideas of our vocations . . . may be shattered.

> The greatest fruit of the night of spirit is the disposition that is willing to accept God on his own terms. As a result, one allows God to be God without knowing who or what that is. Total self surrender and abandonment grow mightily, though in a manner hidden from us.[64]

Finally, despite our attempts to outline a "path," and lest we think we know how this path may unfold, Father Keating reminds us that a path led by the guidance of the Spirit is always a call into the unknown:

> While we may talk of the divine "plan" and outline the stages of the spiritual journey as presented by the great teachers of our tradition, the only thing we can be absolutely sure of in the spiritual journey is that whatever we are expecting to happen will not happen. . . . Sometimes the night of sense begins at once, sometimes the night of sense and the night of spirit are reversed, and sometimes they take place at the same time. If we have read widely and think that things are going to proceed according to our understanding, God will reverse the normal order for our benefit. One way or another, we will have to take the leap of trust into the unknown.[65]

THE NINE ELEMENTS OF SPIRITUAL MATURITY

We now turn to what should be, with deep commitment and hard work, the fruits of becoming a new monastic: spiritual maturity. Growing in spiritual maturity is both the beginning and end of the path, and all steps in between. Knowing what that is allows us to set our spiritual compass pointing true north. For this section, we take the lead of Brother Wayne Teasdale, highlighting his nine elements of a mature interspirituality as laid forth in *The Mystic Heart*. Together these nine elements compose a profound basis from which to understand and perceive what a mature spiritual life looks and feels like. It is more than just an understanding; these nine elements must seep into our bones with the help of our practice. They must become integrated elements of who we are, and they must be brought to bear on our completing of the world. They are the basis of the nine vows of the new monastic, deepening in actuality and in our commitment to them as our path progresses.

The nine elements are (1) actual moral capacity; (2) solidarity with all living beings; (3) deep nonviolence; (4) humility; (5) spiritual practice; (6) mature self-knowledge; (7) simplicity of life; (8) selfless service and compassionate action; and (9) the prophetic voice. Let us look at each in turn, making generous use of Brother Wayne's own words:

Element 1: Actual Moral Capacity

> The first element in a global or universal spirituality, and thus part of interspirituality itself, is a fully operative moral capacity.... Living the spiritual life has a direct relationship to the formation of a moral vision. As we grow in compassion, love, mercy, kindness, gentleness, wisdom, patience, and sensitivity, the meaning of ethics naturally extends beyond simply avoiding certain attitudes and actions. It assumes an interior nature that transforms society's moral code through spiritual wisdom. It becomes part of the consciousness of the individual mystic, and not something externally imposed by society. Ultimately, the work of the individual enlarges the entire culture's moral understanding.[66]

The new monastic does not receive one's moral framework from society. Certainly it does not correspond to what is merely lawful. Too many people in today's world feel that if something is not against the law it is somehow moral. A true moral framework emerges from one's own being, out of the philosophical and spiritual framework one creates within one's journey, and out of one's own mystical experience, in conjunction with one's existential experience of the suffering within life, particularly that of the least among us. It also emerges out of a knowledge of our political systems, our sociological realities, structural evil in its many forms, and the revealed truths of our wisdom traditions. All of this must become internalized for the new monastic, integrated into her being and her path. Recall that it also emerges dialogically, in relationship to all of these realities. Therefore any true moral capacity must be informed by mature knowledge of that which is among us, and this must be substantiated within the core of one's being.

> Thus actualized moral capacity is based on a transformed inner nature. The moral dimension of the spiritual journey has nothing to do with external rules and regulations, but with a fundamental, radical reorientation of the person's inner commitment to be established permanently and concretely in love and compassion. Once we are so established, we have acquired all we can from the ethical guidelines of the various religious traditions. We are then good, merciful, loving, wise, gentle, patient, and compassionate simply because that's what we are in our realized nature, not because any system tells us to be this way.[67]

Element 2: Solidarity with All Living Beings

> The second element in a universal mysticism is a deep realization of the interconnectedness of everyone and everything. . . . This unity undergirding all reality, being, and life creates our sense of solidarity with all living beings, the earth, and the cosmos. . . . [It] is a mystical perception of consciousness.

The new monastic manifests concretely his solidarity with all of life in the intrinsic dialogical nature of his journey. By allowing himself to be constantly informed by the other, he inherently acknowledges both his essential interdependence—that all parts his own Being are intimately caught up with, and formed by, the other—as well as his own uniqueness as a pole of interdependent life. Our solidarity with all of life also has a deep social-activist component, as it requires an encounter with, and a response to, the many injustices in our world:

> This deep feeling of connection is often triggered by the encounter with the world's suffering. . . . As we walk the mystical path, we become more and more aware of our intimate connection with everyone and everything else. And the spiritual life requires that we are ready to respond to the suffering of those we meet along the way because they are connected to us.[68]

Element 3: Deep Nonviolence

> When the spiritual life has put down deep roots, there is a natural, organic evolution into deep nonviolence. . . . The realization of the interconnectedness of all beings brings with it a sense of the utter preciousness of all life. Every being in every species is precious and irreplaceable. . . . The spiritually mature have a natural sensitivity toward all other persons and other creatures, and a profound awareness of the dignity and worth of everyone and everything that is.[69]

Deep nonviolence goes considerably beyond refraining from violence. It is a disposition of the heart. Brother Wayne once said that God is "infinite sensitivity," and the manifestation of this quality of the Divine is deep nonviolence. It is particularly important to embody toward one's apparent enemies. It does not mean that one cannot and should not be firm (as we will see when we come to element nine, the Prophetic Voice), but that one is always holding others in one's heart, always praying for that which is best for all. Particularly for new monastics on a more activist path, it becomes essential to refrain from demonizing "the enemy." The practice of deep nonviolence brings clarity, sensitivity, and wisdom to these difficult arenas. On the other hand, it also calls us into action girded with a moral power that in the end surpasses that of all violence. Martin Luther King Jr. is of course one of the great symbols of this power which pervaded the civil rights movement, as is Mahatma Gandhi in his struggle for a free and united India:

> As we grow in spiritual wisdom, we become more sensitive to the rights of others, including other species. Gentleness, calm, patience, and humility are all aspects of nonharming. . . . Mahatma Gandhi was able to apply this inner resource with great effectiveness in India's struggle for independence. His achievement stands as a permanent monument to the power and depth of nonviolence to change politics and society, to transform conflict into peaceful opportunities to resolve differences.[70]

Element 4: Humility

> The spiritual life is impossible without humility. Humility of heart is a great treasure because it keeps us honest, cutting away self-deception, falsehood, and inauthenticity. It forces us to be real, even when it is uncomfortable. It rescues us from superficiality, and compels us to always be true to ourselves and to others.[71]

We have seen how for the new monastic, and especially for one on an interspiritual path, the path itself is based on increasing degrees of humility. The diminutions of our false self, as well as our relationships with mentors and a community, help to keep us humble. Humility is also not just about bowing our heads, or feeling little, but is about Truth. Therefore, it also entails accepting our gifts, stepping into them in humility, in trust that they will be put to good use in the completing of the world.

> Humility of heart is not about bowing and scraping before others; it is about honesty and self-truth . . . an egoless understanding—as opposed to the false self's projections—of one's own limitations, of where one stands in relation to others on the way. This is the foundation of the spiritual journey, which must be grounded in the truth of ourselves. Thomas Keating has said that "The greatest accomplishment in life is to be who you are, and that means to be who God wanted you to be when he created you." No other accomplishment in life compares to this attainment. The humble man or woman has chosen to be fully who they are.[72]

Element 5: Spiritual Practice

> Spiritual practice, the work of our transformation, is the means of inner growth and change toward human maturity glimpsed in the best of religious experience. . . . Daily spiritual practice is the "technology" of inner change. . . . Spiritual practice shapes our understanding, character, will, personality, attitudes, and actions by enlarging their scope through the light of compassion and love.[73]

Daily spiritual practice is a *sine qua non* for new monastic life. Without it, one could hardly be considered a new monastic. We hope we have emphasized its importance clearly throughout this book, and in many ways, if there was one element we would choose to concentrate on, this would be it, as it is what informs and develops and matures all of the other elements. There are many types of spiritual practice, and we recommended and elucidated a number of practices with varying elements in "Beginnings" when we presented "The Heart of New Monastic Life." One's spiritual practice should consist of a number of different practices meant to develop an integrated spiritual life—not only meditation, or study, or spiritual reading, or communion with nature, or social service, but a synergistic combination of all. For a new monastic, one's spiritual practice also involves the discernment and then carrying out of one's vocation, which, when done properly, tends to integrate all of the above elements. So we see, spiritual practice is much more for the new monastic than spending thirty minutes each day in a particular spiritual discipline. While this is necessary, it is not sufficient—for it is only the beginning. An integrated life which is not separate from one's practice is the true goal of all genuine spiritual practice for the new monastic.

Element 6: Mature Self-Knowledge

> Socrates counseled, "Know Thyself." In the same way, mystics have genuine, mature, honest self-knowledge. They are radically open to acknowledging faults and limitations, and do not shy away from coming to terms with them. . . . Spiritual progress depends on a maturity in our self-understanding. We must know ourselves fully. Humility is the basis of an honest, mature self-awareness that accepts ourselves as we are, without covering up, making excuses, or blaming others.[74]

Mature self-knowledge is an extension of our training in humility. It is also a reflection of our dialogical relationship with others, particularly our community. A true spiritual director can be of immense help in offering us opportunities to confront and recognize hitherto unknown parts of ourselves. They can reflect back to us, often through a symbolic language or a sudden, penetrating insight, inner knowledge of how our being is functioning in relationship to others and the Divine. This knowledge is always humbling, but consists of both negative aspects of ourselves as well as positive aspects.

As we begin to gain self-knowledge, a much greater respect and compassion for others begins to arise. We no longer look down on others, for if grace reveals their faults to us we know only too well our own struggles with these negative inner dynamics. As we begin to accept our own gifts and develop them in service to the whole we also begin to have a much more profound respect for the gifts of others, and we are able to encourage them to develop those gifts. Even more, our passion for completing the world and the corresponding knowledge of the need for each person's unique gifts propels our sensitivity to these gifts of others. We begin to see how our own gifts are most often effective and powerful when in synergistic relationship with the gifts of others.

Mature self-knowledge always leads us deeper into the world, as we begin to discover the interdependent dynamics of our own interior, and let go of those processes which denigrate this inherent beauty. Without this gift, we become islands unto ourselves, unable to relate and interact with other truths surrounding us, and we close ourselves off from the evolutionary impulse of the universe.

> Profound inner change takes root gradually within us as we gain this precious self-knowledge and uncover all the hidden motives that lie buried deep within us. . . . When it reaches its full potential, [it] becomes the basis for very radical inner change. Mature self-knowledge happens when we move beyond denial—denial of our faults and limitations, our buried motives or hidden agendas—and beyond judgment of others, beyond projection on others our own need for inner work. . . . Self-knowledge, like all mystical knowing, gives us an invincible certitude about ourselves and divine matters. This certitude, and the clarity of our understanding, partially accounts for our joy and contentment.[75]

Element 7: Simplicity of Life

> Simplicity of life concerns our relationship with the planet, the natural world, other species, and other human beings. What we do here—how we live our lives, how we use and abuse the earth's resources—is an important moral issue. Simplicity of life is an inner focus on what is necessary. As we grow in mystical consciousness and become inwardly integrated, our life naturally becomes simplified, uncluttered by property and money. . . . Mystics naturally gravitate to simplicity of life, which then is incarnated in their actions by a lifestyle that sets aside wealth and power.[76]

The new monastic strives to simplify his life, both outwardly and inwardly. His life becomes a reflection of his commitments, estranged from the dominant themes and accepted norms of our culture. The new monastic also understands, through experience, the beauty of a fundamental simplicity of life and the freedom it provides to follow the inspirations of the Spirit. It is somewhat of a paradox of spiritual life that as we grow and learn to appreciate the great complexity of life, within that complexity an increasing beauty and order is found. It is by tapping into this that we find a true and honorable simplicity of life, one that can be found within the complex systems of Nature and resonates with her organic unity. This simplicity is also to be found in the manifestation of Sophia, and the beauty with which she synthesizes and reveals herself. Simplicity of life is essential for the new monastic, and holds within it a moral component.

This element of global spirituality is necessary because we must simplify our lives if the Ecological Age is really to take root.

When we voluntarily embrace a simpler lifestyle that does not require squandering our precious resources, degrading the environment, oppressing other species, and depriving the poor, simplicity of life reveals itself concretely as a great generosity of spirit. . . . Simplicity of heart and life require an appreciation of insecurity, vulnerability, marginality, and detachment, which a certain experience of material poverty facilitates.[77]

Simplicity of life also brings clarity to the world of the new monastic. It focuses our attention on what really matters, on what our lives are truly about. It aims to remove so much of the clutter and distractions in our modern life. In this sense it may separate us at first from those around us if they are not also following this path, and are caught up in the cultural milieu of our times and its endless ways to keep our attention off of the profound, and simple, meaning of our lives. But we should not worry too much, for our unity with them will be rediscovered on a much deeper level over the course of our journeys:

Simplicity has a way of focusing our attention on what is absolutely essential; it goes to the core of our being and strips away all the distractions that compete for our attention. It directs us to the utter seriousness of the spiritual journey, and relieves us of any crutches we may have relied on.

Simplicity, as a virtue, knows only what is real. . . . It is not impressed with many things, but with few things used well, especially in service to others. . . . [It] allows us to become single-minded about the inner experience, and not to waste our precious time and energy on useless efforts that only distract us. . . . Simplicity is at once an inner law of the spiritual life, and a basic demand of justice and wise economics.

The spiritual journey is not a game; it is the most ultimate and most real human adventure. . . . Simplicity of heart can make all the difference in terms of living the interior experience *while* relating it to others, to the natural world, to other species and to the community at large.[78]

Element 8: Selfless Service and Compassionate Action

Selfless service and compassionate action together constitute another universal element of interspirituality. Any truly viable spirituality for the third millennium will need to include our commitment to the social dimension. . . . The need is very great in our times. As the rich get richer, the problem of homelessness worldwide has grown to alarming proportions. . . . The spiritual life summons us to selfless service in particular.[79]

We are all called not just to dream about a better world but to act for a better world. That gives us a mandate to experience every person in need, every cry, including the cry of the earth, as a call to be answered. Selfless service and compassionate action are both a spiritual practice and a fruit of our spiritual practice. As a practice it helps us to bear witness to suffering in a prayerful way, letting go of our individual preferences, ideas, and comforts. It allows us to feel the call of each situation, and then respond in a way that utilizes the best of us for others. As a fruit of our practice, selfless service and compassionate action become natural and spontaneous, arising from an inner state of prayer which is often characterized by a deep feeling of interconnectedness with all living beings and the earth. Then we simply respond with the same intimacy and care that we would want someone else to respond to our own cries and heartbreaks.

Element 9: The Prophetic Voice

A further vital component in a universal spirituality, and so in an interspirituality, is the awakened and utterly necessary function of leadership in the area of justice. I call this the operation of the prophetic or moral voice in situations that require witness and response.[80]

In order for things to really change, it is not enough to invest in practices that lead to personal change. It is also not enough to just participate in social service or political activism. Integral change happens on three levels. First, we have to work on changing our selves. Second, we have to incarnate all the deep qualities of the heart that we are developing into our relationships. Finally, we have to realize that our lives and our relationships don't happen in a vacuum; they happen within structures and institutions that often dictate the logic of our lives, relationships, and dreams. A mature spirituality requires us to resist structural evil and speak and act for justice. As Archbishop Desmond Tutu often says, "God has a dream," and our vocation is to actualize that dream so our lives, our relationships, and our institutions can begin to reflect the values of compassion, interconnectedness, and justice.

We no longer have the luxury of ignoring the many challenges to justice in all its forms. We have a universal responsibility to apply the moral or prophetic function wherever we see justice disregarded, threats to world peace, oppression by states against its people or a neighboring nation . . . and the abuse of human rights, the rights of the earth, and other species. This is a critical operation of all spirituality, particularly through the collective voice of religious and spiritual leaders; it is a function desperately needed now, in the Interspiritual Age.[81]

THE EVOLUTIONARY IMPERATIVE

The new monastic can never forget that our path is caught up in more than our own personal journeys. The very nature of our personal journeys changes in this light. It is always caught up in our service to the world. In this evolutionary view, the importance of time and of the historical process emerges, and with it the need for dialogical practices with the other, which we recall includes other people, other religious traditions, psychological, sociological and scientific insights. It is in this way that we complete the world together, and the arena in which we build our own souls is caught up with and even narrowly determined by that much greater opus. The guidance of the Spirit, a vocational emphasis, and the "dark nights" allow us to incorporate this insight into the very depth of our mystical path. We are formed in the crucible of our spiritual journey in a way which serves the whole in the widest expanse possible. And that is the whole point—the entire reason for our journeys in the first place. So we have come full circle. For the new monastic, the spiritual journey is not an avenue to peace or bliss, but is how best to serve. In this, we are literally, though in a mysterious way, bringing God to fruition. We are helping to "complete the world."

We have unique gifts to bring to realization in this adventure. The human condition then, including our weakness, ignorance, and struggles, can be seen as the necessary condition for birthing our particular emergent divine attributes into the greater Kosmos. These attributes of the Divine may have no other way of coming into being but through this incarnational process of becoming. We may not even understand just what these attributes are—the mystery of each human being and humanity's destiny as a whole remain shrouded in secrecy—but we have intuitions of their flowering. We should be able to take pride in the fact that we are here, as *humanity*, experiencing and living and learning, overcoming resistance to the pain and struggle of our maturation, taking joy in our practice.

And it is here—in the world—that new monastics work out the details of their journeys. It is here that we experience the humiliations of our false self. It is here that we partake in the beauty of our own unique unfolding . . . and that of others.

We understand ourselves as beings in the process of becoming, where this process of becoming is ontologically equal and advaiticly intertwined with a transcendent reality existing outside of time. It is this transcendent reality existing outside of time, experienced within the depths of our own being and subsequently cognized as the center of all that exists, that is the basis, foundation, and guarantor of our eventual success in the adventure of becoming. However, for the new monastic, realizations of this transcendent reality are important only inasmuch as they contribute to the process of becoming at the same time. It is important to recognize that the transcendent reality, when it takes us away from this world, can also be an impediment to the process of becoming, which is to say an impediment to its own Self.

An awareness of transcendent, nondual reality can remove all defensiveness in our lives and open us to divine expressions of compassion, love, and wisdom. The insight it brings removes all fear and can allow us to embrace life and live it to its fullest—but it can also become an escape from the process of becoming, removing the suffering and struggle so necessary for incarnation, and creating a widening distance between ourselves and our fellow humans. It is a paradox—that which reveals a preexistent unity can also create a tremendous gap between our lived experience and that of those around us. At the extreme end of this temptation to transcendence one can actually forfeit one's potential to participate meaningfully in the evolution of humankind by becoming too far divorced from the dimensions of time and historical unfoldment.

The experiences of the "dark nights" are safeguards against this temptation, and more. They operate, according to the work of the Spirit, to prepare us for that which we are called to: an integrated entrance into higher stages of consciousness and more mature ways of being—and to the development of our faculties in service of our unique vocations in the world. We can envision our integral psychograph, with its various lines of development through differing stages. The "dark nights" allow the Spirit to work on our individual psychograph, preparing, healing, and developing each line as needed—not necessarily in a way that brings all lines to full development, but in a way where uneven development is much less of a concern, and our development occurs in synergy with our vocation. These "dark nights" are not a glorification of suffering for the sake of suffering itself, but rather lead to an understanding of the sacrifices necessary in order that we may become what is needed—integrated, mature, divine-human beings—aligned with the evolutionary impulse of our entire human family, and designed to manifest our vocation under the direction of this same evolutionary impulse, that which we call the Spirit.

These manifestations of the Spirit have various aspects. One of these was the appearance of Sophia, or ever-present Wisdom. In this aspect the Spirit guides our understanding, synthesizes the various truths of humanity we come into contact with, builds a conceptual framework within our own being, and develops our faculties so that we may continue to move forward on the path in a fruitful and ever-maturing way, serving the larger birth of the fullness of our human family.

Another of these manifestations is as the teleological pull of the Kosmos itself, the very evolutionary impulse that has—in the fullness of time—brought about the human family from stardust. It was this aspect that was of such primary importance in the spirituality of Pierre Teilhard de Chardin, what Ken Wilber calls *Eros*, and what Alfred North Whitehead called "the creative advance into novelty."[82] The new monastic endeavors to cultivate a relationship with this impulse, to be informed by its guidance, and to grow in its discernment. For those on an interspiritual path, this is the foundation of one's Path, the inner drumbeat, which molds one's choices and directs one's actions. This relationship is born in the heart, but is a full-body affair: sensual, intellectual, spiritual, and emotional. In learning to follow the guidance of the Spirit, we are aligning ourselves with the intrinsic teleological pull of the universe itself. As we do so, all of our actions, relationships, even our inner thoughts and the subtle spiritual movements of our being serve the greater birth of our human family, as does the unique path we walk.

Finally, we have seen the manifestation of the Spirit as divine therapist, as the one who transforms us in a mysterious way, who watches over our journey, who takes into account both others and ourselves in the processes of its transforming work within our souls in the "dark nights." Out of this work is born an integrated human being, a divinized human being, who can now serve in whatever way he or she is uniquely called. Its inner work is wedded to a greater plan, of which our vocation is an integral part.

As we walk our spiritual paths with fidelity to this impulse—within us and among us—with uncompromising strength and passion, we maintain the integrity of this transfiguration and can take responsibility for our part in it. We are grateful for this opportunity to give, through our struggle and growth into maturity, unique gifts unto the entire universe. We have faith—faith that something of greater value is being accomplished in us, and through our action in the world.

Then, even in the midst of our greatest defeats, our most horrendous mistakes, and crushing experiences of utter decrepitude, we can take solace in the fact that something greater is being born out of the crucible of our human condition. We can take pride in the fact that we are walking a path and transmuting, slowly but surely, our experience into increasing emanations of divine life. Only we can birth the divine-human woman and man. And they must be birthed, in the blood and sweat and tears of the human predicament. The divine-human is not a preexistent reality, but a creative emergence born of the Spirit, yet in eternal partnership with our own other half, that of the timeless reality of God.

As we come to a close we wish you, the reader, our deepest prayer and humble hope for your journeys. Our prayers are with you. May you continue to consent to the Spirit of guidance present in your heart. May you live in fidelity to its call and direction. May you become transformed and transfigured. May your life become a reflection of Divine Life.

In the end Father Keating expresses for us not just the attainment of this path, but the intrinsic treading of it, for the two cannot be said to be separate:

> It is the freedom to manifest God through one's own uniqueness . . . to be a kind of fifth Gospel: to become the word of God and to manifest God rather than the false self, with its emotional programs for happiness and attachments to various roles, including the most spiritual.[83]

> Our prayer is certain to have an effect on others and to force us to express this love in daily life. We do not have to think about it too much because, when the time comes, we will know what we are supposed to do or it may happen spontaneously. It may also change several times in our lifetimes, especially if we begin this journey early enough. . . . This brings me to the final point: prayer cannot stand alone without action emerging from it. Contemplative prayer without action stagnates, and action without contemplative prayer leads to burn-out or running around in circles. Contemplative prayer sifts our contemplative vision and our ideas about what we should be doing. It enables us to blend the two and to bring the spirit of our contemplative commitment into daily life. . . . Without trying to, but just by being in God as you go about your daily functions, you exercise a kind of apostolate. . . . You may be pouring grace into the atmosphere and into other people. All our activities need to come out of this center.[84]

To manifest God through one's own uniqueness . . . to become a "fifth Gospel" in the world . . . to exercise a kind of apostolate . . . pouring grace into the atmosphere and other people . . . just by going about the business of Life.

For the new monastic, this is the meaning, the culmination, the journey—of one's life . . .

AFTERWORD

By Father Thomas Keating

The inspiration of this book and its presentation of what Rory and Adam call "new monasticism" seems to be a genuine movement of the Holy Spirit. It is distinct from the so-called interspiritual movement, which contains a broad spectrum of attitudes and aspirations. The broader movement manifests good energy, but also expresses different understandings of the term "interspirituality." For some it is a manifestation of spiritual values without being rooted in a specific religion or a religious discipline of a traditional nature. It seeks to embody the desire of transformation into higher states of consciousness, and affirm a commitment to spiritual experience without joining one of the world religions.

The new monasticism values the spiritual goals and traditions of the world religions and respects and welcomes those who wish to persevere in them, but they are free to develop new practices in the light of global and cultural developments. It is now possible for religious persons to interact and learn from each other practices from other traditions that can enrich their own. This dialogue could be a unifying factor for the global community as people and societies continue to evolve. The great obstacle to this kind of human and spiritual growth is the elitist attitude characteristic of most religions, in which they attribute to their respective belief systems the status of the only true religion. This has led to horrendous violence in the course of history as contending religious commitments proselytize or defend their proclaimed superiority.

The fundamental and primary purpose of religion is to start people on the path to transcendence and divine transformation. The monastic vocation epitomizes everyone's vocation to divine union, whether God is perceived as personal or impersonal. Hence the term "monk" presupposes a radical commitment to surrender the ego-self in order to receive the completely gratuitous gift of participation in the divine life of love, peace, compassion, forgiveness, service of others, and wisdom. Without this commitment, particular practices to reduce the obstacles in us to divine union will languish and perhaps foster the opposite dispositions. Since most people are not called or attracted to seek union with God within the structures of traditional monastic life, means of reaching divine union in the context of the immense diversity of life in the world must be created. Contemplative prayer and nonconceptual meditation seem to be the most helpful means of accessing the divine presence and of establishing a relationship with Ultimate Reality in the midst of the ups and downs of ordinary life.

Adam and Rory have recognized the benefits as well as the hazards of trying to create a new set of spiritual practices built on the wisdom of traditional monastic structures, but with great openness to the technological and scientific opportunities of contemporary culture. The chief focus of this new articulation of the varied spiritual disciplines of the ages is the work of remaining continuously in the presence of the Self, that is, of the presence that is named in different ways, but is acknowledged as the Source of all that is and the immense love that treasures every member of the human family from its beginning.

This great love calls for a personal response from humans that leads to the most intimate relationship conceivable. It awaits our consent. This can be offered in everyday life circumstances. The fact of being a creature and created out of nothing, once fully embraced and consented to, is the path to a relationship of communion in love and shared dispositions that leads to Oneness. This Oneness may be what is meant by the terms Heaven, Beatitude, Enlightenment, and Unity with the Absolute. As this transformation into the divine attitudes occurs and unfolds, one begins to manifest the divine presence in all one's activities, including no activity. The transformed, realized, or enlightened human being, in virtue of participating in the Oneness in which all particular things reside, means that human persons are called to cocreate with God and contribute to the transformation of the emerging global society.

SELECT BIBLIOGRAPHY

Bass, Diana Butler. *Christianity After Religion: The End of Church and the Birth of the New Spiritual Awakening*. New York: HarperOne, 2012.

Bastian, Edward W. *Interspiritual Meditation*. Santa Barbara, CA: Spiritual Paths Publishing, 2010.

Bauman, Zygmunt. *Liquid Times: Living in an Age of Uncertainty*. Cambridge, MA: Polity Press, 2007.

Bucko, Adam, and Matthew Fox. *Occupy Spirituality: A Radical Vision for a New Generation*. Berkeley, CA, North Atlantic, 2013.

Collins, Cecil. *The Vision of the Fool and Other Writings*. Enlarged Edition. Edited by Brian Keeble. Ipswich, UK: Golgonooza Press, 2002.

Cousins, Ewert H. *Christ of the 21st Century*. New York: Continuum, 1998.

Dalai Lama XIV. *Beyond Religion: Ethics for a Whole World*. New York: Houghton Milfflin Harcourt, 2011.

Delio, Ilia. *Christ in Evolution*. Maryknoll, NY: Orbis Books, 2008.

——, ed. *From Teilhard to Omega: Co-Creating an Unfinished Universe*. Maryknoll, NY: Orbis Books, 2014.

Ellsberg, Robert, ed. *Modern Spiritual Masters: Writings on Contemplation and Compassion*. Maryknoll, NY: Orbis Books, 2008.

Erricker, Clive, and Jane Erricker, eds. *Contemporary Spiritualities: Social and Religious Contexts*. New York: Continuum, 2001.

Everson, William. *The Birth of a Poet*. Edited by Lee Bartlett. Santa Barbara, CA: Black Sparrow Press, 1982.

Forest, Jim. *Living With Wisdom: A Life of Thomas Merton*. Revised ed. Maryknoll, NY: Orbis Books, 2008.

Fox, Matthew. *Hildegard of Bingen: A Saint for Our Times; Unleashing Her Power in the 21st Century*. Vancouver: Namaste, 2012.

——. *The Coming of the Cosmic Christ: The Healing of Mother Earth and the Birth of a Global Renaissance*. New York: HarperOne, 1988.

Griffiths, Bede. *The New Creation in Christ: Christian Meditation and Community*. Edited by Robert Kiely and Laurence Freeman, OSB. Springfield, IL: Templegate Publishers, 1994.

Harvey, Andrew, ed. *Essential Mystics*. San Francisco: HarperSanFrancisco, 1997.

John of the Cross. *Dark Night of the Soul*. Translated by Allison Peers. London: Catholic Way Publishing, 2013.

——. *The Collected Works of St. John of the Cross*. Trans. Kieran Kavanaugh and Otilio Rodriguez. Washington, DC: Institute of Carmelite Studies, 1991.

Johnson, Kurt, and David Robert Ord. *The Coming Interspiritual Age*. Vancouver: Namaste, 2012.

Jung, Carl G. *Modern Man in Search of a Soul*. Translated by W. S. Dell and Cary F. Baynes. New York: Harcourt, 1933.

——. *The Archetypes and the Collective Unconscious*. Translated by R. F. C. Hull. Collected Works, Vol. 9, Part 1, 2nd. ed. 1968. Princeton: Princeton University Press, 1990.

——. *Two Essays on Analytical Psychology*. Translated by R.F.C. Hull. Collected Works, Vol. 7, 2nd. ed. 1966. Princeton: Princeton University Press, 1968.

Keating, Thomas. *And the Word Was Made Flesh*. New York: Lantern, 2011.

——. *Intimacy with God*. New York: Crossroad Publishing, 1994.

———. *Invitation to Love: The Way of Christian Contemplation*. New York: Continuum, 2002.

———. *Reflections on the Unknowable*. New York: Lantern, 2014.

———. *The Human Condition: Contemplation and Transformation*. New York: Paulist Press, 1999.

King, Ursula. *Teilhard de Chardin and Eastern Religions: Co-Creating an Unfinished Universe in an Evolutionary World*. New York: Paulist Press, 2011.

Ladinsky, Daniel James. *Love Poems from God: Twelve Sacred Voices from the East and West*. New York: Penguin, 2002.

Lanzetta, Beverly. *Emerging Heart: Global Spirituality and the Sacred*. Minneapolis: Fortress Press, 2007.

———. *Radical Wisdom: A Feminist Mystical Theology*. Minneapolis: Fortress Press, 2005.

———.*The Intercultural Challenge of Raimon Panikkar*, Ed. by Joseph Prabhu. Maryknoll, NY: Orbis Books, 1996.

Meditations on the Tarot: A Journey into Christian Hermenautics. Translated by Robert Powell. New York: J. P. Tarcher/Penguin, 2002.

Merton, Thomas. *Conjectures of a Guilty Bystander*. New York: Doubleday, Image Books, 1989.

———. *New Seeds of Contemplation*. New York: New Directions Books, 1972.

Miles-Yépez, Netanel, ed. *The Common Heart*. New York: Lantern, 2006.

Nouwen, Henri J. M. *Bread for the Journey: A Daybook of Wisdom and Faith*. New York: HarperOne 2006.

———. *Peacework: Prayer, Resistence, Community*. Maryknoll, NY: Orbis Books, 2005.

Panikkar, Raimon. *A Dwelling Place for Wisdom*. Louisville: Westminster/John Knox Press, 1993.

———. *Blessed Simplicity: The Monk as Universal Archetype*. New York: Seabury Press, 1982.

———. *Invisible Harmony: Essays on Contemplation and Responsibility*. Minneapolis: Fortress Press, 1995.

———. *Myth, Faith, and Hermeneutics: Cross-Cultural Studies*. New York: Paulist Press, 1979.

———. *The Cosmotheandric Experience: Emerging Relisious Consciousness*. Maryknoll, NY: Orbis Books, 1993.

———. *The Rhythm of Being*. Maryknoll, NY: Orbis Books, 2010.

———. *The Silence of God: The Answer of the Buddha*. Maryknoll, NY: Orbis Books, 1989.

Parker, Palmer J. *Let Your Life Speak: Listening for the Voice of Vocation*. San Francisco: Jossey-Bass, 2001.

Prabhu, Joseph, ed. *The Intercultural Challenge of Raimon Panikkar*. Maryknoll, NY: Orbis Books, 1996.

Pramuk, Christopher. *Sophia: The Hidden Christ of Thomas Merton*. Collegeville, MN: Liturgical Press, 2009.

Schachter-Shalomi, Zalman and Netanel Miles-Yépez. *Foundations of the Fourth Turning of Hasidism: A Manifesto*. Boulder, CO: Albion-Andalus, 2014.

———. *God Hidden, Whereabouts Unknown: An Essay on the"Contraction" of God in Different Jewish Paradigms*. Boulder, CO: Albion-Andalus, 2013.

Stein, Edith. *Essential Writings*. Edited by John Sullivan. Maryknoll, NY: Orbis Books, 2005.

Steere. Douglas, ed. *Quaker Spirituality: Selected Writings.* New York: Paulist Press, 1984.

Teasdale, Wayne. *A Monk in the World: Cultivating a Spiritual Life.* Novato, CA: New World Library, 2002.

———. *The Mystic Heart: Discovering a Universal Spirituality in the World's Religions.* Novato, CA: New World Library, 1999.

Teilhard de Chardin, Pierre. *Christianity and Evolution.* Translated by René Hague. New York: Harcourt Brace Jovanovich, 1974.

———. *Human Energy.* Translated by J. M. Cohen. New York: Harcourt Brace Jovanovich, 1969.

———. *The Divine Milieu.* New York: Harper & Row, 1960; HarperCollins Classic Edition, 2001.

———. *The Future of Man.* Trans. Denny Norman. New York: HarperCollins, 1964; Doubleday Image Books, 2004.

———. *The Heart of Matter.* Translated by René Hague. New York: Harcourt Brace Jovanovich, 1978.

———. *The Human Phenomenon.* Translated by Sarah Appleton-Weber. Brighton: Sussex Academic Press, 2003.

———. *Toward the Future.* Translated by René Hague. New York: Harcourt, 1975.

Valliere, Paul. *Modern Russian Theology: Bukharev, Soloviev, Bulgakov: Orthodox Theology in a New Key.* Grand Rapids: William B. Eerdmans Publishing, 2000.

Vaughan-Lee, Llewellyn. *Alchemy of Light: Working with the Primal Energies of Life.* Inverness, CA: Golden Sufi Center, 2007.

———. *Darkening of the Light: Witnessing the End of an Era.* Point Reyes, CA: Golden Sufi Center, 2013.

Wilber, Ken. *A Brief History of Everything.* Boston: Shambhala, 2011.

———. *Collected Works,* Vol. 6: *Sex, Ecology, Spirituality: The Spirit of Evolution.* 2nd rev. ed. Boston: Shambhala, 2000.

———. *Integral Psychology: Consciousness, Spirit, Psychology, Therapy.* Boston: Shambhala, 2000.

———. *Integral Spirituality: A Startling New Role for Religion in the Modern and Post-Modern World.* Boston: Integral Books, 2006.

———. *The Fourth Turning: Imagining the Evolution of an Integral Buddhism.* Boston:la, 2014.

Wind, Renate. *Dorothee Soelle: Mystic and Rebel; The Biography.* Minneapolis: Fortress Press, 2012.

NOTES

Introduction

1. Teasdale, *The Mystic Heart*, 26.

2. Teilhard de Chardin, *The Divine Milieu*, 24. We have changed the male-centric language (use of "he" and "his") in this passage to reflect gender inclusive language ("we" and "our"). This is the only quotation where we have made changes to the original language, for reasons given in the following section, Man, Woman, and Language. Italics Teilhard's.

3 Teasdale, *A Monk in the World*, 219. Italics ours.

4. V. K. Harber, "New Monasticism: A Feminist's Perspective on an Engaged Contemplative Life," www.scribd.com.

5. Griffiths, *The New Creation in Christ*, 89.

6. Ibid., 91–94.

7. Panikkar, *Blessed Simplicity*.

8. Cousins, *Christ of the 21st Century*.

9. For a short description of the Christian sannyasi, see www.skyfarm.org/Prayer.htm.

10. Teilhard, *The Divine Milieu*, 24. We have changed the male-centric language (use of "he" and "his") in this passage to reflect gender inclusive language ("we" and "our"). This is the only quotation where we have made changes to the original language; italics Teilhard's.

11. For a detailed description of how to do lectio divina, see Keating, *Intimacy with God*, chapter 5.

12. Bucko and Fox, *Occupy Spirituality*, 121, quoting Rrager and James Fadiman.

13. Ibid., 90.

14. Andrew Lawler, "The Ordinary Decency of the Heart," *Sun Magazine*, Issue 389 (2008), http://thesunmagazine.org; interview with Andrew Harvey.

15. According to Wilber, "Kosmos" was originally used by the Pythagoreans, and has been translated as "cosmos," but the original meaning was much vaster in scope, including all of the many realms of Being: "The original meaning of Kosmos was the patterned nature or process of all domains of existence, from matter to math to theos, and not merely the physical universe. . . . The Kosmos contains the cosmos (or the physiophere), the bios (or biosphere), the nous (the noosphere [or the realm of the mind]), and theos (the theosphere or divine domain)." Wilber, *Collected Works, Vol. 6*, 45.

16. Bucko and Fox, *Occupy Spirituality*, 123.

17. Keating, *Intimacy with God*, 111.

18. These vows are based on Brother Wayne Teasdale's nine elements of spiritual maturity, as articulated in *The Mystic Heart* and developed from them by Rev. Diane Berke.

19. Adam Bucko and Zachary Markwith, "One Path, Many Paths: A Dialogue on the Role of Religion in Modern Times," www.sevenpillarshouse.org.

Movement 1: The Manifesto

1. Teasdale, *Monk in the World*, xxiii, xxix, xxxi.
2. Ibid., xxviii.
3. Ibid., 165.
4. Ibid., 159.
5. Ibid., 163.
6. Ibid., 170.
7. Ibid., 171.
8. Ibid., 163.
9. Acts 17:28.
10. Panikkar, *Blessed Simplicity*, 92.
11. Panikkar, *The Cosmotheandric Experience*, v.
12. Panikkar, *Blessed Simplicity*, 7.
13. Ibid., 8.
14. Ibid., 8–11.
15. Ibid.
16. Ibid., 13.
17. Ibid., 8, 20, 28.
18. Ibid., 29.
19. Ibid.
20. Ibid., 33–34.
21. Ibid., 27.
22. Merton, *New Seeds of Contemplation*, 1–5.
23. Panikkar, *Blessed Simplicity*, 45–46.
24. Ibid., 46.
25. Andrew Harvey, ed., *Essential Mystics*, 206.
26. Panikkar, *Blessed Simplicity*, 43, 50.
27. Ibid., 83.
28. Ibid., 60.
29. Ibid., 84–85.
30. Ibid., 55–56.
31. Ibid., 93.
32. Teasdale, *Monk in the World*, 138.
33. Panikkar, *Blessed Simplicity*, 92.
34. Thomas Keating, "Seekers of Ultimate Mystery," *Contemplative Outreach Newsletter* (June 2010): 3–4.
35. "Rise of the Nones," *Time Magazine*, March 12, 2013.
36. Philip Clayton, "Letting Doubters in the Door," *Los Angeles Times*, March 25, 2012, www.latimes.com.
37. Dalai Lama XIV, *Beyond Religion*, xv.
38. Ibid., xi.
39. Teasdale, *Monk in the World*, 175.
40. Teasdale, *The Mystic Heart*, 26.
41. Johnson and Ord, *The Coming Interspiritual Age*, 9.
42. Ibid., 18, 334 .

43. Matthew Wright, Matthew, "Reshaping Religion: Interspirituality and Multiple Religious Belonging" (Masters of Divinity Thesis, Virginia Theological Seminary, 2012).

44. Teasdale, *Mystic Heart,* 26.

45. Teasdale, *Monk in the World,* 175.

Movement 2: Unpacking the Manifesto

1. Cousins, *Christ of the 21st Century,* 84.

2. The full dialogue can be found in Adam Bucko and Zachary Markwith, "One Path, Many Paths: A Dialogue on the Role of Religion in Modern Times," www.sevenpillarshouse.org.

3. Panikkar, *Myth, Faith, and Hermeneutics,* 4.

4. Teilhard de Chardin, *Human Energy,* 49.

5. Schachter-Shalomi and Netanel Miles-Yépez, *God Hidden,* 6–10

6. Ibid., 6, 7.

7. Ibid., 7–9

8. Teilhard de Chardin, Pierre, *The Future of Man,* 122.

9. Teilhard de Chardin, *Human Energy,* 56.

10. Teilhard, *Future of Man,* 105.

11. Ibid., 58, 64.

12. Cousins, *Christ of the 21st Century,* 8.

13. "It is most striking that the morphological change of living creatures seems to have slowed down at the precise moment when Thought appeared on earth," Teilhard de Chardin, *Future of Man,* 5.

14. Ibid., 6.

15. Ibid., 126.

16. Ibid., 153.

17. Ibid., 126, 12.7

18. Delio, *From Teilhard to Omega,* 47.

19. In fact, it does not seem Teilhard had much exposure to the depths of other religious traditions, despite his worldly travels, as Ursula King argues in *Teilhard de Chardin and Eastern Religions.*

20. Teilhard de Chardin, *Future of Man,* 106–7.

21. Ibid., 121.

22. Ibid., 125.

23. Ibid., 61.

24. Ibid., 109–10.

25. Ibid., 112.

26. Ibid., 67.

27. Ibid., 118.

28. Cousins, *Christ of the 21st Century,* 4.

29. Ibid., 6.

30. Ibid., 7.

31. Ibid., 6.

32. Cousins, "Teilhard's Concept of Religion." As quoted in Delio, *Christ of the Evolution,* 11.

33. Cousins, *Christ of the 21st Century,* 5.

34. Ibid., 10

35. Ibid., 9.

36. Ibid., 104.

37. Ibid., 110.

38. Ibid., 9.

39. Philip Clayton, "Letting Doubters in the Door," *Los Angeles Times,* March 25, 2012.

40. "Rise of the Nones," *Time Magazine,* March 12, 2012.

41. "'Nones' on the Rise," *Pew Research and Public Life Project,* October 9, 2012, www.pewforum.org.

42. Bass, *Christianity After Religion,* 49.

43. Ibid., 3.

44. Ibid., 4.

45. Ibid., 5, 6–7.

46. William D. Dinges and Ilia Delio, OSF, "Teilhard de Chardin and the New Spirituality," in Delio, *From Teilhard to Omega,* 166, 169.

47. Ibid., 169–70.

48. The Mother, from "The Mother, Questions and Answers," vol. 9, 1957–1958, *Collected Works of the Mother,* 151–52, as quoted in Johnson and Ord, *The Coming Interspiritual Age,* 212–13.

49. A "meme," according to *Merriam-Webster's Collegiate Dictionary,* is "an idea, behavior, style or usage that spreads from person to person within a culture," a mechanism for carrying forward cultural identity through the transmission of language, gestures, and rituals. It is a word coined by Richard Dawkins of *The God Delusion* fame in a book called *The Selfish Gene.* We are sure he would be ecstatic with our use of his work here.

50. Teasdale, *The Mystic Heart,* 245–47.

51. Ibid., 238–40, 243.

52. Panikkar, *A Dwelling Place for Wisdom,* 97.

53. Beverly Lanzetta, "The Emerging Heart of Global Spirituality, Meditation 2," February 2014, www.beverlylanzetta.net.

54. Teasdale, *The Mystic Heart,* 10, 12.

55. Ibid., 26.

56. Ibid., 12.

57. Ibid., 28.

58. Ibid.

59. Teasdale, *A Monk in the World,* 215.

60. Teasdale, The *Mystic Heart,* 241.

61. Ibid.

62. Teasdale, *A Monk in the World,* 173.

63. Ibid., 187.

64. Teasdale, *The Mystic Heart*, 248. Brother Wayne also uses sannyasa in its traditional context: "The term sannyasa, meaning renunciation, refers to all those seers, sages, ascetics, and yogis over thousands of years who have renounced the world and who have populated India's remote mountain sanctuaries, river banks, forests, and deserts. The term refers to an extremely ancient state, probably considerably older than Hinduism itself."

65. Ibid., 248–49.

66. Teasdale, *A Monk in the World*, 218.

67. Johnson and Ord, *Coming Interspiritual Age*, 9.

68. Ibid., 362.

69. Bastian, *Interspiritual Meditation*, 23.

70. Rami Shapiro, "Describing InterSpirituality," www.spiritualpaths.net.

71. Quotation from the Snowmass Interspiritual Dialogue application letter.

72. Ibid. We will take a much closer look at this interspiritual incarnation in Movement 3.

73. Teilhard de Chardin, *The Divine Milieu*, 24. Italics ours.

74. Lanzetta, "The Emerging Heart of Global Spirituality, Meditation 4," February 2014, www.beverlylanzetta.net.

75. Panikkar, *The Silence of God*, xviii.

76. 1 Corinthians 13:3.

77. 1 Corinthians 2:10.

78. Cousins, *Christ of the 21st Century*, 16.

79. Lanzetta, "The Emerging Heart of Global Spirituality, Meditation 4."

80. Proverbs 8:27.

81. 1 Corinthians 2:11.

82. Panikkar, *Invisible Harmony*, 178. See endnotes 30, 31 for Heraclitus translation citation, 206.

83. Mirabai Starr, "Coming Out as Interspiritual," *Huffington Post*, July 19, 2012, www.huffingtonpost.com.

84. Matthew Wright, "Digging Deep to Holy Water," www.shalem.org.

85. Collins, *The Vision of the Fool*, 96–99.

86. Panikkar, *Myth, Faith, and Hermeneutics*, 9.

87. Delio, *Christ in Evolution*, 101.

88. Panikkar, *The Intra-Religious Dialogue*, 31.

89. Teilhard de Chardin, *Human Energy*, 65.

90. Lanzetta, *The Intercultural Challenge of Raimon Panikkar*, 94.

91. Panikkar, *Intra-Religious Dialogue*, 37.

92. Ibid., xix.

93. Ibid., 25, 37, 38.

94. Acts 17:28.

95. Panikkar, *Intra-Religious Dialogue*, 34.

96. Ibid., xvi.

97. Ibid., 38.

98. Ibid., 31.

99. Delio, *Christ in Evolution*, 99.

100. Panikkar, *Intra-Religious Dialogue*, 31–32.

101. Ibid., 33.

102. Cousins, *Christ of the 21st Century*, 118. Italics ours.

103. Panikkar, *Intra-Religious Dialogue*, xvii.

104. Proverbs 8:2.

105. Proverbs 3:18.

106. Wisdom 9:11.

107. Pramuk, *Sophia: The Hidden Christ of Thomas Merton*, 219.

108. Everson, *The Birth of a Poet*, 20.

109. Teilhard de Chardin, *Teilhard, Human Energy*, 131.

110. Thomas Merton, "Hagia Sophia," as reprinted in Pramuk, *Sophia*, 305.

111. Proverbs 8:35.

112. Proverbs 8:23, 27.

113. Pramuk, *Sophia*, xxvi, xxvii.

114. Ibid., xxiii.

115. Ibid., xxvi.

116. Valliere, *Modern Russian Theology*, 151.

117. Pramuk, *Sophia*, 173.

118. Valliere, *Modern Russian Theology*, 161.

119. Catherine Evtuhov, in Valliere, *Modern Russian Theology*, 261. Also cited in Pramuk, *Sophia*, 235.

120. Pramuk, *Sophia*, 237, 246–47, quoting Bulgakov as cited in Valliere, *Modern Russian Theology*, 336, and Rowan Williams, in *Sergii Bulgakov: Towards a Russian Political Theology* (Bloomsbury, UK: T & T Clark, 2001), 128–29.

121. Pramuk, *Sophia*, 207–8.

122. Teilhard de Chardin, *The Heart of Matter*, 59.

123. Kathleen Duffy, SSJ, in Delio, *From Teilhard to Omega*, 26.

124. Ibid., 28.

125. Pramuk, *Sophia*, 234.

126. Ibid., 235, citing Valliere, *Modern Russian Theology*, 161, n. 40.

127. Proverbs 8:31.

128. Pramuk, *Sophia*, xxii. Here Pramuk is describing Merton's theological method.

129. Ibid., xviii.

130. Valliere, *Modern Russian Theology*, 151.

131. Teilhard de Chardin, *Christianity and Evolution*, 116.

132. Teilhard de Chardin, *Human Energy*, 29–30.

133. Ibid., 162.

134. Ibid., 66.

135. Teilhard de Chardin, *Future of Man*, 189.

136. Ibid., 44.

137. Teilhard de Chardin, *Human Energy*, 63.

138. Ibid., 63, 67.

139. Teilhard de Chardin, *Future of Man*, 45.

140. Teilhard de Chardin, *Christianity and Evolution*, 117.

141. Teilhard de Chardin, *Future of Man*, 233.

142. Keating, *And the Word Was Made Flesh*, 7.

143. Panikkar, *The Rhythm of Being*, 6.

144. Ibid., 19.

145. Ibid., 20.

146. Merton, *Introduction to Christian Mysticism*, 35, 16; as cited in Pramuk, *Sophia*, xxiii.

147. Panikkar, *Dwelling Place*, 88.

148. Collins, *Vision of the Fool*, 94, 116, 124.

149. Ibid., 145–46.

150. Ibid., 148, 156–57.

151. Ibid., 149.

152. Merton, "Hagia Sophia," as reprinted in Pramuk, *Sophia*, 301–5.

153. Everson, *Birth of a Poet*, 19.

154. Ibid., v, vi.

155. The others include Madeleine Delbrel, William Everson, Parker Palmer, Rumi, Dorothy Soelle, the anonymous author of *Meditations on the Tarot*, Thomas Merton, Andrew Harvey, Thomas Keating, Matthew Fox, and more.

156. Everson, *Birth of a Poet*, 20–21.

157. Ibid., 19.

158. Ibid., 55.

159. Teilhard de Chardin, *The Divine Milieu*, 24.

160. Palmer, *Let Your Life Speak*, 4, 10.

161. Everson, *Birth of a Poet*, 18.

162. Ibid., 22.

163. Ibid., 18.

164. Ibid., 35, 37.

165. Ibid., 66.

166. Palmer, *Let Your Life Speak*, 36.

167. Everson, *Birth of a Poet*, 28–29.

168. Ibid., 32.

169. Palmer, *Let Your Life Speak*, 16.

170. Everson, *Birth of a Poet*, 193.

171. St. John of the Cross, as rendered by Daniel Ladinsky, in *Love Poems from God*.

172. Everson, *Birth of a Poet*, 183.

173. Ibid., 167.

174. Ibid., 185.

175. St. Francis of Assisi, "No One Knows His Name," as rendered by Ladinsky in *Love Poems from God*, 39.

176. Forest, *Living With Wisdom*, 174, 175.

177. Everson, *Birth of a Poet*, 30.

178. Mark 6:4.

179. Everson, *Birth of a Poet*, 70.

180. Ibid., 73.

181. Palmer, *Let Your Life Speak,* 42, 44, 50.

182. Ibid., 49.

183. Ibid., 49, quoting Mary Sarton, "Now I Become Myself."

184. Everson, *Birth of a Poet,* 193.

185. *Meditations on the Tarot,* 200, 201.

186. Ibid., 226.

187. Ibid., 227.

188. Madeleine Delbrel, in Robert Ellsberg, ed. *Modern Spiritual Masters,* 56.

189. Collins, *Vision of the Fool,* 35.

190. Fox, *Hildegard of Bingen,* 11.

191. Everson, *Birth of a Poet,* 191.

192. Andrew Harvey, www.andrewharvey.net/sacred-activism/.

193. Thomas Kelly, in Douglas V. Steere, ed., *Quaker Spirituality: Selected Writings,* 310, 311.

194. Stein, *Essential Writings,* 37.

195. Wind, *Dorothee Soelle—Mystic and Rebel,* 1.

196. Teilhard de Chardin, *Christianity and Evolution,* 92.

197. Everson, *Birth of a Poet,* 73.

198. Ibid., 68.

199. Merton, *An Introduction to Christian Mysticism,* 125–26, 129; quoted in Pramuk, *Sophia,* 144–45.

200. Nouwen, *Bread for the Journey,* 136.

201. Keating, *Reflections,* 28.

202. Palmer, *Let Your Life Speak,* 92–93.

203. Panikkar, *Invisible Harmony,* 177.

204. Rumi.

205. Keating, *Reflections,* 95.

206. Henri Nouwen, www.henrinouwen.org/About_HNS/Community/Inspiration.aspx.

207. Nouwen, *Peacework,* 98.

208. Griffiths, *The New Creation,* 96.

Movement 3: A Dialogical Interlude

1. *The Life of St. Anthony,* No. 4, 21, as quoted in Keating, *Invitation to Love,* 61.

2. There was one member, Roger La Borde, who was there from the beginning and who maintains that he doesn't belong to a "tradition." He became part of the group as an apprentice to the original Native American representative, Grandfather Red Elk. Roger doesn't see shamanism as a tradition.

Movement 4: The Path

1. Keating, *Intimacy with God,* 158.

2. Ibid., 117.

3. Ibid., 114.

4. Ibid., 114–15, 118–19.

5. Ibid., 115–16.

6. Ibid., 122–26.

7. Jung, *Modern Man in Search of a Soul*, 197.

8. Ibid., 207, 208.

9. Ibid., 197.

10. Jung, *The Archetypes and the Collective Unconscious*, 23.

11. Jung, *Modern Man*, 202.

12. Ibid., 229.

13. Wilber, *Integral Spirituality*, 53.

14. Ibid., 52.

15. Ibid., 53.

16. "The 1-2-3 of New Monastics" (an initial foray into Ken Wilber's integral framework, with a wish to open a dialogue and apologies for any glaring errors—for those not familiar with Ken's work this may be hard to follow): In the dialogical methodologies we have introduced, dialogical dialogue and dialogical sophiology, we remain aware of a structure/framework being introduced (third person), through *conscious relationship* to the inter-subjective we space among us (second person), which is participated in, informed by, and revealing of, our own uniqueness (first person). It facilitates an emergent phenomenon, born of the coming together of developmental streams, transmissions from higher states and stages, and grounded in an interpersonal, dialogical relationship with the other: people, traditions, science, psychology, anthropology, sociology—that is, wisdom wherever it is found (all partial truths revealed thus far). It partakes of, interacts with, and transforms our bodily energies (physical, subtle, and causal), while being centered in the heart. The emergent quality is none other than the teleological pull of the Kosmos itself—Eros, Sophia, the Spirit—all various guises or aspects of this teleological pull. We learn to tune in and be in relationship with it, to move and manifest its energies through us, and to allow it to introduce and incarnate, within our own worldspace, that which will be most fruitful for the human family.

When these methodologies are participated in at mature levels, for instance among highly developed contemplatives from different paths or traditions, we begin to lay down the faint beginnings of higher-stage Kosmic habits, which can then serve as a teleological pull for the development of lower-level stages, particularly second- tier development, by giving some general direction and energetic pull to these lower- stage formations, making it easier and easier for people to proceed into them (and through them). This is especially relevant for second-tier development. By deepening in particular the intersubjective grooves of even-higher-level Kosmic habits, we create a direction in the teleological pull for lower stages, which will allow those already in a second-tier developmental stage to intuitively move in the world in a way that is paving the road for higher stages, in a much more organic and swift fashion. In other words, instead of bumping around in the dark for what to do with second-tier consciousness, it begins to naturally move in the direction of these higher stage developments. As such, it will have an exponential effect in bringing even more people into second-tier development.

Currently there are a number of groups who are bringing together mature contemplatives from varying traditions for intimate gatherings and dialogues. Many of those who participate feel an intuition to be part of these gathering, but they are often unsure of the actual purpose, beyond simply coming together in dialogue. We feel that these gatherings are doing much to help form some of the higher-stage Kosmic habits, where much of the development seems to be taking place within the subtle energy bodies, as spiritual transmissions and insights are exchanged within an environment of love, wisdom, and acceptance. This begins to form or record higher-level intersubjective worldspace, which can then serve to give further direction and guidance to all lower levels of development. This is a fairly new phenomenon, as it is a function of the convergence of our human family in the modern world which allows for this type of interaction among mature contemplatives from many traditions to occur.

17. Wilber, *Integral Spirituality*, 72.

18. Ibid., 73.

19. This scandal received widespread media attention and was investigated by an independent group of Buddhist teachers who not only verified the many accusations, but found that Sasaki's community continually covered up the activity for decades. For just one article, with links to the independent investigation and other articles as well, see Mark Oppenheimer and Ian Lovett, "Zen Groups Distressed by Accusations Against Teacher," *New York Times*, February 11, 2013.

20. We note here that stages and structures of consciousness are not necessarily the same thing: structures refer to how one views the world in a particular stage, but also contained in this stage are other possibilities, such as the arising of various states of consciousness. For more on this, see Wilber, *Integral Spirituality*.

21. See ibid.

22. Wilber says "in 9 out of 10 cases, those things in the world that most disturb and upset me about others are actually my own shadow qualities, which are now perceived as 'out there.'" Ibid., 120.

23.The "proper interpretation of one's dreams" is an admittedly ambiguous phrase, but a lengthy discussion here of what is meant is beyond the current scope of our work. We refer readers to the work of Carl Jung.

24. Wilber, *Integral Spirituality*, 119.

25. Keating, *Intimacy*, 120.

26. Keating, *Invitation to Love*, 2, 3, 27

27. Ibid., 27.

28. Ibid., 31.

29. Ibid., 29, 32.

30. Ibid., 29–30.

31. Ibid., 30–31.

32. Keating, *The Human Condition*, 18–19.

33. Keating, *Invitation to Love*, 3.

34. Ibid., 3.

35. Keating, *The Human Condition*, 15.

36. Keating, *Invitation to Love*, 40.

37. Keating, *The Human Condition*, 31.

38. Ibid., 23.

39. Ibid., 24.

40. Ibid., 34, 35.

41. Keating, *The Human Condition*, 39.

42. Keating, *Intimacy*, 85.

43. See Schachter-Shalomi and Miles-Yépez, *Foundations of the Fourth Turning of Hasidism*. Also see Ken Wilber, Ken, *The Fourth Turning*.

44. We use the term "magisterium," usually used to refer to the authoritative body of teachings of Christianity and the people who are invested with the authority to decide what is authentic, in the manner used by Reb Zalman Schachter-Shalomi and Netanel Miles-Yépez to represent the general "worldspace" for any religious tradition.

45. Keating, *Intimacy*, 115

46. John of the Cross. *The Collected Works of St. John of the Cross*, 50–52.

47. Wilber, *Integral Spirituality*, 99.

48. Keating, *Invitation to Love*, 84.

49. Ibid., 67.

50. Ibid., 68.

51. Ibid., 68–69.

52. Keating, *Intimacy*, 87.

53. Keating, *Invitation to Love*, 69–70.

54. Keating, *Intimacy*, 90.

55. Keating, *Invitation to Love*, 87.

56. Keating, *Intimacy*, 91.

57. Ibid., 92.

58. Keating, *Invitation to Love*, 99.

59. Jung, *Archetypes and Collective Unconscious*, 42.

60. Ibid., 3, 4.

61. Keating, *Intimacy*, 93.

62. Keating, *Invitation to Love*, 95.

63. Ibid., 96.

64. Ibid., 97–99.

65. Ibid., 100.

66. Teasdale, *The Mystic Heart*, 109, 112.

67. Ibid., 113.

68. Ibid., 114, 115.

69. Ibid., 116–17.

70. Ibid., 117.

71. Ibid., 126.

72. Ibid., 127.

73. Ibid., 128–29.

74. Ibid., 141.

75. Ibid., 142–43.

76. Ibid., 148.

77. Ibid., 149.
78. Ibid., 150–52.
79. Ibid., 152–53.
80. Ibid., 157.
81. Ibid., 158–59.
82. Wilber, *Integral Spirituality*, 236.
83. Keating, *The Human Condition*, 44.
84. Keating, *Intimacy*, 156, 159–60

Index